"Luther is reported to have said that the prophets have a 'strange way of talking.' Anyone who has read Isaiah or Daniel closely knows the truth of these words. Brent Sandy helps us to engage the prophets intelligently and avoid sensationalist readings that take us down a road that obscures God's message. I will recommend this book to all my students."

TREMPER LONGMAN III, ROBERT H. GUNDRY PROFESSOR OF OLD TESTAMENT, WESTMONT COLLEGE

"This book represents the fruition of Dr. Sandy's many years of careful study and thinking on the commonly misunderstood topic of prophetic language. I have benefited from his insights over the years and am delighted to see his work finally made available to a wider audience. Students of the Bible who have been baffled by the prophetic texts of Scripture and their many interpretations will find great relief and helpful guidance in this book. Sandy's presentation makes excellent use of illustrations from the English language to guide the reader in understanding the language of prophecy. The resulting explanations enable the reader to bypass popular sensationalism and reclaim the biblical prophecies as God's Word."

JOHN H. WALTON, PROFESSOR OF OLD TESTAMENT, WHEATON COLLEGE GRADUATE SCHOOL

"Timely, engaging, probing, carefully researched and faithful to the biblical text, *Plowshares and Pruning Hooks* will be helpful reading for students, biblical scholars, theologians and pastors alike. Not all questions are answered, but the right questions are raised. While not satisfying all of his readers, Sandy offers considerable guidance for the beginning student and provides fresh insights for the seasoned scholar. This comprehensive exploration of the language of prophecy   and apocalyptic will prove to be valuable for many."

DAVID S. DOCKERY, PRESIDENT, UNION UNIVERSITY

"Dr. Sandy's book reflects insights gained over long years of careful research. His investigation of the use of imagery, metaphor and stylized language in connection with prophetic literature provides a much-needed correction and direction to a field that is too often plagued by speculative excesses. His command of the subject is ably demonstrated by his own use of imagery in presenting his observations and evidence of the data. "This is not just another book on prophecy. It is a ground-breaking proposal that invites further scrutiny from readers of all persuasions. Geared for a general audience, laymen, pastors and scholars alike will nonetheless profit from its balanced presentation. It will need to be consulted by any serious reader of the Scriptures."

RICHARD D. PATTERSON, DISTINGUISHED PROFESSOR EMERITUS, LIBERTY UNIVERSITY

"With every new major turn of events in the Middle East, many Christians scramble for their Bibles and seek to link the prophecies of the past to the events of the present. Brent Sandy has provided for both the average Bible reader and the serious student of Scripture some careful thinking on how to approach these prophetic texts that so intrigue them. Readers will find *Plowshares and Pruning Hooks* both balanced and challenging. They may not agree on every point, but all of us can appreciate the call for a consistent and careful approach to prophetic texts. This book opens the door for layman and scholar alike to a serious study of prophetic literature and its value as part of the Word of God."

DAVID R. PLASTER, VICE PRESIDENT FOR ACADEMIC AFFAIRS, GRACE COLLEGE AND SEMINARY

PLOWSHARES
& PRUNING HOOKS

Rethinking the Language of Biblical
Prophecy and Apocalyptic

D. BRENT SANDY

InterVarsity Press
Downers Grove, Illinois
Leicester, England

InterVarsity Press, USA
P.O. Box 1400, Downers Grove, IL 60515-1426, USA
World Wide Web: www.ivpress.com
E-mail: mail@ivpress.com

Inter-Varsity Press, England
38 De Montfort Street, Leicester LE1 7GP, England
World Wide Web: www.ivpbooks.com
E-mail: ivp@uccf.org.uk

InterVarsity Press®, U.S.A., is the book-publishing division of InterVarsity Christian Fellowship/USA®, a student movement active on campus at hundreds of universities, colleges and schools of nursing in the United States of America, and a member movement of the International Fellowship of Evangelical Students. For information about local and regional activities, write Public Relations Dept., InterVarsity Christian Fellowship/USA, 6400 Schroeder Rd., P.O. Box 7895, Madison, WI 53707-7895, or visit the IVCF website at <www.ivcf.org>.

Inter-Varsity Press, England, is the book-publishing division of the Universities and Colleges Christian Fellowship (formerly the Inter-Varsity Fellowship), a student movement linking Christian Unions in universities and colleges throughout the United Kingdom and the Republic of Ireland, and a member movement of the International Fellowship of Evangelical Students. For information about local and national activities write to UCCF, 38 De Montfort Street, Leicester LE1 7GP.

Acknolwedgment of the use of outside sources is given on pages 15-17.

Cover illustration: Roberta Polfus

Cover design: Kathy Lay Burrows

USA ISBN 0-8308-2653-X
UK ISBN 0-85111-277-3

Printed in the United States of America ∞

Library of Congress Cataloging-in-Publication Data

Sandy, D. Brent, 1947-
  Plowshares & pruning hooks : rethinking the language of biblical
prophecy and apocalyptic / D. Brent Sandy.
      p. cm.
  Includes bibliographical references and indexes.
    ISBN 0-8308-2653-X (pbk. : alk. paper)
    1. Bible—Prophecies.   2. Bible—Language, style. 3. Apocalyptic
literature—History and criticism.   I. Title: Plowshares and pruning
hooks.   II. Title.
    BS647.3 S36 2002
    220.1'5—dc21
                                                                        2002007714

British Library Cataloguing in Publication Data
A catalogue record for this book is available from the British Library.

P	20	19	18	17	16	15	14	13	12	11	10	9	8	7	6	5	4	3	2	1
Y	18	17	16	15	14	13	12	11	10	09	08	07	06	05	04	03	02			

To the prophets of old who
conquered kingdoms,
administered justice,
were destitute—living in deserts and caves,
were persecuted and mistreated,
were tortured, jeered, flogged, chained,
   imprisoned, stoned, sawed in two:

the world was not worthy of them. (Heb 11:33-38)

May this book be worthy of them.

CONTENTS

List of Figures

Preface

I grew up loving exploration, the kind of exploration where there were no maps and no one told you what to do or where to go. It was one step at a time into the unknown: playing with salamanders in a mud-hole, fingering fungus growing beside a tree deep in the woods, mixing chemical compounds in a high school lab, pulling an octopus from its hiding place among the rocks in the Aegean Sea, deciphering a Greek papyrus written more than two thousand years ago. Perhaps not everyone would share my enthusiasm for all of these kinds of adventure.

I am still an explorer, and this book is about biblical prophecy, an area of current exploration. Many people would have liked to tell me what to do and where to go, but I wanted to figure things out for myself—one step at a time. Perhaps not everyone will share enthusiasm for my discoveries. For some readers, joining in the exploration may be thrilling. For others it may be threatening. But I am simply asking straightforward questions about how to interpret prophecy and letting the evidence take me where it will.

But do we really need another book on prophecy? Yes and no. Books on prophecy of recent decades follow several different courses, like streams and rivulets flowing through the countryside. The biggest stream with the biggest fish purports to tell how prophecy will be fulfilled, often in relation to recent and anticipated events. For example, some prognosticated about Y2K, linking it with the fulfillment of prophecy. (For those who stockpiled supplies, the hype should have produced a few doubts about such punditry.) Another example is the fascination with the latest events in the Middle East. To some people the books detailing how—and sometimes how soon—prophecy will be fulfilled are life-giving water for the thirsty soul.

To others they are contaminated with sensationalism. Certainly if the number of books sold is the measure of success, this stream is crème de la crème.[1]

A much smaller current of books attempts to go against the flow. They challenge the assumption that contemporary events must certainly be the fulfillment of prophecy.[2] Typically, these books fail to attract popular audiences, partly because it is a rivulet easily overlooked. It is not known for big fish. Of course there are other types of books dealing with various aspects of prophecy and eschatology. With all these rivulets and streams of books on prophecy, it may appear that we have little need for another.

QUESTIONS TO BE EXPLORED

There are issues about this prophetic river, however, that have not received sufficient attention. How does the language of prophecy work? What can we discover from prophecies that have already been fulfilled? How were prophecies stated, and how does that compare with the fulfillment? What did the prophets intend the initial audience to understand? How do we determine when a prophet was using a figure of speech? What are people in the twenty-first century to learn from what prophets two thousand and more years ago wrote? What does God really want us to know about the future?

Our field of exploration, then, is biblical prophecy and the related apocalyptic genre. Making our way through this region may mean traveling into uncharted territory. Such is the nature of exploration. New insights usually come from going beyond where others have gone before, rather than from retracing well-worn paths of the past.[3]

Before embarking, you may want to ask about your guide—where is he coming from and what is his agenda? That is a valid question, especially in a field dominated by presuppositions and theological bias. So I will explain. What I offer in this book is a genuine effort to understand biblical prophecy and apocalyptic *biblically*. While it is impossible to read the text of Scripture in a neutral zone, unaffected by culture and theological and hermeneutical moorings, I have intentionally put blinders on.[4] As much as possible my focus has been on the text and its culture rather than on the periphery of what everybody says about the text. The thesis of this book does not stand or fall based on the research of others. I am simply seeking to discover how biblical language functions, how genres differ and how the original hearers would have understood what the prophets said.

GENESIS OF RESEARCH

My interest in prophecy and apocalyptic came about as follows. During graduate school, I read the Jewish apocrypha and pseudepigrapha (the ones identified as such at that time), though not necessarily in comparison with the canonical materials.[5] Later while teaching courses on the culture and history of the New Testament world, I began to note that the apocalyptic material in the book of Daniel uses language in distinctive ways. Two things stood out in my mind. The language in the Jewish apocalypses that I had read earlier was very similar to Daniel's, but more important, the apocalyptic language in Daniel did not seem to line up as precisely as I expected with events that have already been fulfilled. Concurrently, I began to reflect on the language of the book of Revelation. Gradually my interests turned to the hermeneutics of prophecy and apocalyptic. In other words, I did not come into this subject as a theologian seeking to defend a particular form of eschatology. I came as a philologist and historian.

A seminal thought that gave direction to some of my research was the observation (by whom I do not recall) that prophecies in the Bible were generally not understood until after they were fulfilled. I thought that assertion would be important—and relatively easy—to check out. I also had a growing sense that the language of prophecy and apocalyptic was unusual and worthy of closer inspection. My engagement with the genres of the Old Testament increased my awareness of this issue.[6] As the research continued, I began to wonder whether a careful look at prophecy might even mean a paradigm shift in the interpretation of prophecy. Hence this book.

PREPARATORY REMARKS

Before concluding these preparations for the journey, I have a few clarifications. First, about biblical authority. Without apology, this study of prophecy and apocalyptic presumes a high view of Scripture. (As a practical example, long quotations of Scripture are set in italics, while quotations of similar length from extrabiblical sources are set in roman type.) The biblical canon is divine revelation. While I cannot prove that empirically, I make an intelligent choice to operate from that presupposition. But inspiration is a complex issue and must not be treated superficially. For example, the vertical dimension of Scripture must not negate the horizontal dimension: it is both divine *and* human. Even as God incarnate took up residence in human form in a specific place, time and culture, so Scripture itself is incarnational. If not beyond belief, it is at least beyond explanation. How can it be 100 percent divine and 100 percent human at the same time? How could ordinary people fashion literary masterpieces out of their own culture and creativity yet be superintended by the heavenly Spirit? For the human authors, a notion that their words had somehow been dictated from above would have been absurd. At the same time the divine imprimatur is evident from every thought to every word used to express a thought. Impossible? From a purely human perspective, yes, but by the inspiration of the divine Spirit, clearly possible.

This nuanced awareness of biblical authority is important everywhere in Scripture, but especially in the prophetic portions. Evidence abounds for the human activity of the prophets. Yet even with the human element, the divine Word of the Lord is no less authoritative. *Thus saith the Lord.*

Second, about the fulfillment of prophecy. I am focusing on how to interpret, not on what to expect. Though those two questions cannot be separated completely, this book does not attempt to satisfy the common curiosity of how current events fit with biblical prophecy. It is intended, on the other hand, to satisfy a more important curiosity about how to interpret prophecy so that we can make correct decisions about what kind of events *might* fulfill biblical prophecy. The *how* question should be the starting point for everyone anyway.

Third, about limitations. This book is not intended to tell you everything you need to know about prophecy and apocalyptic. Thorough introductions to each genre provide more comprehensive treatment.[7] This book is not intended to comment on all the prophetic portions of the canon of Scripture. Good commentaries can be found that do that. This book is not intended as a complete discussion of eschatology. Theology books take up those questions. However, the conclusions of this book may affect future introductions, commentaries and theologies.

Fourth, about dispensationalism. Though I was schooled in dispensational thought and have been associated with dispensational institutions and denominations, this book does not exist to defend premillennial dispensationalism. Some of my dispensational friends may be disappointed. Nor does it exist to dismantle dispensationalism. Some of my nondispensational friends may be disappointed. My approach has been to set aside theological theories, lest the weighty jargon of the experts encumber my look at the evidence. Surely readers on both sides of the fence (unfortunate term) will recognize ways I have failed. But perhaps both groups of readers will also identify viewpoints they need to rethink.

Fifth, about indecisiveness. This book may seem to pose a lot of questions without answering them satisfactorily. Some readers will find that disheartening. But it is intentional. In my mind one of the problems in the study of prophecy (and perhaps the Bible as a whole) is a tendency to give quick answers rather than to ask reflective questions.[8] Less pontificating and more pondering would be healthier for all of us. Frankly, only after we settle issues of hermeneutics should we begin facing the questions concerning implications for eschatology.

Sixth, about being an explorer. I am not always sure what path I am on or where I belong. While I was in seminary the trail I followed was New Testament and Greek. Then in doctoral work I turned to classical studies, with a passion for anything that would provide backgrounds to the New Testament. I stayed on the path of documentary papyri for several years.[9] Gradually I made my way back to the discipline of New Testament studies. More recently, with my interest in New Testament apocalyptic, it became obvious that I must begin with the Old Testament prophets. Since this book interacts with the newest path in my explorations, I do not claim to be an experienced guide, only a curious explorer. The result is a simple book for simple people honestly asking simple questions about prophecy.

Seventh, about prophecy. In some discussions in this book it will be important to distinguish between prophecy and apocalyptic. In other settings—for the sake of economy of language—the term *prophecy* will be used for both prophecy and apocalyptic.

Our exploration is about ready to begin. If you choose to come along on our forays into the regions of prophecy and apocalyptic, meet down at the river. We will be following it as it meanders toward the west where the sun sets and time stands still.

Acknowledgments

I give credit to many people who have influenced who I am and what I am about. It would be fun to tell their stories and to honor their impact on me as well as on others. Unfortunately, this is not the place for that, especially since the group would be large, including family, teachers, colleagues, students, parishioners and friends. Especially in writing this book I have become indebted to many people, more than can be remembered, leaving debts that cannot be repaid. Readers who were particularly constructive in their criticisms are Dan Reid (IVP), Lee Ryken and Tremper Longman (outside readers), Dick Patterson, John Teevan, Wayne Hannah, Tom Stallter, Dave Plaster and Sam Ochstein. To my student assistant, Dan Kramer, special thanks for the endless hours checking Scripture quotations and references. My greatest treasure is my wonderful wife and family: Cheryl, Jason, Jaron and his wife, Laëtitia. During this book's gestation, they were remarkably patient and willing to help, awaiting a long overdue delivery.

Many of the ideas expressed in this book were formulated in the course of research for papers and articles over the past ten years. Thank you to those who listened and interacted with my developing ideas. The papers and articles are as follows:

"Prediction and Fulfillment in Daniel 8," presented at the Evangelical Theological Society's Annual Meeting, 1992. I traced the relevant historical events and compared them with Daniel's vision.

"Did Daniel See Mussolini?" *Christianity Today*, February 8, 1993. I raised the question whether prophecy was primarily intended "to lay bare the particulars of the future [or] to invade the present."

"Daniel's Apocalyptic Visions: Listener Response to a Literary Form," Evangelical Theological Society's Midwest Regional Meeting, 1993. I examined the issue of orality in the ancient world and how hearers would have understood the imagery of the prophets.

"Hearing the Apocalypse: Illocution and the Function of Apocalyptic," Evangelical Theological Society's Annual Meeting, 1993. I ventured into the illocution of language and ways we may use words that on the surface mean one thing but are really intended to communicate something else. I applied that to apocalyptic and specifically to Revelation 12—14.

"Apocalyptic," coauthored with Marty Abegg, in *Cracking Old Testament Codes*, ed. D. Brent Sandy and Ronald L. Giese Jr. (Nashville: Broadman & Holman, 1995). We presented the distinctive features of the apocalyptic genre and offered guidelines for interpreting apocalyptic.

"An Apology for the Literal Interpretation of Prophecy," Evangelical Theological Society's Annual Meeting, 1995. I examined the fulfillment of the prophecies of the former prophets in 1 and 2 Kings.

"The Language and Imagery of Prophecy," Evangelical Theological Society's Annual Meeting, 1997. I focused on the philosophy of metaphor and the use of metaphoric language in the language of the covenant and the prophets.

"Apocalypse," and "Prophecy, New Testament," in *Dictionary of Biblical Imagery*, ed. Leland Ryken, James C. Wilhoit and Tremper Longman III (Downers Grove, Ill.: InterVarsity Press, 1998).

"'The Prophet That Teaches Lies Is the Tail': Toward a Correct Hermeneutic for the Language of Judgment and Blessing," Evangelical Theological Society's Annual Meeting, 1998. I set forth criteria for determining when a prophet was speaking metaphorically.

"What Does God Want Us to Know About the Future? The Function and Form of Biblical Prophecy," Evangelical Theological Society's Regional Meeting, 1999. I analyzed what Scripture reveals about the intent of prophecy.

"Apocalyptic Imagery in the New Testament," Evangelical Theological Society's Annual Meeting, 1999. I identified twelve thematic features of the apocalyptic genre.

"Apocalyptic: A Suitable Form for Divine Revelation?" Evangelical Theological Society's Regional Meeting, 2000. I addressed the question, "How apocalyptic is the apocalypse?"

"Israel's Future: The Language of Blessing in the Prophets," Evangelical Theological Society's Annual Meeting, 2000. I examined the promises of blessing on agriculture, descendants, a homeland and restoration, and explored the meaning of *forever*.

"Prophetic Imagination and Imagery," Society of Biblical Literature Annual Meeting, 2000. I argued that closer attention needs to be given to the aesthetics and artistry of prophecy if we are to understand the message correctly.

"Interpreting Old Testament Prophetic Language in Matthew: Images and Metaphors," Evangelical Theological Society's Annual Meeting, 2001. I argued against the notion of double fulfillment (bifocal vision) of the Old Testament prophets on the grounds that they generally saw the immediate fulfillment of their prophecies but not the distant fulfillments.

Material from my previous book *Cracking Old Testament Codes*, © 1995 by Broadman and Holman Publishers, is used by permission.

1

WHAT MAKES PROPHECY POWERFUL?

Climb into an eight-person raft for an October trip down the Upper Gauley River in West Virginia, and you will experience power. Millions of gallons of water being released from Summersville Reservoir turn the gorge into a competition between water and rock. The rock wins, and the water alters its course, surging over and around and between boulders and canyon walls. The result is roaring whitewater: massive hydraulics, towering liquid walls, class V rapids—powerful enough to stand your raft straight up in the air, with you and your buddies in it—maybe! Guides prepare rafters for the good and the bad: the rush of adrenaline, the teamwork, the risks. And they need to. Every year the river chews up and spits out hapless victims. But you are there to experience adventure, to behold beauty, to learn respect, to stand in awe, to feel power.

Prophecy is like whitewater, perhaps the most powerful whitewater in Scripture—maybe in all the literature of the world. This is language unmatched in what it beholds and in how it describes the beholden. Words of worship, terror and mercy are unparalleled. Words of beauty, passion and hope are unequalled. Words of adoration, condemnation and salvation are unrivaled.

KODAK MOMENTS

In order to speak to our hearts, the powerful language of prophecy brings God's might and wrath and humankind's sin and doom to life with surrealistic images. It is reality described in unreal ways. Stop and take in the scenery. You will discover four principal subjects that the prophets portray in the language of West Virginia whitewater (see figure 1.1).

The prophets bring four subjects into clearer focus

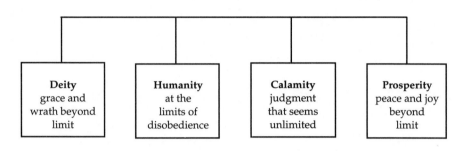

| **Deity**
grace and
wrath beyond
limit | **Humanity**
at the
limits of
disobedience | **Calamity**
judgment
that seems
unlimited | **Prosperity**
peace and joy
beyond
limit |

Figure 1.1. The prophetic focus

Deity. Prophecy beholds God in raw anger—punishing rapids . . . fire
and brimstone. And in soft love—pools of water smooth as glass . . . grace
and peace. It is God at the extreme limit of his attributes. As Isaiah knew
well, to stand too close to the Almighty is to be shaken to the very core (Is
6:4-5). Heavens convulse, mountains crumble, hearts cringe.

Isaiah reports that when God whistles, people come speedily from the
ends of the earth (Is 5:26). His voice thunders and people flee at the sound
of it (Is 33:3). Islands are struck with fear, and the ends of the earth tremble
(Is 41:5). The word of his tongue is a destructive fire. He shakes the nations
in the sieve of destruction (Is 30:27-28). Jeremiah pictures God as a mighty
warrior (Jer 20:11), as a storm swirling down on the heads of the sinful (Jer
23:19), as one who pushes his enemies off cliffs (Jer 51:25). Habakkuk says
that the earth shudders when God shows up: hills collapse, mountains
writhe, sun and moon stand still, and pestilence follows his steps (Hab 3:4-
12). As an advertisement for travel in Manitoba, Canada, says, "If this
doesn't leave you breathless, check your pulse."

God's towering attributes stand out most vividly on the flat landscape
of human helplessness (Is 40:6-31). Nations are but specks of dust on a set
of scales. People are like grasshoppers, potsherds left lying on the ground
(Is 45:9).

Unfortunately, we tend to forget who we are—and more important,
who he is:

Your thinking is perverse!
Should the potter be regarded as the clay?
Should the thing made say about its maker,
"He didn't make me"?
Or should the pottery say about the potter,
"He doesn't understand"? (Is 29:16 NET)

But God is not only about fireworks and sonic booms. He gathers the lambs in his arms and carries them close to his own heart (Is 40:11). He prepares a feast of rich food and a banquet of aged wine for all people (Is 25:6). He bequeaths the most beautiful heritage (Jer 3:19).

Humanity. Prophecy also beholds the naked sinfulness of God's chosen people. They are adulterous, with men thronging to the houses of prostitutes, "well-fed, lusty stallions, each neighing for another man's wife" (Jer 5:7-8). God can put up with no more—he files for divorce (Jer 3:8; cf. 8:10). Like a bride who comes to the wedding but forgot her jewelry—"my people have forgotten me for more days than can even be counted" (Jer 2:32 NET).

My people have committed a double wrong:
they left me, the fountain of life-giving water,
and they have dug cisterns for themselves, cracked cisterns,
which cannot even hold water. (Jer 2:13 NET)

Now why go to Egypt to drink water from the Shihor?
And why go to Assyria to drink water from the River? (Jer 2:18)

"Although you wash yourself with soda
and use an abundance of soap,
the stain of your guilt is still before me,"
declares the Sovereign LORD. (Jer 2:22)

Such idols are like scarecrows in a cucumber field.
They cannot talk.
They have to be carried
because they cannot walk. (Jer 10:5 NET)

Such sinfulness on earth appalls the heavens—they shudder with great horror (Jer 2:12). The creation of the world is undone; it once again becomes without form and void (Jer 4:23; cf. Gen 1:2). Worst of all, God cancels his blessing, love and pity (Jer 16:5-6).

Calamity. If beholding the sinfulness of humanity is not enough to dissuade hearers from joining the parade to destruction, language of impending catastrophe may help. Once having soared with eagles and made nests among the stars (Obad 4), now the disobedient only mumble out of the dust of the ground (Is 29:4). Once having been jars of fine wine, now they are empty, smashed jugs (Jer 48:11-12). Once having eaten from fields rich with produce, now they are dead bodies lying like manure on open fields, like grain that has been cut down but left to rot (Jer 9:22). Once a thriving olive tree laden with beautiful fruit, now they are ablaze with the roar of a firestorm (Jer 11:16). Once a mighty war club, now they are only a burned-out mountain. God's arsenal of weapons of wrath seems to be limitless (Jer 50:25).

> *I will punish them in four different ways. I will have war kill them. I will have dogs drag off their dead bodies. I will have birds and wild beasts devour and destroy their corpses. I will make all the people in all the kingdoms of the world horrified.* (Jer 15:3-4 NET; cf. Jer 16:4)

> *"I will sweep away everything*
> *from the face of the earth,"*
> *declares the* LORD.
> *"I will sweep away both men and animals:*
> *I will sweep away the birds of the air*
> *and the fish of the sea.*
> *The wicked will have only heaps of rubble*
> *when I cut off man from the face of the earth,"*
> *declares the* LORD. (Zeph 1:2-3)

Some of the language of judgment is not so calamitous but is no less vivid. Picture this if you will:

> *I will pull up your skirts over your face*
> *that your shame may be seen.* (Jer 13:26; cf. Is 47:2)

> *No, they have no shame at all;*
> *they do not even know how to blush.* (Jer 8:12)

> *We were with child, we writhed in pain,*
> *but we gave birth to wind.* (Is 26:18)

> *The bed is too short to stretch out on,*
> *the blanket too narrow to wrap around you.* (Is 28:20)

I will put an end to the sounds of joy and gladness, to the glad celebration of brides and grooms in these lands. I will put an end to the sound of people grinding meal. I will put an end to lamps shining in their homes. (Jer 25:10 NET)

"As surely as I live," declares the LORD, "even if you, Jehoachin son of Jehoiakim king of Judah, were a signet ring on my right hand, I would still pull you off." (Jer 22:24)

Prosperity. Prophecy beholds not only calamity but blessed prosperity. The blind will see again. The deaf will hear again (Is 29:18). The sounds of joy and the tambourine will be heard again (Jer 31:4; 33:11). Maidens will dance again, and young men and old as well (Jer 31:4, 13). No one will be without a mate (Is 34:16). The lame will prance like deer (Is 35:6). Livestock will graze freely (Is 32:20). Swords will be made into plowshares (Is 2:4). The moon will shine as bright as the sun, and the sun will become seven times brighter (Is 30:26). Valleys will be lifted up. Mountains and hills will be leveled (Is 40:4). Highways will be built through the wilderness (Is 35:8). Burning sand will become pools of water (Is 35:7; 41:18). Rivers will flow in the desert and on the mountaintops (Is 30:25; 43:20). Trees and flowers will grow in the desert (Is 35:1; 41:19).

As a billboard for God's hatred of sin, prophecy speaks boldly and to the point. Anyone who fails to see the message is terribly near-sighted. And as a sign of God's everlasting love, prophecy speaks tenderly and to the heart. Unfortunately, those who fail to read the billboards advertising God's anger probably miss the signs announcing his love as well. One cannot be understood without the other.

FLASHFLOOD WARNINGS

The perpetual pounding of what the prophets are proclaiming may seem overdone to modern ears, yet the whitewater of the prophets keeps on roaring. God's spokesmen will not give up. Their words crash against the stubbornness of the people again and again. It was as obvious then as now: ordinary and plain language simply was not enough for these prophetic sirens and flashing lights. Flashflood warnings and summons to arms are not announced in unexpressive, humdrum diction. The words of the prophets were poignant and pregnant with meaning, because the subject matter called for the most vivid words possible.

Prophecy was first of all oratory, because the prophets were first of all preachers.[1] In the hearing of crowds and kings they denounced, warned and assured. Not only did the substance of their sermons call for vivid words, the iciness of their audience required burning rhetoric. They needed expressions that would explode in the heads and hearts of their hearers.[2] Isaiah reports, "He made my mouth like a sharpened sword . . . he made me into a polished arrow" (Is 49:2).

While the linguistic elements were the same as for anyone else, the prophets linked words with rhythm, used ordinary words for unordinary ideas (metaphor), gave inanimate objects life (personification), exaggerated to get points across (hyperbole)—all of it resulting in language that was colorful as well as memorable. Though it is from another time and another culture, we still sense some of its power, especially when we hear it rather than just read it.[3] The language is imaginative, etching graphic pictures on our minds. It is conversation, drawing us into dialogue with the prophet. It is invitation—stop and ponder the word-pictures. It is mind-jarring, hope-crushing and heart-rending. It is above all poetic. The prophets were wordsmiths, master carpenters.

> *As men gather abandoned eggs,*
> *so I gathered all the countries;*
> *not one flapped a wing,*
> *or opened its mouth to chirp.* (Is 10:14)

> *Like fluttering birds*
> *pushed from the nest,*
> *so are the women of Moab.* (Is 16:2)

> *You conceive chaff,*
> *you give birth to straw.* (Is 33:11)

> *Though at this time your ropes are slack,*
> *the mast is not secured,*
> *and the sail is unfurled.* (Is 33:23 NET)

> *You heavens above, rain down righteousness.* (Is 45:8)

> *You will drink the milk of nations*
> *and be nursed at royal breasts.* (Is 60:16)[4]

We not only read the prophets, we feel the impact of their bombardment. "The prophet's word is a scream in the night. While the world is at ease and asleep, the prophet feels the blast from heaven."[5] Prophecy needs to be experienced.

STREETS OF GOLD?

For another perspective on the power of prophecy, we need to slow down and think more philosophically. Language originates in humankind's fundamental need to communicate. It is a way to express what humans experience and need to voice. In rudimentary form, words are symbols for the things we want to talk about, such as bodily functions. "My stomach hurts" expresses a human condition. *Stomach* is a symbol that may refer to anywhere in the midsection of the body; *hurts* is a symbol that may refer to any kind of discomfort. But as our knowledge of anatomy and pain increases, these symbols become less and less precise. So as society learns more and more about the world it lives in, language evolves and becomes more sophisticated: vocabulary increases; words become more specific in meanings; grammar develops. "My stomach hurts" might be described more precisely: "An incompetent pyloric sphincter has allowed reflux of biliary acid, resulting in damage and erosion of the gastric mucosal barrier." For most us, now we have gone too far in the other direction with an overly technical description. Nevertheless, language remains a description of what humans experience.[6]

But humans have always been interested in things they have never experienced. If there is life after death, what is it like? We all have attempted to imagine it, but probably all in vain. Sometimes our imaginations run wild. But there is a clear pattern: our ideas about things we have never experienced are largely controlled by things we have experienced. No matter how hard we try, we cannot create the categories of thinking and expression necessary to describe what we have never experienced (see figure 1.2). We long to know about life after death, so we are fascinated by near-death experiences. But do we really know what the experience of moving from this world into the next is like? Likewise, we long to know about the future and are fascinated by a genre of literature called science fiction. But by the term we use to describe it, we admit that we do not expect the fictions to be true.

God's dilemma. When God sat down to write us a letter and to answer a few of our questions, he had a decision to make. How would he communicate to a population of billions that would inhabit this planet? After all, these billions *babel* in thousands of different languages and cultures. When you

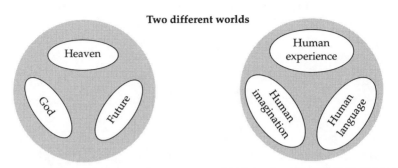

Figure 1.2. Humanity's dilemma

get right down to it, God's choices were limited. Perhaps he could create a new international language and culture that everyone would understand. But we assume he made the best choice: to use already existing languages developed by humans. We are not sure why he chose Hebrew and Aramaic and Greek—they are not superior languages—nor why he chose Palestine—the cultures of that region do not seem especially superior (neither in the past nor currently). However, those particular cultures and languages preserved for all humanity the eternity of the divine Word. For the rest of the world's population, translations, commentaries and other resources will have to suffice--except for those few who go to great effort to learn the cultures and languages of Palestine two to four thousand years ago.[7]

But the other issue God faced was how to describe heavenly concepts in human language.[8] Earthbound creatures have language only to describe things we have experienced or fancied. Certainly our attempts to imagine what heaven is like would be fiction. Since we do not have the categories to describe the spirit world that God inhabits, and since his thoughts are not our thoughts (Is 55:8-9), God's choices were limited. Again we assume he made the best choice: to use already existing language developed by humans. Are human means of communication generally effective? Yes. Are they perfect? No.[9] So would we not conclude that the descriptions of God and heaven and the future in human language have inherent limitations?

The majority of the Bible is in the genre of narrative—stories of people's experiences through which aspects of God's character are revealed little by little. God bridges the chasm between heaven and earth, shows up from time to time, works behind the scenes most of the time—and all the while people are discovering who God is and what he is like.

Second to narrative, as far as quantity goes, is the genre of prophecy. But prophecy is faced with a bigger challenge: to reveal God more directly, to proclaim the attributes of deity, to declare the agenda of eternity, to divulge the passions of the Trinity, and to do that with only the imperfect language of humanity. People must come to fear God and the extent of his wrath. People must come to appreciate God and the extent of his love. People must come to understand God and the otherness of his heavenly realm. The question was how to do that with mere human language.

"Asked to explain a difficult *étude*, Schumann sat down and played it a second time."[10] Performance was better than explanation.

Prophecy's dilemma. In a sense, prophecy was assigned an impossible task. With language limited to what we have experienced, how can God be described?[11] God is the only thing in the universe like himself, and nothing really compares to him. And how can heaven be described? We think only in the material realm, surrounded by tangible objects, but heaven is a place of spirits. And how can the future be described? Changes that will occur in the future are impossible to imagine in the present. Before there was electricity, could people have conceived of televisions and microwaves? Before there were computers, could people have conceived of cyberspace and computer viruses? Before there were test tubes and laboratories, could people have conceived of germ warfare?

Perhaps now it is clearer why prophecy faced a huge challenge. And we can see why the language of prophecy goes out of its way to communicate with power. How does it do it? The short answer is, by means of the creative use of language. It is a performance. A long answer will be developed in the chapters that follow. The result is a very heavenly revelation in very earthly language. "Since poetry is our best human model of intricately rich communication, not only solemn, weighty, and forceful but also densely woven with complex internal connections, meanings, and implications, it makes sense that divine speech should be represented in poetry."[12]

Two radically different worlds find a meeting ground in the words of the prophets. These were human authors that surprise us as literary geniuses and at the same time thrill us as inspired geniuses. "Above all, you do well if you recognize this: no prophecy of Scripture ever comes about by the prophet's own imagination, for no prophecy was ever borne of human impulse; rather, men carried along by the Holy Spirit spoke from God" (2 Pet 1:20-21 NET).

Under divine empowerment, the prophets created metaphors and similes from their world to let us experience what the world of God and heaven is like—as best they could. But Isaiah and Jeremiah and Ezekiel and John could do only so much with the words and categories of earthlings. Will we walk streets of gold? We can be sure heavenly existence is something like what they describe, but if we think it is exactly what they describe, we will have lowered the spirit world of God and heaven to the physical world that we have experienced.

ONE REWARD OR MANY REWARDS?

A significant example of the extensive power of prophetic language is found in the pronouncements to the seven churches in Asia Minor recorded in Revelation 2—3. The language sounds similar to that of the Old Testament prophets.[13] Note a selection of blessing phrases:

> *To those who overcome, I will give the right to eat from the tree of life, which is in the paradise of God. I will give you the crown of life. I will give you some of the hidden manna. I will give you a white stone with a new name written on it, known only to him who receives it. To those who overcome and do my will to the end, I will give authority over the nations. I will also give you the morning star. Those who overcome will be dressed in white. I will make you a pillar in the temple of my God. Never again will you leave it. I will write on you the name of my God and the name of the city of my God, the new Jerusalem, which is coming down out of heaven from my God. I will write on you my new name. To those who overcome, I will give the right to sit with me on my throne.*

The concept of rewards—an important form of motivation in Jewish and Greco-Roman society—runs through the whole of Scripture (from Gen 15:1 to Rev 22:12). Though rewards for Christians were generally spiritual rather than tangible, in some instances the reward offered was a crown: of righteousness, of life, of glory (2 Tim 4:8; Jas 1:12; 1 Pet 5:4; cf. Is 61:3). But even there the genitive case ("of") may designate apposition, suggesting that these rewards also were spiritual: not actual crowns but a crowning with spiritual blessings of righteousness, life and glory.[14] Whatever the intent of *crowns*, the opportunity to receive rewards and, conversely, the fear of not receiving them were effective means of encouragement for holy and faithful living.

Are these for real? In the seven letters to the churches, the way the rewards are described is unexpectedly specific and extravagant. What are
readers supposed to conclude about this treasure room of promises? Will
overcomers have the privilege of eating some Garden of Eden fruit from
the tree of life just as Adam and Eve did? Will they have the privilege of
eating some Sinai desert manna as Moses and the Israelites did—which,
by the way, has been hidden away for thousands of years?[15] Will each overcomer receive a crown, a white stone and a personal star? Will there be a
monumental colonnade of overcomers, each a pillar on the eschatological
temple porch? Will each rule a nation? Will they all sit alongside Jesus on
his eternal throne?[16]

Or is each of these images symbolic? Instead of real manna or white
stones or personal stars, each of these objects may actually designate
something else. But then we want to know what each object symbolizes.
For example, does the white stone refer to a courtroom scene where God
declares faithful followers innocent? That idea is based on the practice of
Roman jury members' casting votes of acquittal with white stones versus
black stones for votes of guilt. Or does the white stone refer to an invitation for faithful followers to the banquet of all banquets? That suggestion
is based on the custom of using white stones as admission tickets for
grand banquets. Or does the white stone suggest the privileged role of
faithful followers as priests? That suggestion is based on the precious
stones in the breastplate of the high priest's attire. This list could go on,
for at least twelve different suggestions have been offered for the meaning of the white stone.[17] But the next phrase needs to be researched as
well—what is the new name written on the stone? And the next phrase
needs to be researched too—why is it known only to him who receives
it? And so on.

While this may seem a tedious and uncertain way to interpret prophecy,
no one said understanding a document written two thousand years ago in
an unfamiliar genre would be simple. It definitely makes entering into the
culture of the people living in Asia Minor in John's day indispensable. In
that regard, an understanding of the literary conventions current then may
suggest a solution. From the study of imagery we observe that prophetic
language freely uses a variety of images to refer to the same thing.[18] In the
case of the rewards of Revelation 2—3, perhaps rather than disassembling
each reward piece by piece to determine its significance, we should keep

them whole and look at their referent collectively rather than individually.

Toward a solution. The reasoning goes like this. The finish line that the universe longs for and the book of Revelation is moving toward is God's future and full presence with the whole of his creation.[19] As it was in the beginning. The anticipation for that cosmic conclusion occurs throughout John's writings, but the climax is expressed by a loud voice from the throne at the end of his last book: "Now the dwelling of God is with men, and he will live with them. They will be his people, and God himself will be with them and be their God" (Rev 21:3). The reality of deity and humanity in perfect unity is underscored in numerous ways throughout the book. It is evident in the son of man standing among the lampstands, which are symbols of the churches. It is evident in the opening of the door to heaven and the invitation for John to "come up here." It is evident in the multitudes representing every nation, singing and serving before God's throne. It is evident in the new Jerusalem prepared as a bride for her husband. It is evident in the Lamb's providing the only light necessary for the holy city. It is evident in the river of life flowing from the throne of God. In John's Gospel Jesus looked ahead to this glorious future before his departure: "And if I go and prepare a place for you, I will come back and take you to be with me that you also may be where I am" (Jn 14:3). "Father, I want those you have given me to be with me where I am" (Jn 17:24).

Since that is where the book of Revelation and the consummation of time are headed, we now have a possible map for understanding the rewards for overcomers. Though expressed in different words, the reward is to experience God's presence in all its fullness (see figure 1.3). For example,

Various images are used to visualize one reward

- Tree of life
- Crown of life
- White stone
- Authority over the nations
- Morning star
- Dressed in white
- Pillar in God's temple
- Name of God
- Name of Jerusalem
- Sit on God's throne

The **reward** is deity and humanity in perfect unity—

Now the dwelling of God is with man.
—Rev 21:3

Figure 1.3. The reward for overcomers

the tree of life recalls the unique closeness Adam and Eve had with God in the Garden. Overcomers will have that same kind of closeness with God. The manna from heaven was God's special provision, and in eating what God rained down from heaven, the people experienced God's presence.[20] Overcomers will have that same kind of closeness with God. To become a pillar in the temple of God is to be in God's presence forever. Overcomers will experience an everlasting oneness with God. So each reward is a different way to visualize the same basic truth. "He who overcomes will inherit all this, and I will be his God and he will be my son" (Rev 21:7).

In line with this thesis, of the twelve options for the significance of the white stone, there is a good possibility: white stones were worn as amulets to represent divine presence. That matches perfectly the author's primary intent of highlighting oneness with God.[21] In turn, this supports the premise that the essential idea of the different rewards was to depict in graphic terms one overall reward: how wonderful the relationship with God will be in the final state.

This proposal for understanding the rewards for overcomers may seem helpful, but it is deficient. The approach has been cerebral almost to the exclusion of the emotional. But prophecy speaks to the heart as much as the head. If we think that by objectifying and exegeting every aspect of prophecy we can grasp the intent, we will have ignored one of the most important features of prophecy. The variety of expressions of future rewards allow us to *preexperience* a small part of what being in God's presence will be like. As an old hymn puts it, "O that will be glory for me!"

As evident from Revelation 2—3, prophetic language communicates with bright lights and a full range of colors. Its subject is photogenic, and images of the subject appear on a large screen with an infinite number of pixels. To read prophecy correctly means to stand in awe of the aesthetics of prophetic artistry and to catch a vision of what heaven will be like.

CONCLUSION

What makes prophecy powerful? Imagine a twentysomething American student describing a whitewater rafting experience to a seventysomething Bedouin patriarch. The American has something exhilarating to tell about, but how can she express it?

The Bedouin ekes out an existence in a water-deprived desert, has barely seen rain, let alone a river, and has no framework for conceiving of millions of gallons of water being released at the base of a huge dam. The Bedouin cannot understand concepts like whitewater, the deafening roar of crashing water, hydraulics and walls of water. He is also baffled by the notion of pumping air inside of cloth, with men (and women!) floating in a boat made of such cloth. He is puzzled by the possibility of people having the leisure or desire to do such a thing.

For the American to communicate with this man of sand—assuming language is not a barrier—she must use things from a Bedouin's world and conjure up images that will let him experience a very different world. The combination of something exciting to describe and something impossible to describe will result in something like the language of prophecy. The power is in what it beholds and in how it describes the beholden.

WHAT MAKES PROPHECY PROBLEMATIC?

T he words of astronaut Jim Lovell calmly radioed from Apollo 13 have been immortalized as a statement of the human condition: "Houston, we have a problem." For millions listening in as the drama unfolded, the question was whether the problem of the loss of oxygen could be solved. Would the three astronauts make it back to planet earth in their little life-boat in space—the lunar landing module—or would the demons of space prevail?

Problems were not new to NASA, nor have they been eliminated. It is a high-tech endeavor with little margin for error. Nor are problems new to the church. They span nearly two thousand years of our history.[1] It is a holy endeavor with uncertainty about the margin for error.

Some problems for the church have been troublesome (the Judaizers), some life-threatening (persecution), some near-disasters (lapses into worldliness). Others have been turning points (the Diet of Worms).[2] Some seem to stay around forever (sovereignty versus free will). Others have largely been solved. For example, regarding the exact nature of Christ's deity, the church struggled for three centuries.[3] But the councils and creeds helped to reach a consensus. And the Trinity has been a defining doctrine of orthodox Christianity ever since.[4] Unfortunately, it took many more centuries for the church to agree that slavery was a plague to society.

But prophecy? Have we reached a consensus yet? Hardly, unless we only consider basic concepts.[5] The truth is, prophecy has inflamed more than its fair share of problems for the church—whether among casual readers or among professional scholars—and has put the church and its members at risk. One risk is disobedience, since there is disregard for clarion calls to unity (Jn 17:20-23; Eph 4:3-6). A second is disbelief, since our unity is supposed to produce belief. A third is discredit, since numerous claims about predictions soon to be fulfilled have proved wrong. A fourth is disinterest, since people have become disenchanted with a subject so confusing. Perhaps we ought to radio our own distress call: *Heaven, we have a problem!*

Why is prophecy a closed book, with people saying, "I read it because it's in the Bible, but I don't understand what I'm reading"? Why do seminarians find the book of Revelation intimidating? Why is prophecy subject to disagreement? Why do churches take sides and divide over eschatology? Why do scholars with similar methods of interpretation fail to agree about significant aspects of prophecy? If anything, in the last one hundred years the haze of confusion hanging over prophecy has become heavier. We long for rays of hope that indicate the fog might be lifting.[6]

So where does the problem lie? Is prophecy itself the problem? Perhaps it is the imagery, language of judgment and visions. Or is the nature of human interpretation the problem? Perhaps it is distance from the world of prophecy, doubt about how to understand prophecy and differences in theological assumptions. The question is, can we do anything to shed light on the apparent problem of prophecy?

PROBLEM 1: PREDICTIVE OR POETIC?

Most prophecy is written in poetic verse.[7] That raises immediate questions: how is poetry different from prose, and how should poetic prophecy be interpreted? Is poetry in the service of prophecy as full of figures of speech as is typical of poetry? If the answer is yes, that creates problems for the reader who expects prophecy to throw the window on the future wide open (see figure 2.1). It became evident in the preceding chapter that prophecy abounds with extreme language: "I will make their widows more numerous than the sand of the sea" (Jer 15:8). The question then becomes, are there some ways that poetic prophecy lays out details of future events? But there is even a more basic problem: it is not always clear what portions of Scripture are predictive. Psalm 22 is a helpful place to begin because it highlights several problems.

Peering through the window of poetry into the future

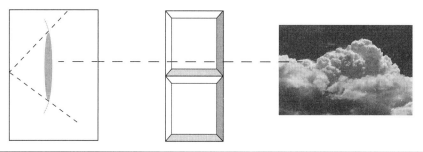

Figure 2.1. The window of poetry

The first problem: is this psalm prophetic? In the context of other laments, it seems that the psalmist was simply expressing his personal tragedy in poetic language. The circumstances were so bad that he felt as if his heart had become softened wax, as if his bones were all out of joint, as if his tongue were sticking to the roof of his completely dry mouth. But in the context of messianic prophecies, the apostle John saw more than a personal lament in Psalm 22. He considered events surrounding Jesus' death to be specific fulfillment of phrases from this prayer of anguish (Jn 19:24; cf. Jn 19:28). And the author of the book of Hebrews quotes Psalm 22:22 as the words of Jesus: "I will declare your name to my brothers; in the presence of the congregation I will sing your praises" (Heb 2:12). Consequently, some argue that Psalm 22 was prophetic, while others have good reason to think that prophecy was not the author's intent at all.[8] Of course this is not the only psalm that creates doubt about whether it is predictive.[9] Furthermore, the prophets themselves may sound like psalmists in some expressions of God's blessings: "He will be like a tree planted by the water that sends out its roots by the stream" (Jer 17:8).

The second problem is the significance of the sobering line that Jesus quoted on the cross—"My God, my God, why have you forsaken me?" (Mt 27:46). By quoting the first line of the psalm, was Jesus identifying with the psalmist's agony and inviting hearers to recall the words of the psalm in light of his suffering?[10] Or was he identifying with the psalmist's faith in the God who will give victory in spite of adversity (cf. Ps 22:22-31)?[11] Or was he making a theological statement about God forsaking God? For some Christians the latter has been a conundrum, so it is worth noting that Jesus may not have intended such a severe idea.

The third problem is the most important one for our purposes. Note the variety of poetic ways the psalmist describes the adversity in his life:

Many bulls surround me;
  strong bulls of Bashan encircle me.
Roaring lions tearing their prey
  open their mouths wide against me.
I am poured out like water,
  and all my bones are out of joint.
My heart has turned to wax;
  it has melted away within me.
My strength is dried up like a potsherd,
  and my tongue sticks to the roof of my mouth;
  you lay me in the dust of death.
Dogs have surrounded me;
  a band of evil men has encircled me,
  they have pierced my hands and my feet.
I can count all my bones;
  people stare and gloat over me.
They divide my garments among them
  and cast lots for my clothing. . . .

Deliver my life from the sword,
  my precious life from the power of the dogs.
Rescue me from the mouth of lions;
  save me from the horns of the wild oxen. (Ps 22:12-18, 20-21)

From a postcross perspective we reflect back on those words and see striking phrases connected with our Lord's passion. Soldiers hammered spikes through his hands and feet.[12] They gambled for his garments.

A precross perspective. Suppose we were told in advance that this psalm would prefigure Jesus' suffering. Hundreds of years or a few decades before Jesus was executed—or even one year before—could we have anticipated which of the phrases would apply to his death?

Now Psalm 22 might look a little different. What about "all my bones are out of joint"?[13] Is that the result of torture? What about "my heart has turned to wax"? Is that a heart attack? Would we have been able to determine in advance how Jesus would die?

Actually, given the wording of Psalm 22, we might have concluded something very different: that Jesus would be subjected to another form of

Roman execution—to be thrown to wild animals in a coliseum. "Roaring lions . . . open their mouths against me, . . . dogs have surrounded me; a band of evil men has encircled me, . . . save me from the horns of the wild oxen."

From the language of Psalm 22, it would have been chancy to anticipate how the Messiah would die and which of the images would apply. But perhaps an even more important question is at stake: would it have been clear to us from Old Testament prophecy that the Messiah would have to die? For the contemporaries of Jesus, even that was lost in the haze.[14]

So what makes prophecy problematic? There are two related problems. First, prophecy may be poetic, and by its very nature poetry is a performance rather than a series of propositions.[15] It is the music of literature. This inherent and enriching ambiguity of poetry limits our ability to interpret it with scientific precision. Second, poetry may not be prophetic. The intent of Psalm 22 was probably not prediction. The psalmist's point was that in the midst of the worst difficulties he could sing a hymn of praise to God (Ps 22:22-31). If Psalm 22 were predictive in some sense, we would not have been successful in determining in advance how it would be fulfilled.

In our culture when someone says, "He beat his opponent to a pulp," we need to know more about the situation to determine the meaning of those words. And when the psalmist writes, "I am in the midst of lions; I lie among ravenous beasts" (Ps 57:4), we may not know to what extent he is describing adversity precisely or poetically. Perhaps we do not need to know. In the case of Psalms 22 and 57, the point is that no matter what the circumstances are, we can find our ultimate refuge in God.

PROBLEM 2: LITERAL OR FIGURATIVE?

Common to human speech are phrases like "set the stage," "get it out on the table," "between a rock and a hard place," "a shot in the dark," "upset the fruit basket," "pave the way," "put your best foot forward," "up your alley," "be a burr under the saddle"—the list could go on for miles! For some phrases the meaning is almost always figurative: "off the cuff," "start from scratch," "beat around the bush," "live high on the hog," "the straw that broke the camel's back." For others the context must reveal whether the meaning is literal or figurative: "a loaded gun," "hit the fan," "slip through the cracks," "on the other side of the coin," "new kid on the block," "turn upside down." We draw from a repertoire of such phrases for several reasons: to be creative, to gain attention and to give a visual sense to what we want to communicate.

Speakers and authors commonly craft their own metaphors: *In the semi-darkness of despair, a flood engulfs me, waves of doubt beat on the shore of my mind. The earth slips from beneath my feet, I float aimlessly in the mire of loneliness. Will tomorrow's dawn again be shadowed by sorrow?*

Examples of biblical figures of speech. The biblical authors were no less interested or adept in using metaphors.[16] Though not as familiar to our ears—because they come from a different time and place—they appear all through the prophetic literature:

- "I will sweep her with the broom of destruction" (Is 14:23).
- "Your neck muscles are like iron and your forehead like bronze" (Is 48:4 NET).
- "He made me into a polished arrow and concealed me in his quiver" (Is 49:2).
- "Your sun will never set again" (Is 60:20).
- "Such people are smoke in my nostrils" (Is 65:5).
- "Circumcise yourselves to the LORD, circumcise your hearts" (Jer 4:4).
- "Egypt will run away, hissing like a snake" (Jer 46:22 NET).
- "In his winepress the Lord has trampled the Virgin Daughter of Judah" (Lam 1:15).
- "My heart is poured out on the ground" (Lam 2:11).
- "He has broken my teeth with gravel" (Lam 3:16).

In these examples it seems obvious that the intended meaning is figurative.

In other examples, however, it is not always obvious when the meaning is figurative:

- "Herds of camels will cover your land" (Is 60:6).
- "I will lead them beside streams of water on a level path where they will not stumble" (Jer 31:9).
- "Look! An eagle is swooping down, spreading its wings over Moab" (Jer 48:40).
- "The sea will rise over Babylon; its roaring waves will cover her" (Jer 51:42).
- "In days to come Jacob will take root, Israel will bud and blossom and fill all the world with fruit" (Is 27:6).
- "I will destroy your mother" (Hos 4:5).

While those may all be metaphoric, certainly everything in the prophets is not:

- "I will hand all Judah over to the king of Babylon" (Jer 20:4).
- "My people will go into exile" (Is 5:13).
- "The LORD will call you back" (Is 54:6).
- "A remnant will return" (Is 10:21).
- "Your people will rebuild the ancient ruins" (Is 58:12).
- "The virgin will be with child and will give birth to a son" (Is 7:14).

Our problem, then, is determining when the prophet is being literal or figurative. It is no small problem. Even the words we use to refer to the issue can create problems. *Literal* may be used to designate the opposite of *figurative*. In a very different sense, it may designate the opposite of *historical* (or *actual*).[17] Yet between these two senses are graduated steps. For example:

> *They will beat their swords into plowshares*
> *and their spears into pruning hooks.*
> *Nation will not take up sword against nation,*
> *nor will they train for war anymore.* (Is 2:4 = Mic 4:3; cf. Joel 3:10)

Degrees of literalness. These words could be understood to say that each person who has a sword or a spear will reshape it by pounding it into a plow or pruning hook (good luck!). That would be a very strict literalness. Or a reader may conclude that "beat" refers to going to a blacksmith who will use fire to soften the iron before refashioning it. Having a blacksmith do it would be a little less literal. Another step away from strict literalness would be for those who have any instrument of aggression to transform it, by whatever means necessary, into an instrument of agriculture. The statement is still literal, though the specific words of the text are pointing to a meaning beyond the surface meanings of the words. Or if we take the author to be saying that political peace will be achieved between all nations—or even simply that God will restore order on the earth—the figurative meaning may be predominant, but all literalness has not been lost. Only when we reach the point of denying that anything will happen as a result of these words have we moved completely away from literal meaning. At that point to be nonliteral would mean to be nonhistorical (nonactual). In other words, the literal or figurative interpretation of Scripture is not a simple black-or-white issue.

Since the Enlightenment and the resulting tendency of some scholars to challenge the literalness of the Bible in the historical sense, many Christians have defended the literal meaning of Scripture. The intent is not to deny that Scripture may be figurative but to affirm that *where it intends to be,* it is historically true. Parables, for example, are not intended to be historically true. Unfortunately, the uses of the word *literal* become confusing, in the minds of both those who make pronouncements and those who hear the pronouncements.[18] For the purposes of this book, it is not a matter of literal opposite the historical sense but literal opposite the figurative sense and the degrees away from the surface meaning. However, because *literal* continues to be a misleading term, substitute terms will be preferred.[19]

All that is to say that readers of prophecy need to be prepared for the picturesque properties of the language (see figure 2.2).[20] The frequency of language that may be figurative raises the question whether metaphor is the rule or the exception. One thing is clear: not only were authors intentional about *what* they said, they were intentional about *how* they said

God's sword

The word of the LORD came to me: "Son of man, prophesy and say, 'This is what the Lord says:

"'A sword, a sword,
sharpened and polished—
sharpened for the slaughter,
polished to flash like lightning!

"'Shall we rejoice in the scepter of my son Judah? The sword despises every such stick.' . . .

"O sword, slash to the right, then to the left,
wherever your blade is turned.
I too will strike my hands together,
and my wrath will subside.
I the LORD have spoken."

The word of the LORD came to me: "Son of man, mark out two roads for the sword of the king of Babylon to take, both starting from the same country. Make a signpost where the road branches off to the city. Mark out one road for the sword to come against Rabbah of the Ammonites and another against Judah and fortified Jerusalem."

Ezekiel 21:8-10, 16-20

Figure 2.2. The picturesque language of prophecy

what they said. Rather than being straightforward or superficial, prophets spoke in terms that called hearers to reflect on the meaning of their statements.

This is a problem facing all interpreters. We often cannot be sure what the prophets meant by what they said—that is, when the surface meaning of the words are the intended meaning and when the intended meaning is one or more steps away from that surface meaning.

So what makes prophecy problematic? Actually, it would be less of a problem if we could determine when a prophet was speaking figuratively, if we knew when to take the words at face value.

In our culture, if someone says, "It was a crushing blow," it may refer to someone's getting hit in the head by a baseball bat, resulting in a concussion or even worse. It may refer to a boxing match's knockdown or knockout. It may refer to any of a variety of physical hits, with varying degrees of effect on the body. We might also refer to a homerun in baseball as "crushing" the ball. But "a crushing blow" may have nothing to do with anything physical. It can refer to a disappointment or to any of a variety of forms of adversity. The point is that words, phrases and sentences with widely used literal meanings may take on figurative meanings, which may end up being used just as widely.

PROBLEM 3: EXACT OR EMOTIVE?

Most prophecy is full of emotion, because the prophets are addressing a desperate situation. If the chosen people insist on continuing in their idolatry, the supreme God will pour out the terror of his wrath. So the prophets speak with great urgency to call the people to repentance. The question is whether emotional language is necessarily exact language. "I've told you a million times" is not exact, but it conveys a powerful message. The hyperbole gets the point across better than an exact figure of the number of times I told you. Of course sometimes an emotional statement can be exact, but the pattern is that the stronger the emotion, the more likelihood of inexactness. Hyperboles, in effect, stretch the truth in order to increase the impact of the words. "The prophets' statements [may be] grossly inaccurate. Yet their concern is not with the facts, but with the meaning of the facts. . . . What seems to be exaggeration is often only deeper penetration."[21]

Examples from the language of judgment underscore this point. Frustrated beyond measure with the apostasy of his people, God speaks:

> *Therefore this is what the Sovereign* LORD *says: My anger and my wrath will be*
> *poured out on this place, on man and beast, on the trees of the field and on the fruit*
> *of the ground, and it will burn and not be quenched.* (Jer 7:20)[22]

> *Through your own fault you will lose*
>   *the inheritance I gave you.*
> *I will enslave you to your enemies*
>   *in a land you do not know,*
> *for you have kindled my anger,*
>   *and it will burn forever.* (Jer 17:4)

> *I will completely destroy them and make them an object of horror and scorn, and an*
> *everlasting ruin.* (Jer 25:9)

> *The fortress will be abandoned,*
>   *the noisy city deserted;*
> *citadel and watchtower will become a wasteland forever.* (Is 32:14)[23]

Can "forever" be emotive? The emotion of the sovereign God shows
through clearly. But there is a problem: what about the words *forever* and *ev-*
erlasting? True, God took away the inheritance of the Israelites and sent them
into captivity, and Jerusalem lay in ruins. But *forever, everlasting?*[24] That suggests that God would never repent of his anger or have mercy on his chosen
people again. But of course God promised that his vengeance would not last
forever—that a restoration would occur. "Your people will rebuild the ancient ruins and will raise up the age-old foundations" (Is 58:12).

There are many other examples of judgment expressed as never-ending. Nathan the prophet confronted David about his sin with Bathsheba
and announced the consequences: "Now, therefore, the sword will never
depart from your house, because you despised me and took the wife of
Uriah the Hittite to be your own" (2 Sam 12:10). This problem may make
some of us feel that we are in quicksand: why are the words *forever* and *ev-*
erlasting in the text if it will not be forever and everlasting? Note that we
are not questioning the truthfulness of the prophets but simply seeking to
understand the intent of their words. (For further discussion of *forever*, see
pp. 45-46, 98-101.)

There are other examples where a prophet's intent may be to express
emotion more than exactness, to speak with poetic license in order to shock
listeners. When Jeremiah thought about the hopelessness of his role as a

prophet, he cursed the day he was born. He cursed the newsbearer of his birth. He regretted that he was not killed while yet in the womb. He even wished that his mother not be blessed and that the newsbearer live with constant trouble (Jer 20:14-18). When God summarized his frustration with the sinfulness of his people, he said there was nothing in the entire history of Israel and Judah but what provoked him to anger (Jer 32:30-31).

Reflecting on the way his people had been unfaithful to him, God warned that they could not even trust each other—that every brother was a deceiver and every friend a slanderer and liar (Jer 9:4-5; cf. Jer 6:12; 8:10). When emphasizing the odds his people would face when confronted with the armies of Babylon, the Lord said that even if every enemy soldier were to lie mortally wounded in his tent, Babylon would still be able to conquer Jerusalem (Jer 37:10).[25] When the defeat of Judah at the hands of the Babylonians was imminent, the Lord announced that he would take vengeance on all the nations where his people were scattered and proceed to destroy those nations completely (Jer 30:11; 46:28). Each example in this paragraph constitutes a potential problem: do the words really mean what they appear to indicate on the surface (see figure 2.3), or are they examples of hyperbole designed to convey intense emotion?

Hyperbole in other contexts. Hyperbole is not unique to the prophets. Regarding the number of Israelites poised to enter the land of Canaan, we read, "Today you are as many as the stars in the sky" (Deut 1:10). Regarding Canaan: "The cities are large, with walls up to the sky" (Deut 1:28). The combined forces of the armies that Joshua faced were "as numerous as the sand on the seashore" (Josh 11:4). Among seven hundred left-handed soldiers, "each . . . could sling a stone at a hair and not miss" (Judg 20:16).

Surface meanings may not be correct meanings

metaphor . . . don't upset the apple cart
beneath the surface . . . *don't stir up trouble*

metaphor . . . my dogs are barking
beneath the surface . . . *my feet are tired*

metaphor . . . you have lived as a prostitute with many lovers (Jer 3:1)
beneath the surface . . . *you are full of idolatry*

Figure 2.3. Metaphor and meaning

When people played flutes and rejoiced, "the ground shook with the sound" (1 Kings 1:40). Waves in a storm "mounted up to the heavens and went down to the depths" (Ps 107:26).

So what makes prophecy problematic? Actually it would be less of a problem if we always knew when the prophets were speaking with emotion more than exactness, if we knew when they were speaking figuratively, if we knew when they were using hyperbole.

In regard to the word *forever* in the context of judgment, two examples of poetry that are clearly hyperbolic should be noted. The psalmist exposes his feelings in a moment of deep dejection:

> *Why have you rejected us forever, O God?*
> *Why does your anger smolder against the sheep of your pasture? . . .*
> *Turn your steps toward these everlasting ruins,*
> *all this destruction the enemy has brought on the sanctuary.* (Ps 74:1, 3)

> *And Jonah reflects on his seemingly unending entombment in the large fish:*
> *To the roots of the mountains I sank down;*
> *the earth beneath barred me in forever.* (Jon 2:6)

In our culture, when someone says, "I'm going to pound you to smithereens," we can be pretty sure those words reflect deep emotion. When we use the word *smithereens*, chances are we do not know the dictionary definition. But that is immaterial to the meaning of the sentence. Likewise when a prophet records these words, "I will sweep away everything from the face of the earth, . . . both men and animals . . . the birds of the air and the fish of the sea" (Zeph 1:2-3), we do not know to what extent he is speaking with deep emotion or with exactness.

PROBLEM 4: CONDITIONAL OR UNCONDITIONAL?

A related problem of prophecy, but with a different solution, is the question of God's promised blessings. The covenant promises are lavish in what they assure the chosen people: agricultural prosperity, a homeland, descendants, influence. On the other hand, Jeremiah was commissioned to warn the people of Judah about the coming disaster of the Babylonian invasion. His words are visual and startling. "A lion has come out of his lair; a destroyer of nations has set out. He has left his place to lay waste your land" (Jer 4:7). It would be an all-encompassing catastrophe, for God could take no more of the people's idolatry. "I will destroy them with the sword, famine and plague" (Jer 14:12).

This kind of talk made Jeremiah a very unpopular prophet. His message was rejected, his body beaten, and his life threatened—and with good reason. He was suspected of being a tool of the enemy: he appeared to be stirring up discouragement among the people. What the other prophets of his day were saying about God's protection seemed to make more sense. Of course Jeremiah considered them false prophets.

One thing that was not in Jeremiah's favor: he had been beating his drum of doom for years, and nothing had happened yet. Also not in Jeremiah's favor: had not God made some wonderful promises about the permanence of his chosen people in the land?

Covenant promises. As far back as the Abrahamic covenant, God announced that the land would belong to Abraham's descendants forever: "The whole land of Canaan, where you are now an alien, I will give as an everlasting possession to you and your descendants after you" (Gen 17:8). Likewise in the Mosaic covenant God offered his people peace and prosperity in the land (Lev 26:6). "For the LORD your God is a merciful God; he will not abandon or destroy you or forget the covenant with your forefathers, which he confirmed to them by oath" (Deut 4:31).

In the Davidic covenant God promised, "Now I will make your name great, like the names of the greatest men of the earth. And I will provide a place for my people Israel and will plant them so that they can have a home of their own and no longer be disturbed. Wicked people will not oppress them anymore. . . . Your house and your kingdom will endure forever before me; your throne will be established forever" (2 Sam 7:9-10, 16; 1 Chron 17:8-9). That theme was reiterated regarding Solomon: "But you will have a son who will be a man of peace and rest, and I will give him rest from all his enemies on every side. His name will be Solomon, and I will grant Israel peace and quiet during his reign. He is the one who will build a house for my Name. He will be my son, and I will be his father. And I will establish the throne of his kingdom over Israel forever" (1 Chron 22:9-10). God spoke through the prophet Ahijah: "I will give one tribe to his son so that David my servant may always have a lamp before me in Jerusalem, the city where I chose to put my Name" (1 Kings 11:36).

So were the words of Jeremiah about the coming destruction out of sync with the rest of prophecy? Especially for people blind to their own disobedience, the words *everlasting, always, forever* made them think that they were safe in the land.

For the people of Judah, in particular, it was certainly more understandable that over a century earlier God had allowed the northern kingdom to be leveled by the Assyrians. During the two hundred years of the northern kingdom's history, apostasy to Canaanite religion was rampant. Furthermore, there were nine separate dynasties that ruled in Samaria. But the southern kingdom was different. Joshua had led the people of Israel into the central hill country almost one thousand years before, and though their presence there was contested, they always prevailed. Consequently it became central to their national identity that their place was in the land.[26] Furthermore, Jerusalem was the home of God's temple. It was the city of peace. And very significantly, the Davidic dynasty had been in control of the southern kingdom for 350 years. God had promised it would last forever. How could it possibly be otherwise? "Though the mountains be shaken and the hills be removed, yet my unfailing love for you will not be shaken nor my covenant of peace be removed. . . . Great will be your children's peace" (Is 54:10, 13; cf. 9:6-7; 55:12). "I will not carry out my fierce anger, nor will I turn and devastate Ephraim" (Hos 11:9).

Jeremiah's problem. Whose side would we have been on—Jeremiah's or the other prophets'? Probably not Jeremiah's! Note his complaint to the Lord: "Ah, Sovereign LORD, the prophets keep telling them, 'You will not see the sword or suffer famine. Indeed, I will give you lasting peace in this place'" (Jer 14:13). Jeremiah was frustrated with the competition, but not only from the false prophets. To the Lord himself he protests, "Ah, Sovereign LORD, how completely you have deceived this people and Jerusalem by saying, 'You will have peace,' when the sword is at our throats" (Jer 4:10; cf. Jer 23:16-22). Jeremiah was in the hot seat. God was revealing to him the destruction coming on his people, while the people were basking in the assurance of previous prophecies. But Jeremiah thought it should really be God in the hot seat: *you have completely deceived your people.* On the surface of things at least, prophecy was in conflict with itself.

But is this the whole story? Can prophecies be conditional? Can prophecies be given in hyperbole? Unfortunately it is not always clear even in retrospect what parts of the covenant were unconditional, what parts conditional or what parts hyperbolic.[27] At least from the surface level of the text, God can appear to change his mind, but conditionality is not always stated.[28] "The LORD will send you back in ships to Egypt on a journey I said you should never make again" (Deut 28:68). Jeremiah records the divine prerogative: "If at any time I announce that a nation or kingdom is to be uprooted, torn down and destroyed, and if that nation I warned repents of its evil, then I will relent and not inflict on it the disaster I had planned. And if at another time I announce that a nation or kingdom is to be built up and planted, and it does evil in my sight and does not obey me, then I will reconsider the good I had intended to do for it" (Jer 18:7-10; cf. 17:24-27; 22:4-5; 26:3). God will curse or bless as he chooses, depending largely on obedience, but not only that.

With the advantage of hindsight, do we now concede that prophecies about peace and permanence in the land were possibly *all* conditional? God blessed the Babylonians abundantly (not based on obedience) and sent them to destroy his people, whom he had promised to bless in the land. Of course God changed his treatment of the Babylonians as well, going from blessing to severe judgment (Jer 50—51).

So what makes prophecy problematic? Actually it would be less of a problem if we could determine when promises of blessing were subject to being conditional, if we knew when prophecies were given in hyperbole, if we knew when to take the words at face value.

In our culture, when someone says, "Tonight we'll go out for pizza and then go bowling," there may be situations in which that would not happen, even though such possibilities were not expressed. Parents may tell their children about something planned for later in the day, but the children's misconduct could result in the privilege's being taken away. A husband may tell his wife about plans for an evening out, but the unexpected arrival of out-of-town guests may change those plans. Unexpressed conditions are common in human communication. Is that true for divine communication as well?

PROBLEM 5: REAL OR SURREAL?

Visions common in Ezekiel, Zechariah, Daniel and Revelation pose special challenges. For example, Zechariah begins his book with a series of eight night visions. Each vision conveys an important truth, but were the things Zechariah saw all imaginary and symbolic? What about a man standing among myrtle trees, with red, brown, and white horses behind him (Zech 1:8)? a man with a measuring line preparing to measure Jerusalem (Zech

2:1-2)? seven eyes on a stone (Zech 3:9)? a solid gold lampstand with seven lamps (Zech 4:2)? a flying scroll (Zech 5:2)? four chariots—red, black, white and dappled (Zech 6:2)? How these visions are to be understood is not easily discerned.

The second of the visions portrays God's vengeance on the enemies who destroyed Jerusalem and carried off its people.

Then I looked up—and there before me were four horns! I asked the angel who was speaking to me, "What are these?"

He answered me, "These are the horns that scattered Judah, Israel and Jerusalem."

Then the LORD showed me four craftsmen. I asked, "What are these coming to do?"

He answered, "These are the horns that scattered Judah so that no one could raise his head, but the craftsmen have come to terrify them and throw down these horns of the nations who lifted up their horns against the land of Judah to scatter its people." (Zech 1:18-21)

Questions about imagery. Any number of questions might be asked about elements of the vision. Why are there four horns? Do they signify four distinct rulers? If so, who? Or do they signify four distinct nations? If so, which ones? Do they signify four distinct scatterings? If so, besides the Assyrian and Babylonian captivities, what were the other two? Were there four scatterings so severe that God's people could not raise their heads?

Why are there four craftsmen? Who or what do they represent? Do they signify four distinct rulers? If so, who? Do they signify four distinct nations? If so, which ones? Whom did they come to terrify? In what sense did they cut off and throw down the four horns? On the other hand, does the number four symbolize completeness, so that the vision is not necessarily referring to four different scatterings and destructions?

We could ask similar questions regarding Daniel's vision: "The goat became very great, but at the height of his power his large horn was broken off, and in its place four prominent horns grew up toward the four winds of heaven" (Dan 8:8; for further discussion of Daniel's vision, see chapter five, pp. 111-20).

Some fundamental questions should be asked before addressing visions like this. At what level are readers supposed to understand the prophetic visions—every detail? the overall picture? Are the elements of the vision surreal rather than empirical realities? Do visions usually stand alone, or is their significance connected with other visions or with the theme of the book?

The point of the vision. In the case of Zechariah, examining the visions in the context of his whole prophecy helps us grasp the meaning of each vision (see figure 2.4). Zechariah was on a mission of encouragement, because God's people were faced with impossible odds. But relief was in sight: God had not forgotten them. The future he planned would be glorious. With that as the theme of Zechariah's prophecy and series of visions, the interpretation of each vision fits into that larger framework. The starting point, then, for understanding the vision of horns and craftsmen is this message: God's people can be assured of God's ultimate protection, which includes the defeat of all enemies.

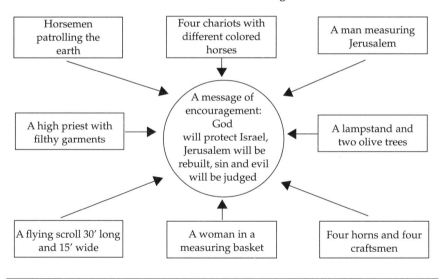

Figure 2.4. Zechariah's visions

It is also essential to recognize the imagery typical of apocalyptic visions. These images are often otherworldly and fantastic. The imagery heightens the prophets' messages by describing judgment and blessing in vivid and surrealistic ways.[29]

So what makes prophecy problematic? Actually it would be less of a problem if we knew when visions were imaginary, if we knew when details in visions were incidental to the main point and only for effect.

In our culture there are many examples of imaginary accounts that we readily accept. From entertainers to storytellers to comedians, the freedom to describe something as if it were true—though in reality it is not—is essential to crafting good stories. It may be obvious to the audience when something is make-believe, but not always. Jesus himself apparently used the technique of fiction in the parables he told, and there are some instances where it is not clear whether his story was parabolic or from real life (e.g., Lk 16:19-31).

PROBLEM 6: ORAL OR WRITTEN?

Prophecy can also be difficult to interpret because of how it was written. This has to do with the process of turning speeches into literature. In the Old Testament both oral and writing prophets were active. If they were writing prophets, however, in most cases they were transforming the oral form of their message into written form. Thus God spoke to Isaiah regarding his oracle: he was to write it on a scroll so that it might be an everlasting witness (Is 30:8).

Unfortunately, ancient orality is too far in the past for those of us in today's world of textuality to understand completely. Print and electronic forms of communication have taken over. We cannot imagine life without the printed page, and maybe not without the computer screen. The world of the Bible, however, was primarily oral.[30] It was extremely rare for individuals to have any literary writings in their possession. Not only would they have been expensive, but it would have been uncommon to make copies for individuals. They may have had documents such as deeds to property and the like, but little else.

Jeremiah purchased a field and was given a deed of purchase, which he signed in the presence of witnesses. As was common with such deeds, it was recorded in duplicate with one part sealed. If someone were to contest what the unsealed portion said—with the contention that it had been surreptitiously altered—the sealed portion could be opened before witnesses and checked for verification. Like many other people of his day, Jeremiah stored this important document in the lockbox of the ancient world, a clay jar (Jer 32:8-14).

How did this world of orality affect the prophets? It often meant speaking and writing so that people would be able to grasp readily what they heard and then to remember it. Prophets apparently preached similar sermons repeatedly, sometimes with similar wording, sometimes with new forms. The challenge before the prophets was to effect change in the thinking of the hearers. That invited creativity—discovering the most effective way to communicate the frequently repeated messages.

From oral to written forms. But once the prophets began recording their prophecies, they likely faced questions about the similarity and dissimilarity of oral and written forms. Some preachers today offer printed copies of their messages. Unless they deliver their messages by reading directly from a manuscript, the preacher must decide: do I prepare a script for what I intend to say in my message? That will preserve the content of the message, but probably not the exact wording (unless I memorize it). Or do I have a stenographer record word for word what I actually say in my message? That will almost certainly be different in style from what I would have written. Or do I write out what I said in the message sometime after the fact? That will preserve the thrust of the message but not the precise turns of phrase. Invariably there are differences between how we speak and how we write.

There is also the issue of lapse of time. If the preacher should wait a week or two before writing out a message—and if he has preached other messages in the meantime—it may be difficult to keep straight the exact flow of the message in question. The longer the lapse between the time something is given orally and the time it is written down, the less likely it is that the precise wording of the oral form will be preserved.

It is even more difficult if the written form is created by someone other than the speaker. An editor was presented with a transcript of a Billy Graham address and told to make it into a chapter for a published compendium. "What worked well as an address to eighteen thousand people proved to have all kinds of gaps, repetitions, etc., that needed to be filled in or repaired as a written sermon. I had to put words in his mouth and even restructure some things."[31]

Two versions of Jeremiah's prophecy. Jeremiah is the best case in point to study this issue of oral and written forms (see figure 2.5).[32] After he had prophesied for twenty-three years (Jer 25:1-3), "this word came to Jeremiah from the LORD: 'Take a scroll and write on it all the words I have spoken to

From oral to written word

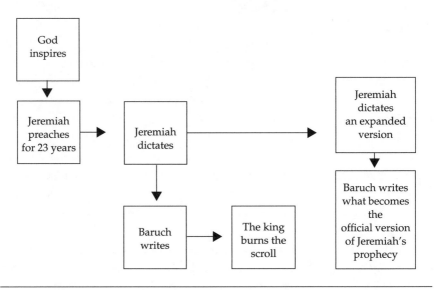

Figure 2.5. Jeremiah 36

you concerning Israel, Judah and all the other nations from the time I began speaking to you in the reign of Josiah until now' " (Jer 36:1-2). Jeremiah summoned Baruch and dictated what he was to write on the scroll.

Baruch then read the scroll in the hearing of the people. Immediately it was considered subversive. And when Jeremiah's words were read to king Jehoiakim, he was furious. It was winter, and firepots were being used to heat the palace. So as column by column of Jeremiah's prophecies was read, Jehoiakim took a knife and cut off the scroll several columns at a time and tossed them into a firepot till the sacred scroll was completely consumed (Jer 36:22-26). The original and only manuscript of what was presumably a sizable portion of the Book of Jeremiah was gone forever.

But all was not lost; in fact, some was gained. "Then Jeremiah got another scroll and gave it to the scribe Baruch son of Neriah. And as Jeremiah dictated, Baruch wrote on this scroll everything that had been on the scroll that King Jehoiakim of Judah burned in the fire. They also added on this scroll several messages of the same kind" (Jer 36:32 NET). In other words, truth was going to prevail no matter how the reigning power would attempt to obliterate it.

Truth crushed to earth shall rise again,
The eternal years of God are hers;
But Error, wounded, writhes with pain,
And dies among his worshippers.
(William Cullen Bryant)

This account underscores important ideas about the process of recording prophecy. The written version of a major portion of Jeremiah's prophecies began as an anthology of twenty-three years of oral versions. Based on what had been word of mouth, Jeremiah dictated what was to become the written word. It was by necessity a representative rather than exhaustive preservation of orality, evidenced by the additional material added in the recension.

Now we hold in our hands—at least in part—the synopsis of twenty-three years of Jeremiah's preaching. The result gives evidence of both oral and written features and may also show the marks of bringing together shorter collections of his oracles.[33] Before the conclusion of the book of Jeremiah, the compiler states, "The words of Jeremiah end here" (Jer 51:64). Thus a later hand had a role in the shaping of the book of Jeremiah. Furthermore, the translation of the Old Testament into Greek reflects a textual source significantly shorter than the Hebrew text, and maybe earlier.[34] All of this is the human side of how Jeremiah's contribution to Scripture came into existence.

Regarding divine authority, the issue is complicated. Shall we assume that the oral form was inspired, since Jeremiah had been proclaiming a message from God? Shall we assume that the written form was equally inspired (or more inspired), since it was a compilation of what Jeremiah had been preaching over all those years (Jer 36:2)?[35] Shall we assume that either the Hebrew text or the Septuagint is inspired, and not both?

I will lay aside those issues for another time; the important point here is the difference between oral and written materials. If there is uncertainty for preachers today regarding how best to prepare printed copies of sermons, the prophets of thousands of years ago would likely have faced a similar tension. Perhaps that explains in part some features of the book of Jeremiah. A chronological order is not followed. Repetition is common. Quick shifts in topic appear frequently.[36] In general Jeremiah's prophecies seem to lack organization, as if various thoughts were compiled rather than carefully structured: "To try to read the book as a whole is undeniably daunting. It lacks the sequence which assists the mind to maintain attention and comprehension. At first sight it is all over the place."[37] Though it is possible that a literary style could account for these features in Jeremiah, in this case it seems to be a byproduct of the original oral composition. This creates problems for interpreters. For many passages it is difficult to determine the larger context as well as the historical setting.

So what makes prophecy problematic? Actually it would be less of a problem if we could distinguish between oral and written features in the prophets, if we could determine the complete context of the prophetic messages.

PROBLEM 7: FULFILLED OR UNFULFILLED?

Prophecy may leave us in doubt about what has already been fulfilled and what is yet to be fulfilled. When the Babylonians destroyed Jerusalem and took the majority of the population captive back to Babylon, it appeared to be the end of the Jewish nation. Even the few who remained behind fled for safety to Egypt. Were God's chosen people gone forever? It probably appeared that way, especially when more than 130 years before—after the Assyrians had deported the majority of the population of the northern kingdom—few if any returned.

Was there no hope? According to the prophets there was hope. God had assured his people that there would be a restoration. Isaiah and Micah speak of a remnant: "Though your people, O Israel, be like the sand by the sea, only a remnant will return" (Is 10:22). "I will make the lame a remnant, those driven away a strong nation. The LORD will rule over them in Mount Zion from that day and forever" (Mic 4:7). Jeremiah develops the idea further: "'The days are coming,' declares the LORD, 'when this city will be rebuilt for me from the Tower of Hananel to the Corner Gate'" (Jer 31:38; cf. Zech 2:1-13). "Do not fear, O Jacob my servant; do not be dismayed, O Israel. I will surely save you out of a distant place, your descendants from the land of their exile" (Jer 46:27). In Jeremiah's prophecies, however, there seem to be mixed signals about the extent of the restoration. He says that some will never return: "None of the remnant of Judah who have gone to live in Egypt will escape or survive to return to the land of Judah, to which they long to return and live; none will return except a few fugitives" (Jer 44:14).

Following the captivity in Babylon, Cyrus granted permission to the

Jews to return to their homeland. Some were more than ready to go. With the leadership of Zerubbabel, Ezra and Nehemiah and with the prophecy of Haggai, the temple and city walls were rebuilt, though not to compare with what had been destroyed. Other captives, however, were not ready to go. Given the comforts of Babylon and the long trek required to return home, as well as the foreboding work that would be necessary to rebuild Jerusalem, many remained in Babylon.

A partial fulfillment of prophecy? This resulted in a problem: had the prophecies of restoration been fulfilled, or was there yet a future restoration that the Jews could count on? Were those who had returned to the Promised Land the extent of the remnant, or were there more to come? Over the next several centuries the question was answered in opposing ways.[38] Some felt confident that the prophecies had been fulfilled. The seventy years of exile were history. God had restored his people to their land. A new temple had been built. Isaiah looked to the future: "Speak tenderly to Jerusalem, and proclaim to her that her hard service has been completed, that her sin has been paid for, that she has received from the LORD's hand double for all her sins" (Is 40:2).

But others argued the opposite. The exile was not over, and God's judgment was continuing. The new temple was not the real replacement. The conclusion was that the true restoration must still be in the future.[39] "I myself will gather the remnant of my flock out of all the countries where I have driven them and will bring them back to their pasture, where they will be fruitful and increase in number" (Jer 23:3).

In Jesus' day the Jews were faced with the same question. The prevailing opinion was that the exile was still in effect. Christians are still faced with that very question. Will there yet be a restoration of Judah to Palestine? A popular opinion is that the creation of the Jewish nation in 1948 is part of the restoration of Israel to the land.

So what makes prophecy problematic? Actually it would be less of a problem if we could determine which predictions have been fully fulfilled, if we could determine whether some predictions may have stages or layers of fulfillment.

These seven problems of prophecy are not intended to be a complete list of the challenges in understanding prophecy. Another one that needs careful consideration is the possibility of cultural differences between the world of the Middle East of more than two thousand years ago and our world of the twenty-first century. For example, underlying the use of hyperbole was an apparent tendency to express ideas in opposites. Hence the two extremes of God's attributes—perfect wrath and perfect grace—are expressed in sharp contrast. But it is too stark for most Western minds.[40] We tend not to tolerate paradox well, since the Enlightenment convinced us that science or some form of higher learning can explain just about everything. We look for easy answers—six simple steps to solve this or that. If necessary, we will oversimplify in order to avoid things we cannot explain.

In contrast, people in the biblical world recognized that life is in many ways unexplainable. So hyperbole was commonly linked with paradox.[41] On the one hand, the vengeance of God's wrath is unfathomable; his anger burns in dense clouds, his lips are full of wrath, his tongue is a consuming fire (Is 30:27); he proclaims war on all who inhabit the earth (Jer 25:29); his judgment will come quickly (Is 60:22); he hides his face from his people, leaving them to waste away (Is 64:7). On the other hand—at the same time and to the same degree—God's love is beyond measure; it will never fail them (Lam 3:22-23, 32); he calls his people precious and honored in his sight (Is 43:4); he is gracious and compassionate and slow to anger (Joel 2:13).

> Come, let us return to the LORD.
> He has torn us to pieces
>   but he will heal us;
> he has injured us
>   but he will bind up our wounds. (Hos 6:1)

The cultural differences between modern Western ways and ancient Eastern ways have only partly been explored.[42] Since all cultural differences have the potential of skewing our understanding of things written in another cultural context, our understanding of prophecy can be limited when we remain unaware of the ancient mindset.

Conclusion

What makes prophecy problematic? To understand the prophetic word correctly, we must recognize that the language of prophecy may be poetic, emotive, conditional, hyperbolic, figurative, surreal, oral and uncertain about fulfillment. These barriers, which stand in the way of correct readings of prophecy, come down to one basic question: when should the words be taken at face value?

Is this question an insurmountable obstacle? If we are to find the answer to that question, we have some big challenges ahead in seeking to follow the river of prophecy to its glorious end. For those who want to become better-informed readers, the chapters that follow offer directional markers for the journey. It may mean a paradigm shift in how we think about prophecy, but since none of us has a corner on the truth, we should welcome enhanced understanding.

But is it correct to say that prophecy is the problem?

Any society can choose to create its own system of communication. As long as it works for them, no one has the right to consider that society at fault if outsiders are left in the dark. It is simply up to outsiders to enter into the culture and ways of thinking in order to understand how that society communicates.

Likewise for prophecy. If we fail to hear the communication as the authors intended and the hearers understood, it is because we are outside in the dark. When God chose to use the forms of communication and culture available in the biblical world, he simply left us with the challenge to enter into that world to understand his revelation. So if prophecy is problematic, whose problem is it?

Unfortunately the zeal to know how—and for some, when—the future will unfold has led interpreters to rush to conclusions. They fail to take time to understand prophecy as the authors intended and the hearers understood. The result is all kinds of speculations and dogmas and denominations and sects. The misinterpretations of the biblical text have been manifold and dangerous and embarrassing. Examples are everywhere, from the Millerites to the Branch Davidians.[43] Even in irenic discussions among evangelicals, different positions on eschatology are described as "rival global solutions" that draw "battle-lines" between themselves.[44]

Heaven, we have a problem! The problem comes at us from every direction—from the nature of prophecy to the nature of humanity. The problem lies both in prophecy and in the interpreters of prophecy. Without doubt, prophecy and apocalyptic provide the biggest challenge in all of Scripture. Can we move toward solving a problem that the church has struggled with for centuries?

3

How Does the Language of Prophecy Work?

A large Southern utility hired a defense attorney because of a lawsuit filed by a small Southern utility. In the course of the trial the attorney for the big utility clearly had the law on his side, and his defense seemed convincing. But he was not prepared for the skill of the small-town lawyer hired by the small utility. Speaking directly to the jury, the lawyer for the prosecution concluded his closing statement as follows: "So now you see what it is. They got us where they want us. They holding us up with one hand, their good sharp fishin' knife in the other, and they sayin', 'you jes set still, little catfish, we're jes goin' to gut ya.'"

At that moment the lawyer for the large utility lost the case. No matter how logical and convincing his defense, the opponent's arresting and emotive metaphor persuaded the jury of the "facts."[1]

The two preceding chapters asked what makes prophecy powerful and at the same time problematic. Hopefully the answer was not hard to miss . . . like giant sequoias standing tall in a forest carpeted with pages from the books in the Bible. Prophecy is powerful and problematic for one tall reason: the creative use of language, poetic expression, arresting and emotive metaphors. If figures of speech were sequoias on the landscape of prophecy, prophecy would be densely forested, and the most common tree in these woods is metaphor. On the other hand, if biblical prophecy had been written devoid of figures of speech, all that the prophets said could be reduced to a few pages. The present chapter explores the significance of the forest of metaphors—as used in language in general, in Scripture everywhere and in prophecy in particular. If we fail to grasp the inherent metaphorical nature of language, we will fail to understand prophecy.

METAPHORS: THE AIR WE BREATHE

A quick fly-over of the history of the study of metaphor takes us back more than two millennia, to the time of Aristotle.[2] He concluded that language can be divided into *logic, rhetoric* and *poetic*, the latter being the proper domain for metaphor. Though Aristotle admired those who were masters of metaphor (*Poetics* 22), he considered metaphor "the seasoning of the meat," not the meat itself (*Rhetoric* 3.1406b). If clarity is the intent, he said, the language of logic is clearly preferable.[3] Despite Aristotle's insights into metaphor, figurative language was then little more than a tool that poets used to craft their literary artifice—rhetorical style that made poetry *poetry*.

Following Aristotle, authors like Cicero, Horace, Longinus and Quintilian advanced the theory of metaphor in small ways.[4] They were concerned with the appropriateness of certain kinds of metaphors for certain occasions. In the centuries since, metaphors have largely been treated as incidental to communication—mere ornamentation for those who want to add finesse and zing to what they say. The consensus was that metaphors could affect emotions, but intelligent discourse did not need them. Metaphors were not considered essential to the structure of communication.

Some fifty years ago, with the research of literary critics, linguists, psychologists, anthropologists and philosophers, metaphors metamorphosed from seasoning to substance, from appetizer to entrée.[5] Instead of simply adding ornamentation, metaphors were recognized as a fundamental operative in society. Metaphoric language is pervasive in the culture of communication as well as in the arts. A metaphor is usually picturesque, expressing ideas in visual images. It increases memorability of concepts and wording. It bonds speakers and hearers and authors and readers together, as the creators of metaphor contemplate how hearers/readers will understand their intent, and hearers/readers reflect on the speakers' meaning and craftsmanship. A metaphor helps convey abstract ideas, many of which cannot be readily expressed without the use of metaphor. A metaphor gives literature elegance. It is a compact way to express thoughts and feelings (and in some cases to bring to mind a whole story).

It is persuasive, in some cases even more powerful than the best reasoning. Perhaps most important, it affects not only how we speak but also how we think.[6] Metaphors are the air we breathe (see figure 3.1).

PARADIGM SHIFT

This new understanding of metaphor charted the course for the research of more recent decades. The reasoning went like this: if language is essentially a medium for expressing a reality, then language is itself metaphorical. And if language is in essence the making of metaphors, then metaphors not only express what we perceive but influence what we perceive.[7]

Take the concepts of birth and death. These are abstractions that we find difficult to grasp. So note how we talk about them and end up thinking about them. When we refer to birth, we may talk of *coming* into this life. A baby is *on the way,* and then we announce its *arrival.* Even more to the point, at the other end of existence, we refer to death in terms of departure.

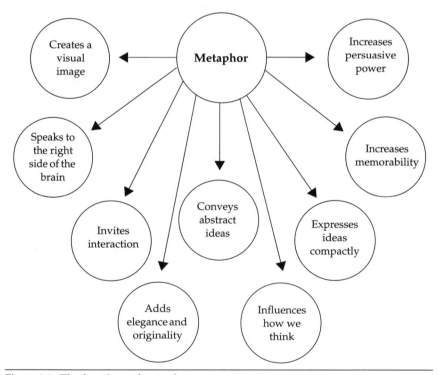

Figure 3.1. The functions of metaphor

As someone is nearing death, we say he is *still with us,* or he is *at death's door.* In some cases doctors are able to *bring him back,* but they may also *lose him.* Sooner or later he will *leave us.* Then we will say he is *no longer with us,* or he is *gone,* or he *passed away,* or he is *among the departed.* We will talk about his *homegoing.*

Though these expressions can rightly be labeled euphemisms, they are metaphors. And these metaphors of departure give us ways to talk about death, but they also influence how we think about the abstraction of death. It is difficult for us to think about death without using the metaphor of departure. For once we create a metaphor for things like life, death, time and love, it may in turn determine how we conceptualize those things.[8] And we cannot separate the metaphor from the reality.

Equally important to note is that the metaphors we use to refer to birth and death may not be technically correct in their description. We use them because they are convenient and meaningful, not because of their precision. In the words of Socrates when nearing death, "I have not convinced our friend Crito that I shall fly hence and leave nothing of me behind. But all the same, Crito, if you can catch me or light upon me, you shall bury me as you think fit" (according to Cicero, *Tusculan Disputations* 1.43.103).

As is evident from metaphors about life and death, one metaphor is likely to attract more metaphors. For another example, an archetypal metaphor—ideas are food for thought—encourages expansions: here's an idea you can sink your teeth into; he devoured the book; I can't swallow all of her ideas; his level of thinking leaves a bad taste in my mouth; this is the meatiest part of the argument.[9]

The prevalence of metaphors in thinking. A good example of how pervasive and formative metaphors are is evident in the following paragraph:

> John lives in a war zone. He is the lone conservative in an apartment full of liberals, and he and his roommates frequently fight over political and religious issues, blasting each other's positions, one volley after another. The common strategy of their skirmishes seems to be that as soon as one sees a gap in another's defenses he charges through to crush his opponent. As a result John seems to have a problem holding his ground against the attacks— especially when his roommates combine forces against him—and he sometimes retreats to nurse his wounds. Once in a while in a counterattack he manages to be on target and shoot down one of their arguments, but it's his own position that more often than not is indefensible. It's unfortunate that

he is destroyed so easily. Since he never seems to win even a single battle, he ought to call for a truce, rather than abandon his position.[10]

The barrage of metaphors in this paragraph is overkill, but even this is not an exhaustive arsenal of metaphors regularly used in describing arguments. Metaphors are so important to how we conceive of arguments that we would find it almost impossible to have an argument without thinking of it in metaphorical language. Words like *fight, opponent, position, strategy, defensive* or *destroy* are hard to avoid when describing an intense argument.

It is noteworthy that metaphoric language, far from being unique to the English language, appears in most languages. For example, metaphors in French are numerous and vivid. Even more important, examining the metaphors of an unknown language underscores an essential point: the meaning of a metaphor generally cannot be understood based on dictionary definitions. Literal translations are rarely helpful. Firsthand exposure to the culture is essential. Note the list of metaphors in French in appendix A. Begin by covering up the third column; then guess at the meaning of the metaphor based on the French or the literal translation given. It will quickly be evident that the meanings of individual words are of little value for recognizing the meaning of metaphors.

FIGURATIVE VERSUS NONFIGURATIVE

Metaphors begin with something nonfigurative and make it figurative by using it to describe something beyond the scope of its normal meaning. That is, metaphors describe x while referring to y. For example: "Some homeowners are sitting ducks for unscrupulous window salesmen." With the reference to ducks (y), a common conception of vulnerability is applied to people (x). The metaphor is effective because "sitting duck" brings to our minds a visual image. The same sentence can be defined another way. A nonfigurative subject (ducks) becomes figurative when it becomes a symbol for a characteristic of another subject (see figure 3.2).

In a sense all language is fundamentally symbolic, since words are simply symbols for actions, objects, emotions and so on. But those symbols remain meaningless without a means of discovering their accepted referents. That is why we need dictionaries—to examine the range of accepted meanings. If we see a billboard for "Cheviot Industries," we will need help to identify the referent for the symbol *cheviot.* Our first thought

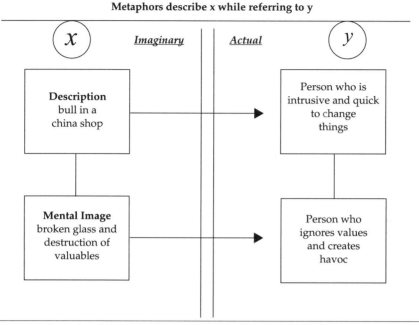

Figure 3.2. Transfer of meaning

may be that it is a family name. But if we check a dictionary, we will read that *cheviot* can refer to a type of sheep, a type of wool or a type of cotton shirting. While we may have expanded the range of meanings for the symbol *cheviot,* depending on the degree of our shared culture, our understanding of its significance may still be limited.

In metaphorical language, nonfigurative words with definitions that are generally well known are used to refer figuratively to something outside the purview of accepted lexical referents.[11] For example: "Let's talk turkey." In this case, most dictionaries are generally not helpful, for the meaning of *turkey* as used in this phrase is not given. Because metaphors may have many unexpected referents, it is impossible for dictionaries to capture all the uses. So metaphors require that we go beyond the dictionary definitions of words. Even if we know what it means to "talk turkey," we may not know why the phrase has that meaning. But that is generally inconsequential. We know what it means and how to use it based on hearing it used in our culture.

It is important to note that metaphors speak truths, but the surface meaning of the words in metaphors speak untruths.[12] "We locked horns when that topic came up." That sentence certainly does not mean what the surface meanings of the words would suggest. Thus there is a sense in which figurative language is always in tension with nonfigurative language, because the former does not play by the rules of the latter. The accepted boundaries of meaning for words in nonfigurative language are inadequate for figurative. By playing the game out of bounds, metaphors extend the meanings of symbols into new areas.[13] Thus recognizing the presence of metaphors is a win-or-lose issue for correct interpretation. For example, the poet's lover says of him, "His legs are pillars of marble," and he says of her, "Your eyes are the pools of Heshbon" (Song 5:15; 7:4). If we fail to recognize the metaphors and use only dictionary definitions, we could be confused about whether this is a relationship between two inanimate objects or two people. The point is, if we force all forms of language to play by one set of rules, we will be hopelessly confused.

ARE METAPHORS INHERENTLY AMBIGUOUS?

Metaphors are often used for things we understand inadequately and find difficult to describe. As noted earlier in this chapter, death is one example. Another example is how the brain works. We have trouble understanding brain activity, so we talk about it in terms more easily understood but certainly less accurate. Take the archetypal metaphor "the mind is a machine." We may say, "I hear the wheels turning; my mind isn't operating at full capacity right now; we're a little rusty on that topic; . . . I've been trying all day to grind out a solution for that problem, but I'm running out of steam."[14]

Metaphors are especially useful for such abstract concepts. The more abstract the concept, the more valuable metaphors become to conceptualize the abstraction. Unfortunately, the ambiguity inherent in something abstract may still be ambiguous when expressed in a metaphor, for metaphors do not eliminate ambiguity. But at least metaphors provide ways for us to think about and converse about things that we find difficult otherwise.

The value of ambiguity. Recognizing that ambiguity is unavoidable in language—that no matter how hard we may seek to be perfectly clear, we cannot be completely—leads to an exploration of the value of ambiguity in deepening and enriching meaning. Ambiguity is a function of metaphor that engages speakers and hearers in a silent dialogue, in contrast to two machines talking to one another. The speaker chooses to use a metaphor, but she must consider whether her hearer will have the insight to recognize the figure of speech and to understand it and whether it will have the desired effect on the hearer. Upon identifying that the speaker is speaking in metaphor, the hearer must consider what he knows about the speaker and the culture they share in determining what the speaker intended to communicate with the metaphors. The result is that both speaker and hearer have penetrated each other's world. This interplay between speaker and hearer happens to some extent in all communication. Language cannot be passive on either side if it is to be understood. Yet when metaphor is employed, the cooperative and pleasurable act of comprehension is enhanced. The use of imagery is then an act of community, for speaker and hearer are drawn closer together in the communicative process.[15] (Looking back over this paragraph, readers should note that they may replace the word *metaphor* with *poetry,* for ambiguity and its function are key elements in poetry.)

Metaphor as a function of community means that hearers who are not a part of the community will be less prepared to identify and understand metaphors. Bridging the language and cultural barriers between the Bible and the twenty-first century is especially urgent for understanding biblical metaphors. For the more metaphorical language is, the less accessible it is to a distant audience (see figure 3.3).

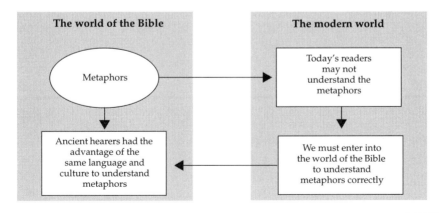

Figure 3.3. The culture of metaphors

SENTENCES AS METAPHORS

Thus far we have been thinking about individual words as metaphors. But we must get beyond a discussion of just words, for meaning is primarily a function of phrases and sentences. The psalmist asks the Lord for deliverance from his enemies—that God would break the teeth and the arm of the wicked (Ps 3:7; 10:15). For readers who think only of the lexical meanings of these symbols, the interpretation will certainly be mistaken. They may even relate Psalm 10 to Psalm 34, where it is stated that the bones of the righteous will not be broken (Ps 34:19-20). That leads to only more misunderstanding. I know of a sincere teacher in a Christian college who erroneously taught, based on these verses, that a broken bone was an indication of sin in the life of the victim.

But just as misguided are readers who recognize the presence of metaphor yet attempt to determine what *break* refers to and what *teeth* and *arm* refer to. What are the referents for those metaphors? The answer is, there are none. But there is a referent for the metaphor as a whole: God's judgment. To break the teeth of the wicked is to judge them. Thus the meaning of metaphors may not be a one-to-one ratio of symbols and referents. When we use the metaphor of climbing on someone's bandwagon, does the metaphorical action we are describing have anything to do with a dictionary definition of a band or a wagon or climbing? Obviously the answer is no. Fortunately for English speakers, there are an increasing number of dictionaries of metaphors, in some cases arranged according to geographical regions.[16]

DOES GOD COMMUNICATE IN METAPHORS?

For over one hundred years E. W. Bullinger's classic volume on figures of speech in the Bible has guided thousands of students in their interpretation of the Scriptures.[17] Classifying two hundred distinct figures of speech and illustrating them with almost eight thousand passages of Scripture—and providing numerous indices and appendices—Bullinger's work has been widely influential. After all these years it has not been replaced. Unfortunately it is almost too detailed, for its technical classifications and amount of information can be daunting. And for those with enough dogged determination to decipher a figure of speech according to Bullinger's categories, the tendency is to think that classifying is equivalent to understanding. But creating an appropriate Latinate name for every imaginable figure of speech does not go far enough.

Nevertheless, basic to Bullinger's compilation of data are important premises. He explains in his introduction that figures of speech break with the normal laws of language for the purpose of "giving additional force, more life, intensified feeling, and greater emphasis. Whereas today 'Figurative Language' is ignorantly spoken of as though it made less of the meaning, and deprived the words of their power and force." He continues, arguing that figures of speech "set forth the truth with greater vigour, and with a far greater meaning . . . indicating to us what is emphatic . . . to call and attract our attention, so that it may be directed to, and fixed upon, the special truth which is to be conveyed to us."[18] These are very incisive comments (see figure 3.4).

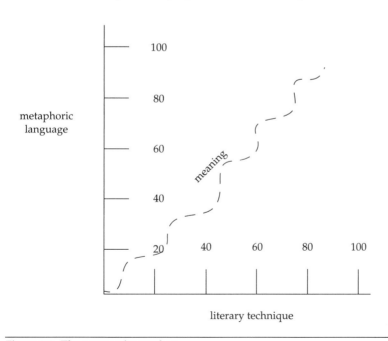

Figure 3.4. The power of metaphor

The prevalence of metaphors in the Bible. While Bullinger's volume is well known, the interpretive significance of his findings is often overlooked, especially with regard to figurative language. Many readers are unprepared

68   PLOWSHARES & PRUNING HOOKS

for the figurative language in the poetic portions of Scripture, let alone elsewhere. But metaphors appear everywhere in the Bible. For example, note a selection from the Pentateuch:

- Canaan is "a land flowing with milk and honey" (Ex 3:17; Num 13:27).
- Moses seeks to persuade his father-in-law to accompany the Israelites through the desert, saying, "You know where we should camp in the desert, and you can be our eyes" (Num 10:31).
- In response to lack of faith, God challenges Moses, "Is the LORD's arm too short?" (Num 11:23).
- In preparation to enter the Promised Land, Moses warns the people, "If you defile the land, it will vomit you out as it vomited out the nations that were before you" (Lev 18:28).
- With the Israelites approaching, the Moabites say, "This horde is going to lick up everything around us, as an ox licks up the grass of the field" (Num 22:4).
- Moses calls the Israelites "stiff-necked" (Deut 9:6) and challenges them to "circumcise [their] hearts" (Deut 10:16).
- Regarding the Israelites' escape from Egypt, God says, "I broke the bars of your yoke and enabled you to walk with heads held high" (Lev 26:13).
- God also reminds them, "You yourselves have seen what I did to Egypt, and how I carried you on eagles' wings and brought you to myself" (Ex 19:4).
- Moses concludes, "But as for you, the LORD took you and brought you out of the iron-smelting furnace, out of Egypt, to be the people of his inheritance, as you now are" (Deut 4:20).

As one would expect, an even greater preponderance of metaphors is found in the poetic portions of the Pentateuch.

- Hagar is informed that Ishmael will be "a wild donkey of a man" (Gen 16:12).
- Jacob's blessing of his sons includes metaphors for their characteristics: Judah is called "a lion's cub"; Issachar "a rawboned donkey"; Dan "a serpent by the roadside, . . . that bites the horse's heels"; Joseph "a fruitful vine near a spring whose branches climb over a wall"; and Benjamin "a ravenous wolf; in the morning he devours the prey, in the evening he divides the plunder" (Gen 49:9, 14, 17, 22, 27).

- In the first Song of Moses, the drowning of Pharaoh's army in the Red Sea is celebrated with lyrics such as "your right hand, O LORD, shattered the enemy"; "you unleashed your burning anger; it consumed them like stubble"; "you stretched out your right hand and the earth swallowed them" (Ex 15:6-7, 12).
- In the Song of Moses at the end of his life, God expresses his judgment on the Israelites' disobedience:

> *For a fire has been kindled by my wrath,*
>   *one that burns to the realm of death below.*
> *It will devour the earth and its harvests*
>   *and set afire the foundations of the mountains.* (Deut 32:22)

Metaphors in poetry. Metaphoric language is evident throughout the Bible, though the highest concentration is naturally in the genre of poetry.[19]

- "As I have observed, those who plow evil and those who sow trouble reap it" (Job 4:8).
- "Even if I washed myself with soap and my hands with washing soda, you would plunge me into a slime pit so that even my clothes would detest me" (Job 9:30-31).
- "God is a righteous judge. . . . He will sharpen his sword; he will bend and string his bow. He has prepared his deadly weapons; he makes ready his flaming arrows" (Ps 7:11-13).
- "For look, the wicked bend their bows; they set their arrows against the strings to shoot from the shadows at the upright in heart" (Ps 11:2).
- "You have made your people experience hard times; you have made us drink intoxicating wine" (Ps 60:3 NET).
- "[Wisdom] is a tree of life to those embrace her; those who lay hold of her will be blessed" (Prov 3:18).
- "The eye that mocks at a father, and despises obeying a mother—the ravens of the valley will peck it out and the young vultures will eat it" (Prov 30:17 NET).

> *If the only home I hope for is the grave,*
>   *if I spread out my bed in darkness,*
> *if I say to corruption, "You are my father,"*
>   *and to the worm, "My mother" or "My sister,"*
> *where then is my hope?* (Job 17:13-15)

In the case of the prophets, poetry was the most common form of expression, and judgment was the most common message. It is sinners in the hands of an angry God.

> *I will be like a lion. . . .*
> *I will tear them to pieces and go away;*
>   *I will carry them off, with no one to rescue them.* (Hos 5:14)

> *Because of their sinful deeds,*
>   *I will drive them out of my house.*
> *I will no longer love them;*
>   *all their leaders are rebellious.* (Hos 9:15)

> *Their blood will be poured out like dust*
>   *and their entrails like filth. . . .*
> *In the fire of his jealousy*
>   *the whole world will be consumed,*
> *for he will make a sudden end*
>   *of all who live on the earth.* (Zeph 1:17-18)

METAPHORS: THE LIFEBLOOD OF PROPHECY

It is not difficult to imagine why metaphors became indispensable for the poetry of the prophets (see figure 3.5).

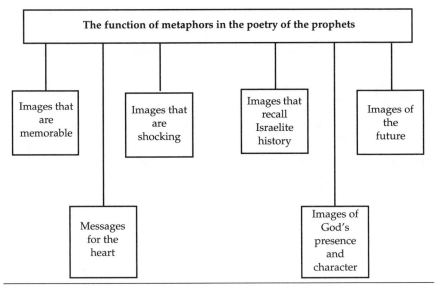

Figure 3.5. Metaphors in the prophets

- Wanting their messages to be remembered long after they spoke, and knowing the limits of simple logic, the prophets painted pictures to make their messages memorable: "I will rebuke your offspring, and spread dung on your faces, the dung of your offerings, and I will put you out of my presence" (Mal 2:3 NRSV).
- Seeking to persuade their apathetic hearers of God's impending judgment, the prophets needed language that spoke to the heart rather than simply cerebral communication: "You stumble day and night, and the prophets stumble with you. So I will destroy your mother" (Hos 4:5).
- Connecting Israel's present failures with the past, the prophets described what God was going to do with images of what he had done: "They will pass through the sea of trouble; the surging sea will be subdued and all the depths of the Nile will dry up" (Zech 10:11).
- Recognizing the mediocrity of their hearers, the prophets gave shock treatment in order to call them back to their senses.[20] "The task of prophetic imagination is to cut through the numbness, to penetrate the self-deception, so that the God of endings is confessed as Lord."[21] "Rend your heart and not your garments. Return to the LORD your God, for he is gracious and compassionate" (Joel 2:13).
- Looking for ways to show them God and what it is like to be in the presence of the Holy, the prophets used metaphoric descriptions for the abstractions of God's presence and character. The intent was to raise the consciousness of God in the hearts of people who were transfixed by the world's values. But without categories of earthbound language to describe the Eternal, this was a special challenge.

> Then the LORD will appear over them;
>   his arrow will flash like lightning.
> The Sovereign LORD will sound the trumpet;
>   he will march in the storms of the south. (Zech 9:14)

- Wanting to explain as clearly as possible how God could and would bless the people—and on the other hand, how he could and would curse the people—the prophets conceptualized that future reality in things common in their own day.

> "The days are coming," declares the Lord,
>   "when the reaper will be overtaken by the plowman

> *and the planter by the one treading grapes.*
> *New wine will drip from the mountains*
> *   and flow from all the hills." (Amos 9:13; cf. Joel 3:18)*

METAPHORS APPROACHING REALITY

While metaphors resonate with the imagination of the hearers to evoke a response, they may seem to become the reality itself.[22] When a metaphor expresses something that is abstract in concrete terms, hearers may come to think of the vehicle as the referent—to ignore the "it is as if" of a metaphor.[23] In other words, the referent and the metaphor may seem to match in domains of meaning rather than just touching or overlapping slightly. For example, the abstract idea of spiritual decay may be described in terms of physical decay. Hearers must beware of missing the metaphor and thinking that physical decay is really the point.

> *Your whole head is injured,*
> *   your whole heart afflicted.*
> *From the soul of your foot to the top of your head*
> *   there is no soundness—*
> *only wounds and welts*
> *   and open sores,*
> *not cleansed or bandaged*
> *   or soothed with oil. (Is 1:5-6)*

So far as the prophets were concerned, the people were asleep in spiritual lethargy and were at risk of never getting up. "Prepare for war! Rouse the warriors. . . . Beat your plowshares into swords and your pruning hooks into spears" (Joel 3:9-10; cf. Is 2:4; Mic 4:3). The prophets were themselves engaged in a war. They were in combat with people who held their ground in the trenches of idolatry. And the weapons were words.[24] There was no better way for the prophets to communicate than through graphic metaphors that were emotive, memorable and persuasive, engaging the hearers in the dialogue while always attempting to transform their thinking.

Surprisingly little research has been done on metaphorical language in the prophets, given its transforming effect on the nature of prophecy.[25] Without poetic technique, prophecy would be little more than tedious diatribe—recitations of failures and dashed hopes, with an occasional offer of hope for the repentant. In poetry, however, their creativity resulted in literary masterpieces.[26] Phrase after phrase reveals a craftsman of words at work. "You have planted wickedness, you have reaped evil, you have eaten the fruit of deception" (Hos 10:13). Agricultural metaphors were especially appropriate, and the genius was to move from the commonplace of everyday life to moral issues with vast consequences.

> *The vine is dried up*
>   *and the fig tree is withered;*
> *the pomegranate, the palm and the apple tree—*
>   *all the trees of the field—are dried up.*
> *Surely the joy of mankind*
>   *is withered away.* (Joel 1:12)

CONCLUSION

How does the language of prophecy work? When people are nearly blind, we increase the font size. When people are nearly deaf, we turn up the volume. When people are mentally handicapped, we use visuals. The audience of prophetic language was sometimes blind, sometimes deaf and often mentally handicapped. The prophet was heaven's prosecuting attorney speaking directly to the defendant: "So now you see what it is. God is holding you up with one hand, his good sharp fishin' knife in the other. And he's sayin', 'unless you repent, little catfish, I'm jes goin' to gut ya.'"

*   *   *

EXCURSUS: DEFINING FIGURES OF SPEECH

We may define metaphors in two ways.[27] The restrictive definition limits the meaning of *metaphor* to two nouns not normally associated together that are often joined by a linking verb. "That man is a thorn in my side," or "Surely the people are grass" (Is 40:7). Other figures of speech accomplish similar associations. *Simile* makes explicit an association of ideas by generally adding *like* or *as*. "I felt as if someone was twisting my arm," or "Even the nations are like a drop from a bucket" (Is 40:15 NRSV). In comparison to metaphors, similes speak more factually: "I feel like biting your head off." Metaphors speak with more emotion: "I am going to bite your head off!" Demetrius *(On Style)* remarks, "When the metaphor seems daring, let it for greater security be converted into a simile. . . . A simile [is] a less risky expression." A more developed figure of speech, *symbol*, may be defined as a metaphor with lasting representation.[28]

Metonymy is arguably a more common figure of speech than metaphors and simile. It is the substitution of a word or words for another. "The Little League coach has a short fuse with those kids," or "The gates of your land are wide open to your enemies; fire has consumed their bars" (Nah 3:13). Whereas metaphor conceives of one thing in terms of another, metonymy more directly has one thing take the place of another.[29] Nevertheless, both metaphor and metonymy result in a figurative sense by defining one thing in light of another. "She ended up with egg on her face," or "When your words came, I ate them" (Jer 15:16).

Synecdoche is an association of a part with a whole or vice versa, when there is close connection between the surface meaning and the intended meaning. In the proverb "The hand that rocks the cradle rules the world," *hand* is synecdoche for mother, and *cradle* is metonymy for infant.[30]

While it is useful to recognize precise definitions for various figures of speech, current scholarship generally uses a less restrictive definition for metaphor, including under the umbrella of metaphor the related figures of speech just mentioned: metonymy, synecdoche, symbol and sometimes simile. In such a case metaphor is defined as follows: "The essence of metaphor is understanding and experiencing one kind of thing in terms of another."[31] "Metaphoric language" is nearly equivalent in meaning to what is meant by "figurative language": words lifted out of their normal context and applied in some aspect of their meaning in another context. "His comment took the wind out of my sails," or "The house of Israel has become dross to me; all of them are the copper, tin, iron and lead left inside a furnace" (Ezek 22:18). *Figure of speech* has a wider designation still, including all the above, plus any unusual arrangement or use of words, including alliteration, parallelism, bracketing, idiom and acrostic.

In this book, *metaphor* is used in the less restrictive definition and is interchangeable with *figurative language*.

4

HOW DOES THE LANGUAGE OF
DESTRUCTION AND BLESSING WORK?

As underscored in previous chapters, the prophets were masters of metaphor. In the language of judgment and blessing, however, additional factors come into play. Imagine these verses of destruction as a public reading of Scripture in a typical worship service:

> I will throw you on the ground,
>   on the open field I will fling you,
> and will cause all the birds of the air to settle on you,
>   and I will let the wild animals of the whole earth gorge themselves with you.
> I will strew your flesh on the mountains,
>   and fill the valleys with your carcass.
> I will drench the land with your flowing blood
>   up to the mountains,
>   and the watercourses will be filled with you.
> When I blot you out, I will cover the heavens,
>   and make their stars dark;
> I will cover the sun with a cloud,
>   and the moon shall not give its light. (Ezek 32:4-7 NRSV)

As is sometimes stated after a Scripture reading, may our hearts be warmed and filled by this beautiful passage of Scripture!

But these verses are hardly uplifting. Why is the language so extreme? It sounds brutal. And it will be, if it is carried out as stated. What is God's spokesman saying?

On the other hand, imagine these verses of blessing read in a typical worship service:

In that day the mountains will drip new wine,
  and the hills will flow with milk;
  all the ravines of Judah will run with water.
A fountain will flow out of the LORD's house
  and will water the valley of acacias. (Joel 3:18)

Now that is much better. Though we may not understand what it means, at least it is not doom and gloom. But this language is also extreme. It sounds like some kind of pie-in-the-sky. And if it is carried out as stated, it will be equivalent to pies dropping out of the sky. What is God's spokesman saying?

The question I have asked before must be asked again: do we take this language at face value? Will God really bring about each of these kinds of judgment and blessing? Will wild animals from all over the earth gorge themselves on sinners? Will rivers of milk flow through the countryside? Those things are certainly possible with an all-powerful God. But it is equally possible that such statements were not intended to be taken at face value.

When a parent says to a child, "I'm going to lock you in your room and throw the key away," or "I'm going to put you on the next flight to Timbuktu," what is the intent? To get the child's attention? To warn of serious consequences? To arouse fear? To threaten? If the child takes the statements at face value, he or she will have reason for fear. Of course the parent might try an opposite approach: "If you are good, I'll buy you an ice-cream cone taller than the Empire State Building!"

This chapter is an exploration of two of the subgenres of prophecy—curses and blessings—in order to improve our eyesight for prophecy.[1] The related genre of apocalyptic will be explored in the next chapter. For now our investigation will take us into key areas for understanding how the prophets expressed God's blessing and judgment.[2] We need to reflect on the limits of human language to describe divine wrath and love. We need to consider how language can function in ways different from the normal meanings of the words. We need to analyze prophetic language in the context of Near Eastern treaties and the Pentateuch. We will find patterns that are precursors to the prophets. Until we begin using these corrective lenses for improving our vision, we will constantly be squinting to see the language of destruction and blessing clearly.

A MOSAIC OF MYSTERY

How is deity visualized in the prophetic books?[3] What is it like for God's holy transcendence to appear on this unholy planet? Or phrased another way, how does a spirit being, unlike anything mortals can imagine, reveal himself in a physical world? A review of some theophanies will suggest that there is no single way to envision God touching our world.

In Genesis 1 God's Spirit hovers over the waters of the unformed earth. In Genesis 3 he walks in the Garden of Eden in the cool of the day, making audible sounds. In Genesis 15 he is a smoking firepot with a blazing torch. In Genesis 28 he appears at the top of a sort of double escalator with angels riding up and down. In Genesis 32 he is a midnight wrestler, and Jacob reports that he saw God face to face. In Exodus 3 he is a burning bush that is not consumed. In Exodus 13 he is a pillar of cloud by day and a pillar of fire by night. In Exodus 19 he is in the midst of a dense cloud at the summit of Mount Sinai, accompanied by booming thunder, flashing lightning and a trumpet that sounds a long blast. God descends in fire, and the volcanic mountain shakes violently, belching forth smoke like a mighty furnace. Then the trumpet sounds an even louder blast. In Exodus 20 Moses encounters God in the midst of thick darkness.

Fast-forwarding to the last book of the Bible: in Revelation 1 the feet of Alpha and Omega glow like bronze in a furnace. His voice resounds like a cascade of rushing water. Out of his mouth comes a double-edged sword. His brilliant face shines like the sun. In Revelation 4 he has the appearance of precious stones with an emeraldlike rainbow encircling him. His seven spirits blaze like bright lamps. In Revelation 5 he is a Lamb with seven horns and seven eyes. In Revelation 14 the Lamb is standing on Mount Zion with 144,000 martyrs. Heavenly harpists play the new songs of eternity. In Revelation 19, with eyes of blazing fire and with too many crowns to count, he rides a white horse. The heavenly cavalry dressed in fine linen follows close on his heels. In Revelation 20 he is seated on a white throne, and earth and sky flee from his presence, because there is no room for them.

In each of these theophanies it is the same God (see figure 4.1). Yet each theophany gives a different description of the same God. Why? Because

God is a mystery. Because human language is too limited to describe the unlimited God. Because there are only approximate ways for us to visualize God's transcendence, and none of them is adequate in itself.[4] If we reflect on the Bible as a whole, the assignment to reveal God is a big challenge. To reveal him in a systematic way is impossible. Glimpses in many different settings and in extreme terms come together in a mosaic of mystery for understanding the transcendent deity. "We have no other language besides metaphor with which to speak about God."[5]

Descriptions of deity

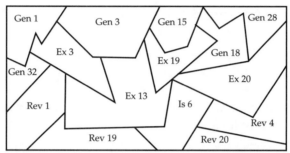

Each appearance or description of God found in different chapters of the Bible is one piece of a puzzle; each piece is unique and adds something to our understanding of God.

Figure 4.1. Pieces of the puzzle

Building on the various ways that God steps into our world, we move on to a related question. What would it be like—instead of God showing up in person—for his attribute of wrath to show up in all its fullness? Can we comprehend that better than we can comprehend God? The prophets suggest an answer, for their descriptions of God's righteous indignation also take on a diversity of extreme forms. Here are some typical ways of picturing God's wrath.

- He will make human beings scarcer than pure gold (Is 13:12).
- He will turn streams into pitch and dust into burning sulfur (Is 34:9).
- He will make oppressors eat their own flesh and drink their own blood (Is 49:26).
- "I will give their wives to other men and their fields to new owners" (Jer 8:10).

- "Fathers will eat their children, and children will eat their fathers" (Ezek 5:10).
- God will become a lion and will tear his people to pieces and carry them off, with no one to rescue them (Hos 5:14).
- He will drive them out of his house and no longer love them (Hos 9:15).
- He will cause their little ones to be dashed to the ground and their pregnant women to be ripped open (Hos 13:16).
- He will hunt them down and summon serpents to bite them and swords to slay them (Amos 9:3-4).

Wow! For humans to do such things would be considered barbaric. But what about God? Apparently the worst-sounding judgment that can be expressed in human language is inadequate to picture God's perfect wrath. In addition to the examples above, there are many other ways God's wrath is described, some less graphic and others equally graphic. (Read, for example, the book of Amos or Zephaniah.)

A corresponding question must be asked as well. What would it be like for God's attribute of love to pour forth a fullness of blessing? The prophets answer this question too.

- He will turn all mountains into roads (Is 49:11).
- His chosen people will be so revered that foreign kings and queens will lick the dust at their feet (Is 49:23).
- His people will "drink the milk of nations and . . . feed at the breasts of kings" (Is 60:16 NET).
- "They will sparkle in his land like jewels in a crown. How attractive and beautiful they will be! Grain will make the young men thrive, and new wine the young women" (Zech 9:16-17).
- Those who live in Jerusalem, even the feeblest among them, will become like David (Zech 12:8).
- "On that day living water will flow out from Jerusalem, half to the eastern sea and half to the western sea, in summer and in winter" (Zech 14:8).
- Of course there are many other ways God's blessings are described, some less graphic and others equally graphic. (Read Isaiah 43:1-7 or Hosea 11:1-4; 14:4-8 for examples.)

The variety and extremity of these expressions of God's wrath and love suggest something important: diverse descriptions of judgment and blessing are the only way to portray the full range of God's attributes, but even then our depth of vision is limited. The reason is not difficult to see: normal human language is simply inadequate to express the heights of God's love and the depths of his wrath. So the best the prophets can do with his attributes is the same as what they do with descriptions of his transcendence: offer a mosaic of mystery—glimpses of the attributes of God. Part of the explanation, then, for wild animals running all over the earth gorging themselves on sinners, and rivers of milk flowing through the countryside, is the inherent limitation of human language to describe the inherent majesty of God's love and wrath.[6] The best way to conceive the inconceivable about God is to picture him acting in very extreme ways.

Form Versus Function

Another clarification will help us understand extreme and unusual language of destruction and blessing: the function of language may prevail over form. As emphasized in chapter one, prophetic language is scripted to have the greatest impact possible on hearers.[7] It was a rhetoric of persuasion calling for repentance. Prophets preached stirring sermons and followed that by writing powerful poetry.[8] Language was pressed into service for gut-wrenching messages. Mission Impossible was to dismantle the dominant consciousness of contemporary culture. This prophetic mantle was being passed along from Moses to Malachi, and it was a huge challenge. Consequently we must be sensitive to ways the prophets responded to the task. Grasping the distinction between what a prophet said and what he meant is an important part of interpretation.

What a speaker intends to communicate is known as *illocution* or *speech acts*.[9] Because a word may have meaning that transcends its dictionary definition, illocution must be carefully considered. Only when the function of what is said is clear can the language be understood.[10]

Multiple intentions of the same words. Understanding the intent of the sentence "I need a glass of water" requires more than a grammar book and dictionary. Those same words in the same order function in different ways. Spoken to a nurse by someone being prepared for surgery, the sentence may be equivalent to saying, "My mouth is dry." The patient knows that a drink will be permitted only after surgery. But spoken to a waitress in a restaurant, "I need a glass of water" may be a request for a specific response from the server. It would be equivalent to saying, "Please bring me a glass of water." Spoken by someone stranded in a desert, "I need a glass of water" may be a desperate expression of hopelessness. It would be equivalent to saying, "I'm dying." The real function of "I need a glass of water" varies according to the speaker's intent.

Illocution can be analyzed from three perspectives: what speakers intend to express based on their perspective on the subject, how the communication is expressed and what impact the communication has on hearers. Language may be informative as a channel for the exchange of data or ideas between people. But more often speakers intend their communication to have a particular impact on listeners. A wife telling her husband about a busy day caring for three children may say something like this: "Today I lost my sanity. Everything imaginable went wrong. I was so mad at the little dinosaurs I wanted to bite their heads off. I'm going shopping. And I may never return." The vividness of her language, with its metaphors and hyperbole, reveals intense emotion beneath her words. Her communication is much more than informative. She is probably eliciting sympathy and prompting her husband to take action that would ease her stress. She is at least clearly stating that the children are his responsibility for the rest of the evening.

Speech acts. Communication often is performative.[11] The intent is to produce some action in the hearer. On the surface the frustrated mother is not asking her husband to do anything, but in reality she is. By children and parents, teachers and preachers, words are used to produce change in hearers. There are numerous examples. If someone says, "I think it's going to rain," that may be intended as advice to carry an umbrella or to close the car windows (see figure 4.2). If someone compliments us, we may respond, "Flattery will get you nowhere," because we sense a hidden agenda in the comment. Research suggests that there is a close connection be-

The same words spoken in different contexts may have different functions

Oh no, it's going to rain.	(= We're going to get wet.)
Oh no, it's going to rain.	(= I won't get the lawn mowed.)
Oh good, it's going to rain.	(= I don't have to mow the lawn.)
Oh good, it's going to rain.	(= My garden will get watered.)
Hurry up, it's going to rain.	(= We must finish painting quickly.)
Relax, it's going to rain.	(= We'll do the painting another day.)

Figure 4.2. Illocution

tween emotion and cognition: emotions can shape what we believe.[12] As demonstrated in chapter one, much of prophetic language is emotionally charged. It is designed to influence our beliefs.

Most important to understanding illocution is noting how words are used in ways different from what is found in a dictionary. Two people greeting each other may have an exchange of words such as "Good morning." "How are you?" "Fine." "Have a good day." Here it is irrelevant whether the person is fine and whether the wishes for a good morning and a good day are sincere. In this case the function of the exchange of words is to establish contact. Contrary to the claim of some who fail to understand the function of language, it is not deceptive to respond with "Fine" even if the events of the day have been unbearable, since the accepted function of "Good morning" and "Fine" is the courtesy of friendship. The dictionary definition of words may have little bearing on their function. Whether the speaker chooses to say "Good morning," "Hello," "How are you?" or "Greetings," the effect is little different.

Illocution in the prophets. If human language functions this way, does it necessarily mean the prophets said things that meant something different from what those words would normally mean?[13] Of course any figurative language fits this category, but there is more to it than that. For example, God says that he will not hear the prayers of his people: "And when they cry out to me for help, I will not listen to them" (Jer 11:11 NET). He instructs Jeremiah not to pray for his people (Jer 7:16; 11:14; 14:11). At one point God says he no longer loves his people: "Because of their sinful deeds, I will drive them out of my house. I will no longer love them; all their leaders are rebellious" (Hos 9:15). The function of these statements obviously does not correspond with the dictionary definition of the words. (Other examples of illocution will be discussed later in this chapter.)

Many students of the Bible overlook the implications of illocution, failing to realize that the words of Scripture are often more than merely informative. The *function* of statements in the Bible can be as important for understanding their meaning as the *content* of the statements. But if the illocution of a communication is not shared by the author and the hearer, then the hearer will not recognize the author's intended meaning. Ignorance of illocution leads to exegetical fallacies. Awareness of illocution will help guide interpreters to correct understandings of Scripture.

LANGUAGE OF LOVE, LANGUAGE OF WRATH

To understand the prophetic illocution of announcements of judgment and blessing, the most important insight comes from the Pentateuch. God announced amazing blessings and terrifying curses through his spokesman Moses. "If you follow my decrees and are careful to obey my commands . . . your threshing will continue until grape harvest and the grape harvest will continue until planting, and you will eat all the food you want and live in safety in your land" (Lev 26:3, 5). On the other hand, "If you remain hostile toward me and refuse to listen to me, I will multiply your afflictions seven times over, as your sins deserve. I will send wild animals against you, and they will rob you of your children, destroy your cattle and make you so few in number that your roads will de deserted" (Lev 26:21-22). But the language of curses and blessings actually originated in ancient Near Eastern culture. If we understand how this language functioned, we will understand the prophets more clearly.[14]

In a society where agreements under oath were subject to being broken, various curses were invoked on potential violators. An example is treaties between a king and a vassal state. The stipulations of the agreement were stated, the gods witnessing the treaty were listed, and the king's curses on violators of the treaty were announced. The result was a distinct genre for enacting treaties, all designed to ensure the allegiance of the vassal. The most striking element of the genre is the announcement of terrifying consequences on any who disregard the treaty. Since this language was intended to encourage compliance with the terms of the agreement, the treaties were often posted publicly for all to see.

Curses in the Ancient Near East. The Aramaic inscriptions of Sefire provide good examples of threatening curses, if a treaty should be violated.[15]

Just as a calf is cut in two, may he be cut in two, and may his nobles be cut in two. Just as a harlot is stripped naked, may his wives be stripped naked, and the wives of his offspring, and the wives of his nobles.

May the city become a mound to house the desert animal: the gazelle and the fox and the wild-cat and the owl; may this city be mentioned no more; may it be sown with salt and weeds and may it not be mentioned again.

Should seven nurses anoint their breasts and nurse a young boy, may he not have his fill; should seven mares suckle a colt, may it not be sated; should seven cows give suck to a calf, may it not have its fill; should seven hens go looking for food, may they not kill anything.

Other examples come from the vassal treaties of Esarhaddon. In this language of malediction, every conceivable adversity is wished in the most graphic of terms on any who do not comply with the terms of the treaties.[16]

May he fell you with his swift arrow; may he fill the plain with your corpses; may he feed your flesh to the eagle and jackal.

May your wives lie in the lap of your enemy before your eyes; may your sons not possess your house; may a foreign enemy divide your goods; may birth be cut off from your land; may the cries of little children in the streets and squares be rare.

May he submerge your land with a great flood; may the locust devour your harvest; may there be no mill or oven in your houses; may no grain be poured out for grinding; instead of grain, may they grind your bones and those of your sons and daughters; may your finger-tips not dip in the dough.

May the earth not receive your corpses; may you be food in the belly of a dog or pig; may anything good be an abomination to you; may tar and pitch be your food; may the urine of an ass be your drink; may duckweed be your covering.

The illocution of these threats is obvious. By imagining the worst possible consequences, kings sought to strike fear in the hearts of potential violators. Of course the chance that things this bad could happen was remote. Yet respect for the gods meant that these things could not be discounted completely. The gods, after all, were called in as witnesses.

Curses and blessings in the Old Testament. The treaty of all treaties was the covenant between God and his people (the same word is used in the Old Testament to designate an international treaty as to refer to the covenant). Mentioned first with Noah (Gen 6:18), developed more fully with Abraham (Gen 12:2-3; 17:1-14), and presented in full regalia with Moses (Ex 19:3-8), the message of the covenant came down to two choices: obey and be blessed, disobey and be cursed.

See, I set before you today life and prosperity, death and destruction. For I command you today to love the LORD your God, to walk in his ways, and to keep his commands, decrees and laws; then you will live and increase, and the LORD your God will bless you in the land you are entering to possess.

But if your heart turns away and you are not obedient, and if you are drawn away to bow down to other gods and worship them, I declare to you this day that you will certainly be destroyed. You will not live long in the land you are crossing the Jordan to enter and possess.

This day I call heaven and earth as witnesses against you that I have set before you life and death, blessings and curses. (Deut 30:15-20)

These two coordinates of the Old Testament determine a person's relationship with God: God will bless his people, but only if they are faithful to him. God will judge his people, but only if they are unfaithful to him. Retribution theology like this is usually associated with the covenant. The blessings will be incredible. The judgment will be totally opposite and just as incredible. A middle-of-the-road option is nowhere to be found (see figure 4.3).

The covenant with God offers two options

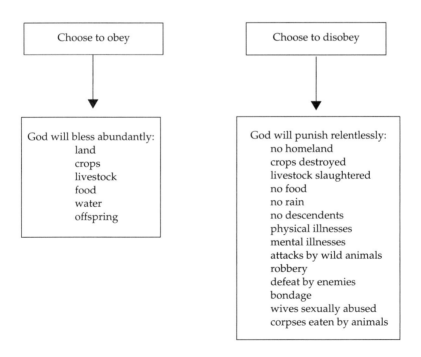

Figure 4.3. Abundant blessing or relentless judgment

Leviticus 26 and Deuteronomy 28 in particular display God's perspective on the obedience and disobedience of his people. These two chapters constitute the most extensive scorecard of blessings and curses in the Pentateuch. Most prominent is the ever-intensifying compendium of judgment on disobedience, from agricultural failure to grave illness to enemy siege to cannibalism to being sent back to Egypt into slavery. The intent is to "formalize, articulate, and enforce the relationship between Israel and the Lord."[17] Following the basic structure of the genre of treaties, the book of Deuteronomy climaxes in chapter 28, mentioning first the telltale blessings from a beneficent king. Since obedience is the key to a good life and prosperity, those who comply with the covenant can expect the best.

> You will be blessed in the city and blessed in the country. . . .
>
> The LORD will grant that the enemies who rise up against you will be defeated before you. . . .
>
> The LORD will send a blessing on your barns and everything you put your hand to. . . .
>
> All the peoples of the earth will see that you are called by the name of the LORD, and they will fear you. The LORD will grant you abundant prosperity—in the fruit of your womb, the young of your livestock and the crops of your ground—in the land he swore to your forefathers to give you. . . .
>
> The Lord will make you the head, not the tail. . . . You will always be at the top, never at the bottom. (Deut 28:3-13)

That list of blessings, however, is only a brief forerunner to what follows: a marathon list of merciless curses, spiraling downward into every kind of chaos. Judgments almost beyond imagination take center stage, invoking all possible disasters on every person who might dare to contemplate disobedience. The consequence of obedience, which is blessing and prosperity, may seem to get short shrift. The consequence of disobedience, on the other hand, which deprives people of everything that is needed or desirable, may seem to get too much shrift.

> The LORD will send on you curses, confusion and rebuke in everything you put your hand to, until you are destroyed and come to sudden ruin. . . . The Lord will strike you with wasting disease, with fever and inflammation, with scorching heat and drought, with blight and mildew, which will plague you until you perish. . . .

The Lord will afflict you with madness, blindness and confusion of mind. . . .

You will be pledged to be married to a woman, but another will take her and ravish her. . . .

You will plant vineyards and cultivate them but you will not drink the wine or gather the grapes, because worms will eat them. . . . You will have sons and daughters but you will not keep them, because they will go into captivity. . . .

You will eat the fruit of the womb, the flesh of the sons and daughters the Lord your God has given you. Even the most gentle and sensitive man among you will have no compassion on his own brother. . . . The most gentle and sensitive woman among you . . . will begrudge . . . the afterbirth from her womb and the children she bears. For she intends to eat them secretly during the siege. (Deut 28:20-57)

Several things about this language of judgment are noteworthy.

The first observation is the literary technique. Carefully constructed symmetry is evident in parallel blessings and curses. You will be blessed so that "your enemies will come at you from one direction but flee from you in seven," while you will be cursed so that "you will come at them from one direction but flee from them in seven." Metaphor is prominent. "The sky over your head will be bronze, the ground beneath you iron." Hyperbole is used to heighten the impact of the threats. "The Lord will turn the rain of your country into dust and powder; it will come down from the skies until you are destroyed. . . . In hunger and thirst, in nakedness and dire poverty, you will serve the enemies the Lord sends against you."

A second observation is the barrage of curses that seems never-ending. In the whole scope of curses and blessings there are thirty different themes,[18] each a specific way that obedience will be blessed and disobedience will be judged: abundance of crops versus no crops, abundance of livestock versus no livestock, fertile land versus infertile land, abundance of food versus no food, abundance of descendants versus no descendants, good health versus illness, freedom versus bondage, victory over enemies versus defeat by enemies, dominion over animals versus wild animals that attack, and so on. (See appendix B.)

A third observation is the deliberately intimidating language, designed to be overwhelming. In every conceivable way, Deuteronomy 28 describes God liquidating his people from the face of the earth for their disobedience. And in case a means of destruction was overlooked, "the Lord will pour out on you every kind of sickness and plague not mentioned in this book of instruction until you have perished" (Deut 28:61 NET). After so many curses, that almost falls on deaf ears.

A fourth observation is that the curses are specifically directed toward an agriculturally based population. The people of Israel would not necessarily always be agriculturally based, but these curses are representative of the kind and severity of God's judgment.

A fifth observation is that some of the curses seem self-contradicting, at least on the surface. At one point it is announced that because of drought and famine there will be nothing on the vine and there will be nothing to eat or drink. But subsequently we read that worms will eat all the fruit of the vine, enemies will come and eat all the fruit, and people will begrudge food to one another. So, reading the text superficially, drought and famine do not eliminate all the crops after all. It is also announced that the disobedient will perish from illnesses that cannot be healed and their corpses will be food for birds. But subsequently it states that they will plant vineyards, bear children and serve other gods. Yet these are not really contradictions if we get beneath the surface and understand the point of the statements.

There is yet another way that the curses may seem contradictory: in the multiple death sentences on the disobedient. For example, "The LORD will send on you curses, confusion and rebuke in everything you put your hand to, until you are destroyed and come to sudden ruin. . . . The LORD will plague you with diseases until he has destroyed you. . . . The Lord will strike you with wasting disease . . . until you perish. . . . Your carcasses will be food for all the birds of the air and the beasts of the earth. . . . The LORD will afflict you with the boils of Egypt . . . from which you cannot be cured. . . . He will put an iron yoke on your neck until he has destroyed you." In this litany of curses everyone gets destroyed numerous times. The relentless language of extreme consequences for sin sends people to hell again and again. In modern terms it would be parallel to our saying, if you do not follow all the commands and decrees of the laws of this land, you will be sent to the gallows and to the electric chair and to the gas chamber and to the firing squad and to the guillotine and to be flayed alive!

TENTATIVE CONCLUSIONS

Based on the exploration thus far into the language of destruction and blessing, some conclusions can be posited for issues such as which lens will give clearer vision for seeing our way through the prophetic corpus. How does the language of the covenant relate to the genre of curses in ancient Near Eastern treaties? Are we to take the language of destruction at face value? What is the illocution of the language of destruction and blessing? The following elements are essential to arriving at correct answers (see figure 4.4): God's covenant with his people and their disobedience, the warning that God's judgment will be severe, the inadequacy of human language to describe the depths of God's wrath, the challenge to hearers to take all this seriously, and imaginative language picturing punishment in the worst possible ways. Putting the elements together, we can draw the following inferences.

1. Parallels between God enforcing his covenant with the Israelites and kings enforcing treaties with vassals suggest that the language of judgment in Leviticus 26 and Deuteronomy 28 comes from the same cloth as the genre of malediction in the ancient Near East. Kings called down judgment on all violators, announcing every imaginable curse of the most extreme kinds, in order to ensure compliance with the terms of the agreement. Likewise God's spokesmen announced judgment of the highest degree on the disobedient, warning all violators of the covenant that there would be deathly consequences.

2. The pattern in the language of judgment was apparently to announce every conceivable adversity in the most graphic of terms. This was language designed to get the hearers' attention, to warn of serious consequences, to arouse fear, to imagine what it would be like to be sinners in the hands of an angry God. "The LORD will bring you back in ships to

Keys to understanding the language of judgment

❧ Hyperboles of harsh language were common in the ancient world.

❧ Human language is inadequate to describe God's wrath.

❧ God's wrath was visualized in extreme language.

❧ Fixed phrases of judgment were applied to varying situations.

❧ Words may function beyond dictionary definitions.

Figure 4.4. Language of judgment

Egypt, by a route that I promised you would never see again" (Deut 28:68 NRSV). So were these hollow threats? No, for God did discipline the Israelites in line with the ways stated, and he still judges disobedience. The flip side is that no one knows in advance which of the specific kinds of judgment mentioned in the curses God will use, or whether he will use methods not even mentioned. The intent of the language was not to specify the details of destruction that would come in the near or distant future.

3. God's judgment must be visualized in diverse ways if its totality is to be expressed. The limitations of human language to describe God call forth many different expressions of his wrath. The point was not to announce the precise and only forms it would take. We do not need to know the details of how God will judge. But everyone needs to understand God's stance on disobedience and the kind of severe vengeance he has in store for the disobedient.

4. This visualized language of judgment is actually a form of metaphor. It is describing the whole of God's judgment, but it refers to it by its parts. Technically it is synecdoche. It is a painting portraying condemnation, and each specific is a brush stroke on the larger canvas. It is the language of hyperbolic metaphor.[19]

5. What has been stated regarding the language of judgment applies in similar fashion to the language of blessing. Though the latter receives much less press, the blessings of obedience are just as real.

This discussion of how God's wrath and love are expressed, particularly in the Pentateuch, provides essential background to the language of the prophets. The prophets will say many of the same things in the same ways.

THE VISUALIZED LANGUAGE OF PROPHECY

The concept of covenant, which is clearly established in the Pentateuch, permeates the whole of the Old Testament. But it is especially prominent in the prophets. Without the covenant there would be no prophets, for their primary role was to be covenant enforcers. They used covenantal language and enlarged it to apprehend violators of the covenant and call them back to the God of Moses.[20] And with the ever-increasing crisis in God's relationship with his people, the enforcers were kept busy. "Judah has broken faith. A detestable thing has been committed in Israel and in

Jerusalem: Judah has desecrated the sanctuary the LORD loves, by marrying the daughter of a foreign god" (Mal 2:11). The role of the prophets was to blow the whistle and cry foul. Something needed to be done. Unfortunately the game had already gotten out of hand. Even though the prophets blew their whistles loud and long and charged after the offending players, the pandemonium continued. It would be up to God to eject the offending players from the game. "The world is a proud place, full of beauty, but the prophets are scandalized, and rave as if the whole world were a slum."[21]

The prophets offered two options, even as the covenant had two options (see figure 4.3, p. 85). Those who complied with the rules of the game would be blessed richly. Those who did not would be damned horribly. The prophets' oracles of salvation were for the obedient. Their oracles of judgment were for the disobedient.

The denouncements of apostasy and predictions of indescribable catastrophes became standard fare, with clear similarities to malediction. Meanwhile, the oracles of salvation promised incredible hope if repentance came before it was too late. Josephus (*Antiquities* 1.14) sums up the message of the prophets with the observation that those who obey "prosper in all things beyond belief" and those who do not end up in "irretrievable disasters." The adjectives of Josephus are telling. The prophets speak in metaphorical language precisely because the hope is "beyond belief" and the judgment is "irretrievable."[22]

The nature of the language of destruction and blessing is best illustrated if we examine recurring themes in the Pentateuch and prophets. It will allow us to test the tentative conclusions suggested above. In so doing we will discover additional insights into how this language functions. The most prominent motifs of destruction and blessing are as follows.

Land and productivity (see pp. 214-16). "The LORD will make you abound in prosperity, in the fruit of your womb" (Deut 28:11 NRSV). The language of blessing on the land is an unexpected flashback to what it was like in the Garden of Eden: seed-bearing and fruit-yielding trees in abundance, barns overflowing with produce. The painful toil of cultivation and the sweat of pulling out thorns and thistles are replaced with an abundance of produce without effort. These blessings for obedience are articulated in such lofty language that the consequences of the Fall (Gen 3) seem to have been reversed. That was in striking contrast to the Israelites' forty years in the desert, where trying to eke out an existence would have been etched in memory. Now they are offered vineyards and olive groves that they did not even plant (Deut 6:11), grain already harvested and in storage (Lev 26:10), flowing streams and underground springs gushing up in hills and valleys (Deut 8:7). In the hyperbolic language of blessing, the Edenic curse is canceled. The prophets take the imagery a notch higher:

- "The desert shall rejoice, and blossom like the rose" (Is 35:1 KJV).
- "Every valley shall be lifted up, and every mountain and hill be made low" (Is 40:4 NRSV).
- "I will make streams flow down the slopes. . . . I will turn the desert into a pool of water" (Is 41:18 NET).
- "He will make her deserts like Eden, her wastelands like the garden of the Lord" (Is 51:3).

This was music to the ears of weary desert travelers. But just as graphic were the curses:

- If you become corrupt and do evil in the eyes of the Lord, "you will soon utterly perish from the land that you are crossing the Jordan to occupy" (Deut 4:26 NRSV).
- If you do not obey the Lord your God, "you shall be plucked off the land that you are entering to possess" (Deut 28:63 NRSV).
- "The riverbed will be parched and dry. The canals will stink; the streams of Egypt will dwindle and dry up" (Is 19:5-6).
- "'I will take away their harvest,' says the Lord. 'There will be no grapes on their vines. There will be no figs on their fig trees. Even the leaves on their trees will wither. The crops that I gave them will be taken away'" (Jer 8:13 NET).

With many other extreme consequences, the violators of the covenant are called to reconsider their disobedience.

Descendants (see pp. 216-17). In a patriarchal society, it was the epitome of the good life to be surrounded by an abundance of offspring, to have a "full quiver." Thus Abraham is promised descendants like the dust of the earth, "so that if anyone could count the dust, then your offspring could be counted" (Gen 13:16). "I have made you the father of many nations. . . . I will make nations of you, and kings will come from you" (Gen 17:5-6). "You shall be the most blessed of peoples, with neither sterility nor barrenness among you" (Deut 7:14 NRSV). When Rebekah is chosen to become

Isaac's wife, a blessing is given: "Our sister, may you increase to thousands upon thousands" (Gen 24:60). Just before entering the Promised Land, Moses announces, "The LORD has increased your numbers so that today you are as many as the stars in the sky. May the LORD, the God of your fathers, increase you a thousand times more" (Deut 1:10-11). The hyperbole is obvious.

On the other hand, the language of judgment threatens to deprive the disobedient of all descendants. Offspring disappear by a variety of horrible means, from wild animals eating them, to parents eating the fruit of the womb and—most demoralizing of all—a mother eating her own afterbirth (Deut 28:56-57). Both Isaiah and Jeremiah use imagery of descendants. Isaiah informs God's covenant people that if they had only been obedient, then their descendants would have been numberless as grains of sand, and their name would never have been cut off or destroyed (Is 48:18-19). But they were not obedient and they were destroyed. The quiver full of descendants never reached the hyperbolic proportion that was possible. Thus the blessing evaporated because of disobedience. Where are the Israelites who signed the covenant in the blood of circumcision? Are they listening?

Homeland (see pp. 217-18). Almost equal in importance in ancient society to having descendants was being in a homeland. Thus God promised Abraham that his descendants would possess the land from the river of Egypt to the Euphrates (Gen 15:18). But the land quickly became an object of God's judgment when he proclaimed such curses as all the soil of the land being burned out by sulfur and salt, leaving nothing planted, nothing sprouting, and the earth unable to support any vegetation (Deut 29:22-23). "On that day every place where there used to be a thousand vines . . . will become briers and thorns" (Is 7:23-24 NRSV). "The earth will be completely devastated and thoroughly ransacked" (Is 24:3 NET). Cain's curse as a fugitive and wanderer on the earth was not unlike the Israelites' curse of being deported from their land—essentially a form of disembodiment. This language of dispersion is prevalent in the curses of the covenant. "I will scatter you among the nations. . . . You will perish among the nations; the land of your enemies will devour you" (Lev 26:33, 38).

If the Israelites would perish in their dispersion, it meant there was no hope of restoration. But after an infinity of invective against anyone who would disobey the law of the Lord, Moses offers a ray of hope: even if you have been banished to the most distant land under the heavens, if you and your children return to the Lord your God and obey him, he will bring you back to the land of your forefathers, and you will take possession of it (Deut 30:2-5).

If we fail to understand the illocution of this language, the judgment of destruction via dispersion can leave people with Western analytical minds scratching our heads. We read that if the Israelites do evil in the eyes of the Lord, they will perish quickly and certainly be destroyed (Deut 4:25-26). But we read that they will be scattered to the ends of the earth. Then we read that they will be destroyed during the time of their captivity. Yet they can be restored to the homeland (Deut 4:27-31)! Apparently we are not supposed to read this language using our Western analytical minds. Instead we must recognize the illocutionary technique of describing judgment and blessing in every conceivable way and in the most graphic of terms.

It is not surprising that Isaiah and Jeremiah both have much to say about captivity and restoration. Isaiah catches us off-guard with an image of dispersion: "He will wind you up tightly into a ball and throw you into a wide, open land" (Is 22:18 NET). Jeremiah is not satisfied with simple captivity: God's chosen people will be scattered among the nations until they are completely destroyed (Jer 9:16). The prophets repeatedly pronounced the judgment of captivity on the Israelites.

But the prophets also pronounced the judgment of captivity on Gentile nations. "I will disperse the Egyptians among the nations and scatter them through the countries" (Ezek 29:12). Isaiah uses the language of dispersion for all the inhabitants of the whole earth—they will all be sent into captivity (Is 24:1). He also turns the idea of captivity against the enemies of the Israelites, saying that they will go into exile too (Jer 30:16). For the Israelites judgment by captivity certainly came to pass. But for the Gentiles? the Egyptians? What was their deportation?

This points to another factor in the language of judgment. In the prophets' announcing dispersion for the Egyptians, as well as for the inhabitants of the whole earth and all the enemies of the Israelites, we have evidence of *fixed language.* Describing the extrication of people from their homeland was a stock way of expressing God's judgment. Homer Heater explored the role of destruction language in the prophets and found eight stock motifs: cities and people cursed as objects of horror to passersby, cities completely desolate, cities as haunts for wild animals, cities that no one passes through anymore, destruction to match Sodom and Gomorrah, summons for enemies to attack, scattering everywhere, and removal of sounds of joy. He concluded that the virtually identical language applied to Jerusalem, Babylon, Edom and Hazor demonstrates that the language is ritualistic and stereotypical. "The language of destruction . . . speaks generally and hyperbolically of devastating defeat and destruction without requiring detailed fulfillment."[23] That is a significant insight into the language of judgment and blessing. Not only were God's spokesmen using every imaginable way to express judgment, but some forms of that language had become stereotypical (see pages 148-49).

Restoration (see p. 218). Beginning in Deuteronomy and continuing through the prophets, words of restoration balance out the words of dispersion. Yahweh will gather you again from all the nations where he scattered you. Then Yahweh your God will restore your fortunes (Deut 30:3). "I will bring your children from the east and gather you from the west. I will say to the north, 'Give them up!' and to the south, 'Do not hold them back'" (Is 43:5-6). Without the hope of restoration, God might have come across as a God of wrath alone.

> I will restore the fortunes of my people Israel,
>   and they shall rebuild the ruined cities and inhabit them;
> they shall plant vineyards and drink their wine,
>   and they shall make gardens and eat their fruit.
> I will plant them upon their land,
>   and they shall never again be plucked up
>   out of the land that I have given them,
>   says the LORD your God. (Amos 9:14-15 NRSV)

But several issues are not clear. Is the language of restoration a hyperbolic way of assuring the people of God's future blessing? What is the basis of restoration? Is repentance a prerequisite? "The LORD your God is merciful; he will not abandon you or destroy you or forget the covenant with your forefathers" (Deut 4:31). In most contexts restoration is promised without condition. In others the restoration depends on recommitment to the terms of the covenant (Deut 30:1-4). In any event, to understand the free-flowing language of restoration—new wine will drip from the mountains and flow from all the hills (Joel 3:18; Amos 9:13)—we must recall the imaginative language of blessing in the covenant:

- "Your threshing will continue until grape harvest and the grape harvest will continue until planting. . . . I will remove savage beasts from the land and the sword will not pass through your country. . . . Five of you will chase a hundred [enemies], and a hundred of you will chase ten thousand, and your enemies will fall by the sword before you. . . . You will still be eating last year's harvest when you will have to move it out to make room for the new" (Lev 26:5-10).

- "The LORD will make you the head, not the tail. If you pay attention to the commands of the LORD your God . . . you will always be at the top, never at the bottom" (Deut 28:13).

The language of restoration seems similarly hyped: "The reaper will be overtaken by the plowman and the planter by the one treading grapes" (Amos 9:13). Covenantal language is everywhere poetic, even when not in verse, speaking to our emotions and leaving us with a profound sense of mystery. Our heads may not understand, but our hearts get the message loud and clear. In the end God will bless in ways beyond explanation.[24]

Desolation (see pp. 218-19). "I will turn your cities into ruins and lay waste your sanctuaries" (Lev 26:31). "The whole land will be a burning waste of salt and sulfur" (Deut 29:23). The most common motif of judgment in the prophets is desolation: Damascus will become a heap of ruins, its towns will be deserted forever (Is 17:1).

> *I looked on the earth, and lo, it was waste and void;*
> *and to the heavens, and they had no light.*
> *I looked on the mountains, and lo, they were quaking,*
> *and all the hills moved to and fro. . . .*
> *I looked, and lo, the fruitful land was a desert,*
> *and all its cities were laid in ruins*
> *before the LORD, before his fierce anger.*
>
> *For thus says the Lord: the whole land shall be a desolation;*
> *yet I will not make a full end.*
>
> *Because of this the earth shall mourn,*
> *and the heavens above grow black.* (Jer 4:23-28 NRSV)

Cities strong and populous will be overgrown with thickets or inhabited by jackals, and not a soul will dwell there, nor will an Arab even dare to pitch a tent (Is 13:20). Your sacred cities have become a desert; even Zion is a desert, Jerusalem a desolation, a wasteland forever (Is 32:14; 64:10). Much of this language is again stock imagery for judgment: Babylon and the cities of Damascus, Memphis, Tyre and Jerusalem are described as desolate forever.[25]

Acclamation (see p. 220). In contrast to desolation, the motif of acclamation describes people coming to the Holy City from the ends of the earth. The mountain of the Lord's temple will be chief among the mountains; all the nations will stream to it (Is 2:2). "Those who were perishing in Assyria and those who were exiled in Egypt will come and worship the Lord on the holy mountain in Jerusalem" (Is 27:13). "They will come from afar— some from the north, some from the west, some from the region of Aswan" (Is 49:12). "Nations will come to your light, and kings to the brightness of your dawn" (Is 60:3).

Related to acclamation are descriptions of highways and roads paved through deserts and across hills that have been leveled, allusions to a reversal of what was experienced at the time of the exodus (see p. 221). In light of the other paradigmatic language of prophecy, these words of acclamation are likely part of the stock language of blessing. Note that regarding Babylon, acclamation is reversed as judgment: the nations will no longer stream to it (Jer 51:44).

Exposure (see pp. 221-22). "Your corpses shall be food for every bird of the air and animal of the earth, and there shall be no one to frighten them away" (Deut 28:26 NRSV). Almost identical wording occurs in the former prophets, beginning with David and Goliath and their taunts (1 Sam 17:44, 46). The same language of judgment is heard again in regard to Jeroboam, Ahab, Jezebel and others at the time of the divided monarchy (e.g., 1 Kings 14:11). Of the rest of the prophets, Jeremiah and Ezekiel use the form frequently, applying it to Judah or Jerusalem (in Jeremiah) and to Judah, Egypt and Gog (in Ezekiel). In some cases the phrases are almost exactly as they appear in Deuteronomy. But the prophets are not bound by a particular formula. Jeremiah takes the idea of exposed and unburied bodies and develops a metaphor of reapers leaving behind unwanted sheaves (Jer 9:22). Ezekiel expands on the metaphor in an apocalyptic scene with the hordes of Gog being sacrificed to birds and wild animals on the mountains of Israel (Ezek 39:17-20). All of this makes it likely that we have another stock image used to express judgment. But exposure is not necessarily always and only metaphoric—witness the case of Jezebel. However, the consistent repetition of almost identical forms of the imagery within various settings of judgment strongly suggests that the language may be stereotypical.

Forever (see p. 222). A very important word for understanding much of prophecy is the adverb *forever,* and its significance needs to be considered carefully. Interesting questions arise about what it means. One semantic domain of *forever* can designate something that is true presently and lasts indefinitely into the future, without interruption and without end. "Your statues are forever right" (Ps 119:144). This meaning is the first to come to mind when we hear the word *forever.* For example:

- "All the land that you see I will give to you and your offspring forever" (Gen 13:15).
- "I will give your descendants all this land I promised them, and it will be their inheritance forever" (Ex 32:13).
- "I will allow your dynasty to rule over Israel permanently" (1 Kings 9:5 NET).

But the occurrences of *forever* within the covenants do not seem to fit that designation. It simply has not been forever, at least in the sense of being permanent from the time it was spoken. Since it has not been forever, what does *forever* mean?

It is common for *forever* to be thought of as something very different, though many are unaware of how they have transformed the word to suit their purposes. In this case, *forever* may or may not begin immediately, may be interrupted for long periods of time, and may achieve its perpetuity only in the distant future, when time essentially will no longer matter anyway. Note the promise to David:

- "Now I will make your name great, like the names of the greatest men of the earth. And I will provide a place for my people Israel and will plant them so that they can have a home of their own and no longer be disturbed. . . . I will also give you rest from all your enemies. . . . Your throne and your kingdom will endure forever before me; your throne will be established forever" (2 Sam 7:9-11, 16).
- "For this is what the LORD says: 'David will never fail to have a man to sit on the throne of the house of Israel, nor will the priests, who are Levites, ever fail to have a man to stand before me continually to offer burnt offerings, to burn grain offerings and to present sacrifices'" (Jer 33:17-18).

But in what sense has David's throne endured forever? In what sense have sacrifices been offered forever? There have been major interruptions: the destructions of Jerusalem by the Babylonians, by the Seleucids and by the Romans. It is certainly a curious way to think of *forever* if it only means part of the time.

One way of dealing with the issue of *forever* allows for interruptions in the near future and sees the perpetuity fulfilled in the not-distant future: this solution transfers the designee from Israel to the church. But that solution is necessary only if the real intent of *forever* is overlooked.

1. A semantic domain for *forever* may designate perpetuity in the present world, with no notion of its being without end. It is simply the notion of continuing. For example, "may my lord King David live forever" (1 Kings 1:31; cf. Neh 2:3; Dan 2:4; 3:9; 6:21); "these stones are to be a memorial to the people of Israel forever" (Josh 4:7).

2. *Forever* may be used in hyperbole, especially in poetic literature:

- "Night and day [Edom] shall not be quenched; its smoke shall go up forever" (Is 34:10 NRSV).
- "In my anger a fire is kindled that shall burn forever" (Jer 15:14 NRSV; cf. 17:4).
- "I will kindle a fire in [Jerusalem's] gates; it shall devour the palaces of Jerusalem and shall not be quenched" (Jer 17:27 NRSV).
- God's people have been "making their land a horror, a thing to be hissed at forever" (Jer 18:16 NRSV).
- Regarding his submarine ride in a big fish, Jonah reports, "I went down to the land whose bars closed upon me forever" (Jon 2:6 NRSV).

3. Most important, there is yet another use of *forever,* though no dictionary suggests this domain for either the Hebrew or the Greek form or for our English word. Fortunately, as English speakers we are already acquainted with the illocution. We might say to someone who has just done us a fine favor, "I will never forget what you have done for me."[26] In so doing we are not making a declaration in line with a dictionary definition of *forever.* We definitely are not saying that there will be no interruption and no end to our thinking about what that person has done for us. Nor are we conscious of hyperbole. A literalist might say that we should never make such a statement because we cannot guarantee that it will be true. That same literalist might say it is wrong to answer "fine" if someone asks in passing how we are doing (see discussion above). But that misses the point of the function of language. *Forever* has a legitimate function not described in dictionaries, and the functional definition may be even more important than the nonfunctional one.

What then is the illocution of *forever* in the statement "I will never forget what you have done for me"? (It is inconsequential whether we say "I will forever remember" or "I will never forget.") *Forever* serves to intensify the verb it modifies, *remember*. Sweethearts say "I love you forever" to express depth of commitment.[27] Thus a nearly equivalent statement to "I will never forget what you have done for me" would be "I will surely remember what you have done for me." But that loses something. By saying "I will never, ever forget," we actually make a stronger statement of the depths of our appreciation. It could be called an element of mystery that makes the statement even more powerful. Tell two sweethearts to substitute "I surely love you" for "I will love you forever," and they will feel that they have lost something.

Now we must test this functional definition within the scope of the Pentateuch and prophets to see whether it has validity in helping us understand Scripture correctly. Is *forever* used to add a sense of pregnancy to language, or a sense of power and emotion and mystery, rather than a simple indication of perpetuity? When Balaam pronounced an oracle against the nation of Amalek, he said that they would "perish forever" (Num 24:20 NRSV). When Jonathan confirmed with David a plan to send him a signal by shooting three arrows, he said, "As for the matter about which you and I have spoken, the LORD is witness between you and me forever" (1 Sam 20:23 NRSV). When a slave agreed to be a household slave, the law said, "he shall be your slave forever" (Deut 15:17 NRSV; cf. Philem 15). When Moses recorded the long list of curses on disobedience, he said that these curses "shall be among you and your descendants . . . forever" (Deut 28:46 NRSV).

Applying this concept to prophetic statements is of course the real point. As noted above, in poetry *forever* may be expected to be hyperbole, but does that mean it is merely a literary device for the sake of being literary? Probably not. The function of the hyperbole is to increase the impact of a statement on the hearers, to add intensification to the meaning of the verb.

- Damascus will become a heap of ruins, its towns deserted forever (Is 17:1).
- "The fortress will be abandoned, . . . citadel and watchtower will become a wasteland forever" (Is 32:14).
- "My anger and my wrath will be poured out on this place, . . . and it will burn and not be quenched" (Jer 7:20).

- "I will bring upon you everlasting disgrace—everlasting shame that will not be forgotten" (Jer 23:40).

It is clear that in this genre of the language of destruction, the illocution of *forever* is *not* transtemporal perpetuity.[28]

The same can be said for *forever* in the language of blessing:

- "The effect of righteousness will be quietness and confidence forever" (Is 32:17).
- "They will possess it forever and dwell there from generation to generation" (Is 34:17).
- "Israel will be saved by the LORD with an everlasting salvation; you will never be put to shame or disgraced, to ages everlasting" (Is 45:17).
- "As for me, this is my covenant with them. . . . My Spirit, who is on you, and my words that I have put in your mouth will not depart from your mouth, or from the mouths of your children, or from the mouths of their descendants from this time on and forever" (Is 59:21).
- "[Jerusalem] will be inhabited forever" (Jer 17:25).
- "I will make an everlasting covenant with them; I will never stop doing good to them" (Jer 32:40).
- "Judah will be inhabited forever and Jerusalem through all generations" (Joel 3:20).

Returning to the first and most obvious semantic domain of *forever*—presently true and indefinitely true—we must not allow that to be a determinative definition. Building interpretations of prophecy around one of several domains of the word is a fallacy. *Forever* may designate perpetuity only within earthly existence, it may be hyperbolic, and it may designate *surely* in the sense of intensification.

Shortness of time (see pp. 222-23). Opposite to the concept of a long period of time are words in the prophets designating a short period of time. The immediacy of curses and blessings may be expressed with "in a single day," "suddenly," "soon" or "swiftly." As with the word *forever,* semantic domains found in dictionaries will not suffice. For a functional definition, it is not difficult to see that words for brevity and swiftness add intensity as well. Impending judgment is that much worse if it is imminent. Words for swiftness raise the bar. It will be severe, and it will be sudden and unexpected. This is the nature of the language of power, speaking to the nonanalytical right side of the brain.

If this insight is applied to Revelation 1:1; 22:6, for example, a problem is resolved swiftly. Expressions of brevity or imminency in the prophets must be interpreted beyond the range of dictionaries. They generally intensify the severity of judgment.

CONCLUSION

Will wild animals from all over the earth gorge themselves on sinners? Will rivers of milk flow through the countryside? Will God disgrace his people forever? We now have a much clearer sense of how to understand such statements in the prophets. We know that prophets speak frequently with metaphors and hyperboles. We know that picturing God's wrath and love requires various levels of extreme language. We know that the prophets' statements may have an illocution that goes beyond the normal meanings of the words they use. We know that it was customary in the biblical world to warn violators by invoking the worst imaginable consequences. We know that the language of destruction and blessing cannot generally be understood if we look only at the surface of the statements. We know that specific terms of judgment were used to express unspecified realities of judgment. We know that stereotypical language can be used to describe God's wrath. We know that the primary point of the language of destruction and blessing is to help us understand God and his holy perspective on blatant disobedience. If we do not know these things, then we will misunderstand the language of judgment and blessing.

I began this chapter with a public reading of Scripture that was full of metaphor. I conclude with a metaphoric benediction:

> May the roads rise up to meet you;
> May the winds be always at your back;
> May the sun shine warmly upon your face,
> And the rains fall softly on your fields.

5

HOW DOES THE LANGUAGE OF
APOCALYPTIC WORK?

In this chapter we will read the last page of the story first. It is definitely a story worth reading, for it recounts some of the most unexpected developments ever to occur in the course of world events. Shock waves were felt from the coastlands of the Mediterranean to the heartland of Mesopotamia. Also unexpected: these events from world history were captured in advance in the book of Daniel.

After reviewing highlights of international politics in the Mediterranean world of the fourth through the second centuries B.C., we can compare the end of the story with the beginning—that is, the historical events with what Daniel's apocalypse envisioned was going to happen. In order to understand the language of apocalyptic, we must review the period of world history relevant to Daniel 8 and then examine Daniel's language. We may be surprised at what we discover. It should provide helpful information for future explorations of apocalyptic.

Though some argue that the highly developed apocalyptic genre in Daniel dates the book to the second century B.C. and therefore does not anticipate events in the fourth century, the working hypothesis underlying this chapter is that the book of Daniel, while apocalyptic, was written in the late sixth century.[1] This is not ruling out the possibility that a human author under divine inspiration could follow a custom of his day and write prophecy after the fact using a pseudonymous name, but we would want clear evidence before coming to that conclusion.[2] Some people think they have that evidence, others do not. Regardless, even if Daniel were a pseudonymous second-century writing, the conclusions of this chapter about the nature of apocalyptic language would still hold true.

The second part of this chapter will compare findings from Daniel 8 with apocalyptic language in the New Testament. Analyzing the meaning of the vision of the woman, the dragon and the beasts in Revelation 12—13 will be a good test of our understanding of the apocalyptic genre.

DAVID AGAINST GOLIATH

The story we are reading climaxes when the famous conqueror Alexander the Great expired in Babylon in 323 B.C. Fifteen years earlier the giant in world politics was the Persian king. The question that was impossible to consider then was what kingdom would ever rise to power and threaten the supreme might and organization of the Persian monarchy. Macedonia was barely a blip on the radar screen.

In a few short years, however, Alexander and his army marched out of Macedonia and across the continent as far as the Indus River, taking almost everything in their path. The world reeled from an endless stream of shocking headline news. Who could explain how the mighty Persian empire collapsed so quickly and unexpectedly? In a speech in Athens in the summer of 330, the orator Aeschines reflected on the current political events reverberating throughout the Mediterranean world, especially the near-end of the Persian kingdom:

> What strange and unexpected event has not occurred in our time? The life we have lived is no ordinary human one, but we were born to be an object of wonder to posterity. The Persian king . . . who had the arrogance to write in his letters that he was the lord of all men from the rising to the setting sun, surely is he now fighting for his own safety rather than for the domination of others? (Aeschines III *Against Ctesiphon* 132-34)

With the death of Alexander, an even more perplexing question was being asked: who and what would be the successor of Alexander and his loosely held together kingdom?

Backing up, in 338 B.C. Greece was united politically for the first time in history, a league of states with a single leader and a common enemy. Before that point it had seemed unlikely that unity would ever be achieved among all the individual Greek city-states. But when an outsider, Philip of Macedon, Alexander's father, became the master of all of Greece by his victory at the battle of Chaeronea, the formerly independent-minded Greeks had no choice but to capitulate.[3] At the peace conference that Philip convened the same year in Corinth, all the Greek states except the then insignificant Sparta acquiesced to him as the sovereign of Greece. The "universal peace" proposed by Philip was readily accepted, while the common enemy of the newly unified Greece was already obvious. With the encouragement of Philip, the Federal Council declared war on Persia and gave him the office of General with unlimited powers.[4]

But this would be David against Goliath. How could the upstart Greek coalition take on the mighty Persian empire? Nevertheless, Philip began preparations and sent preliminary forays into Asia Minor. However, his hegemony was ended by a suspicious assassination.[5]

Alexander's success. When Alexander succeeded his father, he quickly established himself as the second governor over Greece. He then undertook what his father had hoped to do, a major campaign against the Persian kingdom.[6] Incredibly, in eleven quick years Alexander led his ever-bulging army through Anatolia, Syria, Egypt, Mesopotamia, Persia, Parthia and much more. Against all odds—at least based on the Greek versions of the story—Alexander defeated everything the Persians could throw into his path. Each of the battles proved decisive for Greek domination. For the first time, much of the East came under the control of the West.

Alexander was an opportunistic conqueror, but he was probably not nearly as much of a genius as tradition gives him credit for.[7] He died at thirty-three while dreaming of other frontiers to conquer. Whether his death should be considered premature is debatable, since his skills as a conqueror were not matched by skills as an administrator. Part of that incompetence was giving little forethought to what would happen if he were to die prematurely. Thus when he succumbed to a mysterious illness, it threw his army, his family, his generals and his kingdom into chaos—a chaos that lasted for more than forty years. The final pages of the story are full of never-ending intrigue—rival generals vying with each other for parts of Alexander's domain, if not hoping to gain control of all of it.[8]

The fragmenting of Alexander's dominion. Within a week of the death of Alexander, at least ten of his former generals laid claim to or were assigned as rulers of the former satrapies of the Persian empire.[9] For more than twenty years, certain aspiring generals sought to gain control of the whole empire and to be the next Alexander. But the governors of the satrapies began calling themselves kings: Antigonus in Asia, Demetrius in Greece, Ptolemy in Egypt, Cassander in Macedonia, Lysimachus in Thrace, Zipoetes in Bithynia, Mithradates in Pontus and Seleucus in Syria. That meant there was little prospect of a single empire. Though these Hellenistic kingdoms were mere fragments of Alexander's kingdom, some were very successful politically. Culturally, each was a curious blend of diverse ethnic groups and cultures, for west was meeting east as never before. And the world has not been the same since.

All these Hellenistic kingdoms were keeping ancient cartographers busy. Borders shifted this way and that, and territory exchanged hands as one kingdom conquered another. Eventually three kingdoms prevailed: the Ptolemies in control of Egypt and many of the Aegean islands and coastlands, the Seleucids in control of Syria and varying parts of Asia, and the Antigonids in control of Greece and Macedonia. In addition to the three prominent kingdoms, various minor monarchies controlled small areas of Alexander's former empire: for example, Pergamum, Bithynia, Pontus and Paphlagonia, Galatia.[10]

The Seleucid kingdom was especially notorious, at least from the standpoint of the Jewish people. Under the fourth Seleucid king, Antiochus Epiphanes (175-164 B.C.), the expression of Jewish faith was suppressed and the temple in Jerusalem defiled. Eventually the Jews revolted in the famous Maccabean revolt beginning in 166 B.C.

With this summary of how the story ends, it is time to examine how it begins. The anticipation of the formative events of the fourth through second centuries B.C. is preserved in Daniel 8. It is a unique perspective in a unique genre; it is a vision with the characteristics of apocalyptic literature. Before looking in detail at the vision, *apocalyptic* needs to be defined.

DISTINCTIVE FEATURES OF APOCALYPTIC LITERATURE

Depending on how the literary forms of the Old Testament are apportioned, there are ten different genres.[11] But drawing lines of demarcation is difficult, like categorizing books in a bookstore. There may be general headings like Homemaking, Sports, Religion and Travel, or more specific headings like Cooking, Decorating, Team Sports, Olympics, Eastern Religions, Self-Help, International Travel and State Parks. Regardless of the headings, all the books in the bookstore have some features in common.

Under the individual headings the books have even more in common—usually in proportion to how specific the category is. But the number of headings is somewhat arbitrary. Furthermore, not every book fits neatly into a single category. So it is with biblical genres.

Books in the Old Testament under the heading of prophecy have features in common with the other thirty-nine books and have many things in common with each other.[12] But the genre of prophecy may be broken down further into at least three specific headings: oracles of salvation, announcements of judgment and apocalyptic. The first two have much in common, while the third, apocalyptic, has more distinctive characteristics.

Prophecy	Apocalyptic
Laments the sinfulness on the earth and *urges repentance.*	Asserts that the ever-present *wickedness is beyond hope.* The only solution is total destruction: the earth is going to melt with searing heat.
Reveals *God's displeasure with his people*—their irreverent attitudes and idolatrous conduct.	Assumes that *the readers are themselves displeased* with the evil around them and are anxious for God to provide a solution.
Calls the people of God *back to obedience* to God.	Calls for the few remaining faithful to *persevere until the end:* in the face of difficult odds they are to keep their robes pure.
Announces that God is going to *judge sin and offer salvation,* usually to be accomplished through natural means or human agents.	Announces that God himself is going to *intervene and judge the world* through supernatural means: he will ride out of heaven on a white horse and rule the nations.
Presents its message as *direct speech from God:* "Thus says the LORD."	Presents its message in graphic *images, visions and symbols.* The message is sometimes shrouded in mystery: for example, the title on one figure's forehead is "Mystery, Babylon the great, the mother of prostitutes and of the abominations of the earth."
Predicts both *immediate and distant judgment* and salvation.	Focuses primarily on *final solutions.* The situation is too serious for short-term answers. The only hope is for God to bring the history of man's sinfulness to conclusion and to establish a solution that will last for eternity: there will be no more night, and they will reign forever and ever.

Figure 5.1. Prophecy and apocalyptic

Oracles of salvation and announcements of judgment are usually poetic. Messenger formulas, such as "Thus saith the LORD," appear in both to introduce divine speech, such as "I will heal your land." Prominent everywhere are figures of speech. But specific to announcements of judgment are indictments against the people for their disobedience, providing justification for the language of judgment. Likewise, specific to oracles of salvation are affirmations of God's commitment to his people and assurances of future blessing.

Apocalyptic, however, can be an entity unto itself and tends to have a message different from prophecy (see figure 5.1).[13]

Though the typical characteristics of apocalyptic content are not difficult to grasp, its striking differences in technique leave many readers bewildered. While prophecy is figurative and poetic, apocalyptic is visionary and fantastic. While prophecy proclaims God's acts of judgment and blessing, apocalyptic pictures a completely different world of never-seen-before examples of good and evil. In some senses apocalyptic authors are like political cartoonists. They sketch the course of world events and the prominent leaders of the world in figurative, graphic and even bizarre ways. As a result, readers are often left puzzled by what they encounter:[14]

- jaw-dropping scenes of animals, rivers, mountains and stars that jump off the page with movielike special effects (Dan 8:2-14; Zech 6:1-7)
- natural catastrophes producing cosmic chaos throughout the universe, ushering in the dreadful day of judgment (Is 24:18-20; Ezek 38:19-22)
- pernicious and disruptive evil contributing to constant crises and producing a seemingly hopeless pessimism with the course of current events (Is 57:3-13; Dan 7:19-25)
- an underlying determinism resting in the unquestioned conviction that somehow God is maintaining sovereign control (Is 25:1; 26:1-4)
- ecstatic expectation that God will intervene and suppress all evil forces working against his predetermined plan (Zech 14:3-9; Mal 3:1-5)
- ethical teaching aimed at giving courage and comfort to the faithful and confirming them in righteous living (Is 56:1-2; Zech 7:9-10; 8:16-17)

- visions of celestial scenes and beings with an otherworldly perspective (Dan 10:4-19; Zech 3:1-10)
- heavenly interpreters explaining the scenes in language that may be figurative (Ezek 40:3-4; Dan 8:15-17)
- a dualistic perspective that categorizes things into contrasting elements such as good and evil, this age and the age to come (Dan 12:2; Zech 1:14-15)
- visions presented in a very stylized structure, with events and time organized in numerical patterns and repetition of similar sets (Ezek 38—39; Dan 9:24-27)
- foundational to all the above, God's promise to act in the last days to restore his people and establish a new and glorious world order (Is 27:12-13; Zech 8:1-8).[15]

Apocalyptic appears in many forms and in many places, both within the canon of Scripture and in extrabiblical writings.[16] It was a Jewish phenomenon, though subsequently adopted by Christians. In some cases, however, it is difficult to decide what qualifies as apocalyptic, because there is uncertainty about how many characteristics of apocalyptic are required for a text to be considered apocalyptic.[17] The apocalyptic genre can have as many as twenty-eight distinguishing characteristics, but no single text contains all of them, and some texts not considered formally a part of the apocalyptic genre have some of them.

A ROLLER-COASTER RIDE

Perhaps the most important point to understand about apocalyptic is its function. It takes readers on a fascinating journey, inviting us "to enter a whole world of imagination and to live in that world before we move beyond it."[18] Apocalyptic addresses a serious crisis of faith. If God is truly in control, why has he allowed things to get so bad here on this earth? In reply, apocalyptic boldly proclaims that God has not turned his back on the world. Just the opposite: God is going to intervene radically and unexpectedly and introduce a solution that will solve all problems. To bring that intervention and solution to life, the visionary characteristics of apocalyptic are especially appropriate.

When faced with severe adversity such as the Jews experienced at the hands of the Assyrians or Babylonians or Syrians (or the Nazis), many responded by calling on God for salvation. When relief failed to come, patience wore thin and doubts about God's control and mercy arose. People understandably lost sight of the bigger picture of how God might be at work in the affairs of this world. They became preoccupied with the immediacy of their misfortunes.

Largely in response to this kind of crisis, apocalyptic literature gives its readers a roller-coaster ride into the future and into God's presence. There are heart-pumping thrills as those faced with crisis get a glimpse beyond the problems of the present. The lofty heights of the ride—so unlike anything known on this earth—help the persecuted put their misfortunes in perspective. What they are braving is relatively insignificant in the bigger picture of things. But the roller-coaster also takes the riders down in valleys of gloom and despair. The g-forces of the present dilemma are not going to get any better, at least immediately. If anything, wickedness will increase until it reaches a level unknown in human existence.

But there is good news. The stage is being set for God's sudden intervention. He is in control and will win the fight once and for all. He will introduce an eternal solution that will provide peace on earth. The prospect of coming to the end of this roller-coaster ride and getting off is exhilarating.

The effect of the language of apocalyptic on those who hear is dramatic (see figure 5.2).

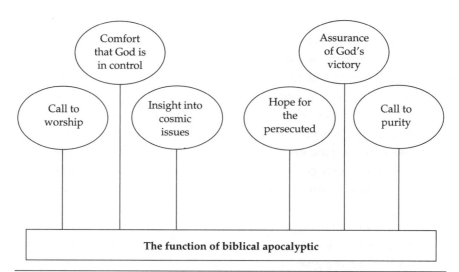

Figure 5.2. What apocalyptic communicates

- It is worshipful, as the faithful are reminded how great God is. Apocalyptic is a call to stand in awe of the sovereign Lord of the universe.
- It is comforting, as the faithful are given new hope that this evil world will eventually come to an end. Apocalyptic is a promise of a new age when God's will *will* be done on earth as it is in heaven.
- It is spell-binding, as scenes of heaven reveal the cosmic battle between good and evil. Apocalyptic assures the faithful that what they are experiencing is simply part of a larger conflict between God and Satan.
- It is a battery charge to increase the saints' resolve. Apocalyptic suggests that if persecution becomes so intense that it results in death, the faithful will be much better off, given what they have to look forward to.
- It is exhilarating to imagine God's personal visit to the earth to correct all wrongs, punish all the wicked and create a radically new world. Apocalyptic announces that the Lamb will once again stand on Mount Zion and every knee will bow in adoration.
- It is a challenge to ethical purity, for the things of this world are temporal and tainted by sin. Apocalyptic promises that those who remain faithful will eventually be honored with the glory of the new heaven and earth.

DID DANIEL HAVE 20-20 VISION?

We are finally ready to reflect on the events of the fourth through second centuries B.C. in light of the vision of Daniel 8. The language and motifs confirm the chapter's identification as apocalyptic: a vision and a trance; animals with unusual characteristics engaged in mortal conflict; the wind, the stars and the host of heaven; messages from the holy ones; mathematical symbolism; a heavenly interpreter; a coming period of wrath; and instructions to seal up the vision.[19]

The vision depicts a powerful ram with two long horns, one longer than the other. The ram is more powerful than all other animals—that is, until a goat appears on the horizon. The goat has one horn between its eyes and approaches from the west, without touching the ground. The goat attacks the ram and shatters its two horns, knocking it to the ground and trampling on it. Then the goat becomes very powerful, until its large horn is broken off. In place of the one horn, four horns grow, and out of one of the four horns a small horn grows. This horn becomes very powerful and prosperous, to the point of setting itself up to be as great as the prince of the host, and to the point of doing away with the daily sacrifices (Dan 8:3-12). But within twenty-three hundred mornings and evenings, the temple is going to be reconsecrated.

Interpretation and fulfillment. The vision is interpreted for Daniel by a heavenly messenger. The two-horned ram is identified as the kings of Media and Persia, the goat as the king of Greece, and the great horn as the first king. The four horns that replace the broken horn of the goat are identified as four kingdoms that will arise from the nation of the goat. And out of one of the horns comes another horn, which causes astounding devastation and destroys the mighty men and the holy people. The latter horn is destroyed, but not by human power (Dan 8:19-25).

If we assume a sixth-century date for the vision, the fulfillment of the predictions is stunning. As noted above, no one living in the sixth, fifth or even fourth century could have anticipated that an army from Greece could conquer the Persian empire, a vast kingdom that had been united for centuries under Persian rule. In addition to the comment by the orator Aeschines on the Persian king fighting for his life (p. 104), Demetrius of Phalerum, an Athenian statesman contemporary with Alexander the Great, reflected on the unlikelihood of the events of his time:

> Can you imagine that fifty years ago if some god had foretold the future to the Persians or their king, or the Macedonians or their king, they would have believed that the very name of the Persians would now be lost, who at one time were masters of almost the whole inhabited world, while the Macedonians, whose very name was formerly unknown, would now be masters of it all?[20]

Furthermore, who could have anticipated the split of Alexander the Great's empire into multiple parts? Or a foreign leader's stopping the daily sacrifices in Jerusalem?

Questions to ponder. The juxtaposition of the historical developments of the Hellenistic world with Daniel's visions raises questions about prediction and fulfillment. How well would the ancient hearers have understood the apocalyptic visions and the celestial interpretations provided by the apocalypse? Would they have grasped the details about how the Persian empire would come to a dramatic demise? Would they have had any idea how a Greek kingdom could replace it? Note the following hazards if the ancient hearers had tried to predict what was going to happen based on the vision of Daniel 8.

1. The interpretation of the vision identifies the two-horned ram as the kings of Media and Persia. But Persia had only one king when the Greeks conquered it. Is this a problem? The solution may be to regard the reference to kings as a figure of speech. Then the expression "kings of Media and Persia" refers by synecdoche to the kingdoms of Media and Persia rather than to the kings. For Daniel, sixth-century Medo-Persia more nearly fit the symbol of a two-horned ram, but by the time it was fulfilled, the relationship of symbol and referent was less direct.[21] Would this have been clear before the vision was fulfilled? Or would hearers have expected two kings to be ruling the Medo-Persian empire at the time of fulfillment, since the ram in the vision had two horns and was interpreted as the kings of Media and Persia?

2. Though the goat that overthrew the ram is identified in the interpretation of the vision (Dan 8:21) as the king of Greece, by synecdoche *king* must refer to kingdom, for it was much more than the king of Greece in a personal confrontation against the kings of Medo-Persia.[22] Furthermore, as typical of symbolism in other prophetic literature (e.g., Nah 3:13-18; Zeph 3:3), the metaphor is mixed: both the goat and the horn are symbolic of king.

3. The description in verse 4 of the ram's conquering to the west, north and south with no one powerful enough to resist does not take account of the expansion of the Persian empire to the east. Esther 1:1 reports that Ahasuerus ruled over 127 provinces from India to Ethiopia.[23] More noteworthy, the description in the vision suppresses the Greeks' successful resistance to Persian invasions in 490 and 480-479 B.C. To say that no one was powerful enough to resist the might of the Persian empire clearly highlights the Persian power, though it is an overstatement.[24] Is this a problem? It depends on how precise we expect apocalyptic visions to be.

4. The conquering horn identified as the first king, Alexander the Great, was not the king of Greece. Though he was the king of Macedonia and was addressed as king by his army and referred to in the sources as king, his title as leader of the league of Greek states was *hēgemōn*. Is this a problem? It might be considered a moot point. Alexander was so powerful that people thought of him as a king, the Macedonians called him king, and he led

a pan-Hellenic army. In 1 Maccabees 1:1, for example, an editorial comment on Alexander's succession to the throne of Darius says that Alexander had previously been the king of Greece. However, though the Hebrew term *melek* has a broader meaning than "king," Daniel's vision could have made a distinction between governor and king by referring to Alexander as the *pechah* or *sar* of Greece. Apparently the vision was not concerned with that level of precision in political terminology.[25]

5. The designation of Alexander as the *first* king—or in this case, *hegēmōn*—of Greece also needs comment. Alexander's position as the leader of the league of Greek states was identical to his father's, making him the second sovereign of Greece.[26] If we understand *first* to denote a priority in position rather than in time, the difficulty is resolved. From the viewpoint of people living outside Greece and Macedonia, Alexander was in effect the first king.

6. The description of the goat's victory over the ram mentions only one battle, thus collapsing a succession of decisive defeats of the Persians by the Greeks into the battle of Gaugamela, east of the Tigris, in September 331 B.C. Though the Persian king Darius escaped, this battle was the biggest blow to Persian control. The battle at Issus was also an important victory for Alexander, since he captured the royal family and many of the Persian nobles.[27] But it is not part of Daniel's vision, unless the reference to breaking the two horns of the ram alludes to the battles of Issus and Gaugamela. This reference to the breaking of the ram's horns, however, would be expected to designate the death of the king, since the breaking of the great horn of the goat denotes the death of Alexander (Dan 8:8; cf. 8:25). But the two broken horns of the ram do not symbolize the death of Darius, since he was not killed at the battle of Gaugamela. The meaning of the breaking of a horn is veiled, therefore, shifting according to the context. The freedom of apocalyptic to shift meanings fits well with its tendency to be allusive rather than precise. Would this have been clear before the vision was fulfilled?

7. When the great horn of the goat was broken, a reference to the death of Alexander, Daniel saw four prominent horns come up. These are subsequently interpreted as four kingdoms that arose out of Alexander's nation. But the breakup of Alexander's kingdom did not result in four kingdoms that conveniently match Daniel's vision. The complexity of the successor kingdoms has not dissuaded commentators—beginning as early as Hip-

polytus (4.26) and Jerome[28]—from trying to find, in the historical circumstances of the Hellenistic period, four kingdoms that work as referents for
Daniel's vision.[29] But in so doing they misrepresent the complexity of the
struggles of the successors and miss the significance of the four kingdoms.[30] While it is possible to find a brief window of time when there were
four main kingdoms, that begs the question. *Four* is not a designation for
the number of Hellenistic kingdoms. Daniel's use of the number four has
a better explanation.

The motif of four successive kingdoms is important in four visions recorded by Daniel (Dan 2:38-44; 7:2-19; 8:8, 22; 11:2, 4). A succession of four
occurs elsewhere in the Old Testament as well (Zech 1:18-21; 6:1-8). It is
also attested in extrabiblical sources.[31] The eighth-century B.C. Greek poet
Hesiod describes four ages that he associates with four metals of declining
value. An Akkadian cuneiform text describes the rise and fall of four empires. The fourth Sibylline Oracle has a ten-generation scheme divided
into a sequence of empires based on a second-century B.C. source with four
nations. A second-century B.C. Roman author describes the first four kingdoms of the world as the Assyrians, the Medes, the Persians and the Macedonians. And in a Zoroastrian text a tree is pictured with branches of four
different metals, representing four eras to come. In Daniel the figure of
four kingdoms principally signifies the increasing chaos growing out of
degenerating Gentile rule, while the orderly sequence of the kingdoms
may also suggest the sovereignty of God's control.[32]

The motif of four is also important in the phrase "the four winds of
heaven" (Dan 8:8). The Lord pronounces judgment on Elam: "I will bring
against Elam the four winds of heaven from the four quarters of the heavens; I will scatter them to the four winds" (Jer 49:36). The four winds of
heaven as a motif of destruction appear in Daniel 7:2, where the four
winds stir up the sea from which the four beasts arise, and in Daniel 11:4,
where Alexander's kingdom will be divided to the four winds of heaven.
The figure of the four winds, then, underscores the devastating destruction on the horizon.

There is yet another sense in which four seems especially appropriate
for the vision in Daniel 8. Though Alexander's vast empire was not divided up into four parts, it was divided in the four directions of the compass.
Thus the number four in relation to kingdoms suggests the successive
stages of decline in Gentile rule and the universal scope of that rule, and

in relation to winds it suggests the severe judgment that the Lord is bringing on the earth. The number four of the four horns and four winds of
heaven in Daniel's vision and of the four kingdoms of Gabriel's interpretation did not reveal, therefore, the number of kingdoms to succeed Alexander. But the number four was significant as a symbol. Would all this
have been clear before the vision was fulfilled?

8. When Daniel introduces his vision (Dan 8:2), he places it in Susa in
the province of Elam. Though commentators have suggested that Susa is
significant in that it was the capital of the kingdom that Daniel was about
to see conquered, there has not been a good explanation for the significance of Elam. But the pattern of allusions in Daniel's visions open the
door for the meaning of Elam. In the prophecies of Jeremiah and Ezekiel
(Jer 49:34-38; Ezek 32:24-25), Elam is a place devastated by the Lord's anger.[33] The coming destruction is bad news. But there is hope in the midst of
the bad news. The Lord says, "I will restore the fortunes of Elam in the
days to come" (Jer 49:39). Likewise the holy messenger tells Daniel (Dan
8:14) that the sanctuary will be restored to its rightful place. Thus the imagery associated with Elam is especially relevant to the vision of Daniel 8,
from impending destruction (Dan 8:2) to the hope of restoration (Dan
8:14). Would this have been clear before the vision was fulfilled?

9. The vision of the little horn (Dan 8:9-14) is full of allusions that cannot
be precisely identified with fulfillment in Antiochus Epiphanes. Why is
Antiochus referred to as a little horn? In what sense did he grow great toward the east? Who is the host of heaven? Who is the prince of the host?
What is referred to by the overthrowing of the sanctuary? Since multiple
explanations are suitable for these allusions, is our inability to identify the
clear referent for each symbol—with the advantage of hindsight—a problem? Not if we understand the imprecision typical of apocalyptic descriptions.

10. The interpretation of the little horn (Dan 8:23-25) helps in our understanding but still leaves us wondering, even after the fulfillment of predictions about the little horn. We have the advantage of hindsight, and
commentators still struggle to resolve some of the allusions in Daniel's visions.[34] Was all of the description fulfilled in Antiochus Epiphanes, or are
there two or more stages of fulfillment? Is a still-future Antichrist being al-
luded to? If so, where does the prediction switch from Antiochus to Antichrist?

Apocalyptic as a Soft-Focus Lens

This look at ten potential hazards in interpreting one of Daniel's apocalyptic visions leads us to ask, How much of this would have been clear before the vision was fulfilled? How does the language of apocalyptic work? What was the function of the vision and the interpretation? The following questions will point to clearer understanding of apocalyptic.

Are the details in the vision allusive and symbolic or precise and explicit? What about the two-horned ram standing beside the Ulai Canal, with one horn longer than the other, or the goat with the prominent horn, attacking and shattering the two horns of the ram? Or the goat's large horn that is broken off, with four horns replacing it? Or a little horn that increases in power and throws down some of the starry host and tramples on them? Allusion and symbolism seem to characterize these aspects of the vision. No kingdom is specified, no person is specified, no heavenly creatures are specified. Generally, the images lack precision.[35]

However, allusion and symbolism are not the same. Both are forms of metaphor, for when mentioning one thing they actually refer to another. But in symbolism something material or easier to comprehend represents something immaterial or harder to comprehend.[36] Though the point of contact between the two subjects may be small, it is generally well defined and enduring. In allusion the correspondence is less defined or precise. For example, the vision states that no one is able to resist the power of the two-horned ram. The ram is a symbol for Persia. The inability of anyone to resist is an allusion to Persia's power to conquer at will; it is not precise, for the Greeks successfully resisted. Another example is the four kingdoms split off from Alexander's empire. Four is an *allusion* to division of the empire, since the number of divisions was not precisely four. Yet in another sense, four is symbolism for the decline in Gentile rule and severe judgment coming on the earth.

Were some of the details added for effect, rather than being allusive or symbolic? For example, what about the various ways the goat's defeat of the ram is described? The goat charges at the ram in great rage, it attacks the ram furiously, it strikes the ram, it shatters the ram's two horns, it knocks the ram to the ground, it tramples on the ram. The vision adds that the ram is unable to stand against the goat and that none can rescue the ram from the goat's power. Is each of these descriptions of the defeat of the ram significant, or are they just different ways to visualize the same event? If each is significant, in what sense did Alexander and his army defeat the Persians in these different ways? What does the trampling on the ground refer to that is different from the other ways the defeat is pictured? What about the shattering of the horns? Does another kingdom attempt to rescue the "ram" from the power of the "goat"? Or are these details simply imaginative ways to describe the basic idea with great visual impact?

In the interpretation of the vision by the angel Gabriel, are all the allusions in the vision made more specific? The two-horned ram is identified as the kings of Media and Persia; the shaggy goat is identified as the king of Greece, with the large horn as the first king; the four horns are four kingdoms; the little horn is a mighty king in the latter part of the reign of the four kingdoms—the destroyer of the mighty men and the holy people, who would take his stand against the Prince of princes. Many of the details, however, remain elusive even with interpretation. As noted above: more than one Persian king? a Greek "king"? the "first" Greek king? four kingdoms? the destroyer of the mighty men and the holy people? the Prince of princes?

If we had been early hearers of Daniel's prophecies—for example, living in Jerusalem in 400 B.C.—would we have come to correct conclusions about what the vision predicted? Given that the ram is interpreted in the vision as the kings of Media and Persia, we would have expected the vision to be fulfilled at a time when the Persian empire had dual kingship, with a Median king and a Persian king. Since the goat is interpreted as the king of Greece and the horn as the first king, we would have expected the vision to be fulfilled when Greece was a kingdom under its first king. (In 400 B.C. we would have expected that if anyone could create a kingdom in Greece it would be Sparta, a *polis* ruled by kings, for Sparta had just been victorious over Athens in the Peloponnesian Wars.) Since the great horn of the goat is broken and replaced with four horns, interpreted as four kingdoms, would we have expected numerous successors of Alexander to fight among themselves for more than forty years for control of various parts of the empire, never really settling into four clearly defined kingdoms?

There are two responses to the hypothetical question of what we would have expected as residents of Jerusalem in 400 B.C. If we were transported across time from the twenty-first century but remained ignorant of the culture and genres of the biblical world, we would make fools of ourselves trying to interpret Daniel 8. On the other hand, if we had lived among the people at that time and learned their culture, we still would not have known exactly what to expect from Daniel's vision. Perhaps we would have at least known not to try to anticipate the details of how the vision would be fulfilled.

What is the point of the vision? The questions above about anticipating the details of political events of the fourth through second centuries raise the issue whether the point of the vision is in the details or the overall impact.

The primary message of the vision of Daniel 8 is not difficult to grasp. Persia, the world empire under which many Jews lived during the time of dispersion, was going to be destroyed. This was good news. The kingdom of Greece, which was going to conquer Persia, would be more vast, more powerful and more evil, resulting in even more trouble coming upon God's people. This was bad news. God had placed a time limit on evil—twenty-three hundred mornings and evenings—and was going to make right the wrongs that had been committed. This was good news. The implications of these political events were important to the Israelites trapped in a dispersion of adversity. The message: do not give up hope. God is in control. Be encouraged. God knows all about the evil and will do something about it. Be patient. The situation may get worse for a while, but in the end all injustices will be rectified.

Daniel, however, was overwhelmed by the bad news. After the vision and interpretation had concluded, he was physically ill for several days (Dan 8:27). Even after he returned to his normal duties, his dismay continued. With the vision of more trouble on the horizon for his people, and with the trouble becoming even worse than before, he was devastated. Fortunately, Daniel would receive other visions to put chapter 8 in perspective:

> There shall be a time of anguish, such as has never occurred since nations first came into existence. But at that time your people shall be delivered, everyone who is found written in the book. . . . Those who are wise shall shine like the brightness of the sky, and those who lead many to righteousness, like the stars forever. (Dan 12:1, 3 NRSV)

Did the original hearers of Daniel 8 understand everything about how the vision was going to be fulfilled? No, that would have been impossible and beyond the intent of the vision. Would it have all made sense to them after the events occurred? Yes, because they understood the nature of apocalyptic language. Do interpreters today—long after the fulfillment—understand the vision and fulfillment of Daniel 8? That depends on our understanding of how apocalyptic works. It also depends on our understanding of the cultural roots of the imagery.[37]

A PREGNANT WOMAN, A DELIVERY AND A DINOSAUR

The book of Revelation is a goldmine of apocalyptic imagery (or for some explorers a minefield of exegetical embarrassment). Revelation 12—13 provides a good sample, since "the visions in chapter 12 form the theological heart of the entire book."[38] Imagine a combination of the movie genres of *Star Wars* and *Jurassic Park*. A very pregnant woman appears on the screen robed in shimmering rays of sun, crowned with twelve galactic stars, her silken feet resting on a full moon as if it were a footstool. From a distance, a *Tyrannosaurus rex*-sized dragon gallops at breakneck speed toward the woman. It is seven-headed, seven-crowned and ten-horned. Its color: an unearthly red. With saliva streaming from hungry lips, the dinosaur pants in anticipation of gorging itself on the son about to be born.

The woman convulses, shrieking in pain, and gives birth to a son. Suddenly a phenomenon never before seen occurs. Like a bolt of lightning rising from the earth, the son is lifted heavenward. In fury and desperation the dinosaur lunges at the woman who has failed to hand over her son. But she sprouts eagle's wings and flies arrow-fast into the desert. Not ready to give up, the dinosaur belches forth a putrid river, intending to sweep the woman into the sea. But the earth comes to her rescue and opens its mouth to swallow every drop of the wicked slime.

Immediately war breaks out on the outskirts of heaven. The chief angel Michael and his heavenly companions mount a full-scale attack on the dinosaur and his companions, preventing their escape back into the dark jungle. Quickly the dinosaur is struck down by Michael's blood-red sword. But it is more than a simple defeat. The dinosaur and his demons are hurled to the earth, never to rise again.

A voice of many waters, speaking in poetic verse, is then heard throughout the universe of galaxies and birthing stars:

> *Now have come the salvation and the power and the kingdom of our God,*
>   *and the authority of his Christ.*
> *For the accuser of our brothers,*
>   *who accuses them before our God day and night,*

has been hurled down.
They overcame him
  by the blood of the Lamb
  and by the word of their testimony;
they did not love their lives so much
  as to shrink from death.
Therefore rejoice, you heavens
  and you who dwell in them!
But woe to the earth and the sea,
  because the devil has gone down to you!
He is filled with fury,
  because he knows that his time is short. (Rev 12:10-12)

The dinosaur, now confined to the earth and threatened by ultimate defeat, is only enraged all the more. It marches off in search of all the rest of the woman's offspring. But the dinosaur pauses on the seashore to commission one of its kind. A beast arises out of the depths, also ten-horned with seven heads. This time there are ten crowns and a blasphemous name on each head. The beast is an otherworldly combination of leopard, bear and lion. He is granted everything the dinosaur possessed: power, throne and authority. Every living creature on the earth takes note of the unlimited power of beast and dragon and falls prostrate in awe. From distant oceans, islands rush to worship the new gods.

The beast, arrogant in his worldly might, slanders the one and only God, his throne and all who inhabit his holy presence. Because God's saints are obstacles in the beast's path, he sallies forth with every imaginable war device for the attack. Fortunately the time is limited to forty-two months. Yet it is a hellacious period because every tribe, people, language and nation is being tyrannized by the beast. All those whose names are safely in the book of life are abhorred, since the whole earth worships the beast while they refuse.

One would think that one dinosaur and one grotesque beast would be enough. Incredibly, there is another. This beast comes out of the pits of the earth instead of the sea. With only two horns, he looks more like a lamb. But that does not mean he is less of a black sheep than the beast that preceded him. For by calling down blazing fire from heaven, he betrays the populace with his sleight of hand and enlarges the worship of his predecessor. After setting up a monumental image of the sea-beast, the earth-beast breathes life into the statue, and it begins killing anyone that refuses to worship its excellence. The tyrannical second beast is not satisfied, however, to regiment only religious life. He manipulates the economy too, by requiring his emblem to appear on the forehead or hand of anyone who wants to buy, sell or trade. The mark is 666.

Interpreting the amazing vision. With a vision of such enigmatic and symbolic proportions, any chance of correct interpretation may seem remote.[39] However, since vivid scenes like this are typical of apocalyptic, we can draw on similar examples to make our way through the maze. We begin by looking for indicators of the primary message of the vision. If we are able to discover more than that, so much the better. But we must not begin with the specific lest we fail to grasp the global.

Hints about the significance of the vision appear several times. In Revelation 12:10 it is good news that "the accuser of our brothers . . . has been hurled down." In Revelation 12:17 the dragon makes war against the woman's offspring, identified as those who obey God's commandments and who hold to the testimony of Jesus. In Revelation 13:7 the beast makes war against the saints in order to conquer them. In Revelation 13:10 a text is quoted from Jeremiah making it clear that persecution and death can be expected, and then the statement appears, "Here is a call for the endurance and faith of the saints," or "This calls for patient endurance and faithfulness on the part of the saints" (NRSV and NIV). A careful hermeneutic seeks to discover what the author intended and what the listeners needed to hear, and those parallel lines of investigation are not hard to follow in this passage.[40] The function of the vision was to explain why the saints were faced with trials and how to handle them.

This ethical dimension of Revelation 12—13 is tightly woven throughout the fabric of apocalyptic. Hearers confront an intensity of evil in the world around them. Many are experiencing firsthand the effects of that evil, in the form of unjust persecution. Their faith and lifestyles are being tried by fire. They should respond in faith and hope.

An apocalyptic sermon. The vision of the woman, the dragon and the beasts is really an apocalyptic sermon with an important message (see figure 5.33). The evil in this world may be beyond belief (visualized in the form of a dragon and beasts), but the days of it are numbered (Rev 12:12, "he knows that his time is short"; Rev 13:5, the beast is given forty-two months to exercise his authority). The persecution that hearers are

An apocalyptic sermon:
God's perspective on persecution

- Persecution is a *small part* of a big picture:
    a cosmic battle rages between good and evil
    Jesus was a victim (Rev 12:4)
    Jesus' followers are victims (Rev 13:7)

- Persecution is a *big part* of our sanctification:
    God is preparing his bride for a star-studded wedding
    "This calls for patient endurance"
    "This calls for faithfulness"

- Persecution is a *doomed part* of the future:
    God will soon destroy all evil in every corner of the universe
    "The accuser of our brothers has been hurled down"
    "They overcame him by the blood of the lamb and by the word of their testimony"

Figure 5.3. Revelation 12—13

experiencing in a hostile environment is not meaningless but is part of the cosmic struggle between good and evil (Rev 12:7, "there was war in heaven"). God's Son was caught up in that struggle too, and he understands how difficult life is for his faithful ones (Rev 12:4, "the dragon stood in front of the woman who was about to give birth, so that he might devour her child"). The struggle continues into the present with Satan's attacks on God's people (Rev 13:7, "he was given power to make war against the saints and to conquer them"). Though it may not appear so now, God is ultimately in control (Rev 12:14, "the woman was given the two wings of a great eagle, so that she might fly to the place prepared for her in the desert"). In the end God's kingdom is going to prevail over every form of evil (Rev 12:10, "now have come the salvation and the power and the kingdom of our God"). In the meantime, hearers may face extreme persecution (Rev 12:11, "they did not love their lives so much as to shrink from death"). The only recourse is to remain faithful and to wait patiently, given how evil the kingdom of this world is and how inevitable is its destruction (Rev 13:10, "this calls for patient endurance and faithfulness on the part of the saints").

The apocalyptic sermon does not end there (see Rev 14). With the struggle with evil fading into the background, the narrator now sees what happens to the saints who are victims of the persecutors. Standing on the heavenly Mount Zion is the Lamb with 144,000 saints, and they are blessed with the glorious sound of harpists and a new song. God considers them his "firstfruits," for they kept themselves pure and followed the Lamb to a martyr's death. In place of words of blasphemy on the head of the beast and on the hands or foreheads of those who worship the beast, the 144,000 have the Father's name on their foreheads. Three angels spring into action to underscore the decision that all people must make, whether to worship the beasts or to take a stand with the Lamb. Going forth on the earth, one angel calls people to repentance, one announces the fall of the world's greatest kingdom, and one warns against worshiping the beast and his image. Then appears the statement, "This calls for patient endurance on the part of the saints who obey God's commandments and remain faithful to Jesus" (Rev 14:12). A voice from heaven follows: "Write: Blessed are the dead who die in the Lord from now on" (Rev 14:13).

This continuation of the vision confirms the ethical dimension of this centerpiece of the Apocalypse. The knowledge that even in death God's saints are recipients of his blessing encourages them to persevere. The future does hold promise of God's grace. Though he will vent his wrath on the corruption of this world, just as surely he will honor those who keep themselves pure.

Deciphering details. With that understanding of the primary significance of the vision, what can we determine about the specifics? Is each detail symbolic in some way? Is anything in the vision predictive of subsequent events? Moving from the general to the specific, we become increasingly uncertain about the meaning of the details. That is not unexpected, given the allusive nature of apocalyptic visions. For much of the vision is an earthly way to think about a heavenly reality, or a present way to think about a future reality. So given our earthly and present limitations, we cannot expect to understand the meaning of each detail. It is also expected with the nature of apocalyptic language that some details may simply be for effect; stated another way, some details may be make-believe. Parables of Jesus used characters he created for the point of illustration; apocalyptic may do the same. We must proceed cautiously, therefore, in considering whether the details of an apocalyptic vision are precise, allusive, symbolic, predictive, imaginary or a combination.

The woman in the vision will serve as a case in point. The supernatural description makes this image more than the mother of Jesus, though there may be an allusion to Mary. Is the mother symbolic for Israel, or the

church? Depending on which one, what is the meaning of being clothed
with the sun, using the moon as a footstool and being crowned with
twelve stars? Do these details function simply to give the woman an otherworldly appearance, or are they symbolic of something in particular?
What is the meaning of her crying out in pain? What is the meaning of the
flight into the desert and the threat of the dragon's river and the earth's
opening its mouth?

Though Israel is most commonly claimed to be the referent for the
mother, it is probably best to consider that an allusion as well. The woman
is also connected to the church (Rev 12:17), but that correspondence is an
even more distant allusion. So there is not a singular symbolism for the
woman, and thus the imagery remains unclear. There is no evidence to
suggest the woman is predictive of a future figure. Perhaps the mother
functions more loosely in the vision. She is an imaginary protagonist for
the antagonist, the dragon. Thus there is allusion but no symbolism.

Uncertainty about the significance of the mother does not apply to her
son, however. This part of the vision more nearly matches reality. He will
rule the nations with an iron scepter, though just what that means is not
completely clear. It is surprising that he appears in the vision at only one
point. It is also puzzling that he is snatched up to God, as if before the
dragon (Satan?) could harm him.

If we assume the dragon is symbolic for Satan, the two beasts may be
allusions to earthly powers operating under his control. There is no basis
for precise identification, but for the original hearers some of the descriptions of the beasts would have had correspondence to Roman emperors:
they spoke blasphemy against God and yet were worshiped as gods. But
lest we become too definite in identifying these details, we must focus primarily on the function. This description serves "to create a high boundary
between good and evil empires, whether the contrast be between past and
present emperors or divine and demonic powers."[41]

Alert readers of the summary of the vision provided at the beginning of
this section may have noted some embellishment. To heighten the impact
of the vision, I filled in the narrative in certain ways. I described the mother's feet as silken and the moon as her footstool. I referred to the dragon as
a dinosaur, since in our culture oversized dinosaurs are easier to visualize.
I added to the mother's shriek of pain a convulsing of her body (cf. Is
26:17). I referred to the war in heaven as on the outskirts of heaven. Bor-

rowing an idea from the Old Testament prophets, I said that islands came from the ends of the earth to worship the new gods. And so on. It appears that a similar kind of visualization happened in the original composition of an apocalyptic vision—all under divine inspiration. The effect of the vision is heightened by graphic touches added by the narrator. Details may have no particular significance other than to give the account more emotive power.

There is a certain amount of futility, therefore, in trying to determine the significance of all the details of apocalyptic visions. Not only is it not always possible, it can distract us from seeing the significance of the vision as a whole. Though it is perhaps a valid pursuit in technical commentaries, the result for most interpreters is too much focus on the trees and failure to see the forest.

The function of the vision and the book. Most certainly we are on thin ice if we think the vision in Revelation 12—13 is primarily predictive of specific future events. If it is in any way, it is unlikely that we can determine in advance how and what might be predictive. Apocalyptic visions often do not yield to attempts in advance to decipher details of fulfillment. Instead of being futuristic, the function of this vision is to provide encouragement and resolve. As a whole, the book of Revelation is more than simply informative—it is performative. The Apocalypse begins with the letters to the seven churches, which are a call to doctrinal and ethical purity. The book concludes with the same focus. In Revelation 22:7 a blessing is promised to those who would keep or obey the words of the prophecy; in Revelation 22:14 the hearers are encouraged to wash their robes so that they may have the right to the tree of life; and twice in the closing verses of the book the imminence of these events is assured, so that the saints are called to endure patiently and remain faithful. And in the middle of the book the message is the same: the vision of the woman, dragon and beasts gives the community of Christians on earth God's perspective on their confrontation with the cult and power of the kingdom of this world, and it calls them to persevere.

> The primary purpose of the book is not to impart information. It is rather to call for *commitment* to the actions, attitudes, and feelings uttered. It is thus primarily commissive language. In particular, it is expressive and evocative language. It makes no attempt to report events or to describe people in a way that everyone could accept. Rather, it provides a highly selective and per-

spectival view. Like a poem, it presents and interprets some aspect of reality, expresses a response to it, and invites the reader or hearer to share in the interpretation and response.[42]

Yet there is a high level of excitement in the Apocalypse as the scenes unfold. On the horizon is a radically new world order in which God will reign in peace. It is a promise that is both present and futuristic—already and not-yet. God is already victorious over all evil forces, and in that day he will dispose of them once and for all.

But there remains a sense in which apocalyptic is mysterious. What all this means is not completely clear. To remove that quality is to change the atmosphere of the genre that makes it what it is. "We do not make contact with the prophet's mind by reducing each figure in his narrative to some empirical equivalent."[43] To read the Apocalypse with a microscope, ever striving to decipher the significance of the most minute detail, defrauds the genre of its intended function. To hear apocalyptic, to feel its emotive language, to sense its mystery is to hear it aright.[44]

It is noteworthy that hearing was precisely the way the first hearers received the message of the Apocalypse. Unfortunately the orality of the ancient world and the implications of that orality are often overlooked. But until the invention of printing, people rarely read a piece of literature, because personal copies were almost nonexistent. If someone read, it was in a public setting in the hearing of others. Hence almost all reading was done aloud. More than reading, many people recited or retold stories and pieces of literature. Studies on the Apocalypse in particular demonstrate that the author crafted it specifically for ease of memorization and recitation.[45] Understanding the orality of the Apocalypse underscores the point that correct interpretation pays more attention to the overall impression of the visions than to the individual details. Hearing the Apocalypse enacted orally in one sitting gives hearers a distinctive sense of the message of the book.

CONCLUSION

Apocalyptic paints impressionistic pictures. Stand back and look at the picture. What is the overall effect? What did the artist seek to convey? But be careful not to stand too close. Impressionism uses dabs and strokes of paint that individually may be peculiar but in the larger context combine to depict scenes of unusual vividness and emotion. The artist's intent cannot be understood if viewers stand close enough to see the individual brushstrokes.

From the vision in Daniel 8 we learned that while apocalyptic may seem on the surface to describe the future in detail, in point of fact it does not. Some details may in the end match up with a precise event, but it would have been impossible to see that in advance. From Revelation 12—13 we learned that an apocalyptic vision may actually be a sermon in disguise. We must not focus on deciphering the bizarre details and miss the underlying message.

Reading apocalyptic, then, is best done from a distance. Like ancient hearers, we need to take in the sweep of the narrative. Apocalyptic uses allusions and symbols that may be peculiar but in the larger context combine to depict scenes of unusual vividness and emotion. But the message can easily be missed if the strokes of the painter's brush are scrutinized individually. What did the author intend to communicate? What did the audience need to hear? The truth comes through vividly when we view it from a distance.

How does the language of apocalyptic work? It tends to be more allusive than precise, more impressionistic than realistic, more fantastic than literal. Consequently we will not understand the parts of the story until we have read the last page.

6

HOW HAVE PROPHECIES BEEN FULFILLED?

Prediction and prophecy are like green beans and beans. Green beans is only one species of beans; prediction is only one species of prophecy. When people say "beans," some think only of green beans, while others think only of refried pinto beans. When people say "prophecy," some think only of prediction. But Moses was a prophet: "Since then, no prophet has arisen in Israel like Moses" (Deut 34:10). Samuel, Nathan, Elijah and Elisha were prophets. Jesus was a prophet. And the primary role of these prophets—and of all prophets—went beyond prediction.

This chapter and the following one focus on the question of prediction in the prophetic books. In what sense is prophecy predictive? The present chapter examines pronouncements that have been fulfilled, especially as announced by the former prophets. The previous chapter on apocalyptic underscored how apocalyptic visions were fulfilled. What we learn from completed pronouncements will help us understand things yet to be completed. These insights will be applied to unfulfilled prophecy in the next chapter.

Actually I should keep this chapter as short as possible, lest we forget that prediction is only one species of prophecy. But brevity here will disappoint most readers, because we are trapped in the web of a culture that wants to know the future.

THE PROPHETIC MISSION

A prophet was a winged messenger between heaven and earth—if you will, the Mercury of the Bible. Privileged to have an audience with God and to hear his passionate perspective on the affairs of humanity, prophets flew on winged sandals to the throne rooms of kings and to the gates of cities. The message was urgent: the God of the thunderbolt was out of sorts and awash with unfathomable wrath, because his chosen people were no longer considering him their chosen God. Idolatry had replaced piety. Unless kings and subjects started marching to the beat of the divine drum, a fullness of fury was going to scorch the earth. All hell would break loose. But there was good news. The fury could be replaced by mercy. Getting in step with God's ways would mean forgiveness, and the driest of deserts would suddenly blossom with love. However, no one seemed to be listening to the good news.[1]

Given the extent of lawlessness in the land, God needed his messengers to be prosecuting attorneys. The human perspective on life had gone crosswise to the divine perspective, and God needed someone to denounce the defiance. The well-to-do were taking advantage of the poor, and God needed someone to point fingers at injustice.[2] Everyone was doing what was right in their own eyes, and God needed someone to charge the criminals with crimes of disobedience. The prophets would be that someone—God's prosecutors. Their role was to enforce the historic covenant between God and the Israelites.[3]

So the prophets warned of earthquakes and tsunamis of divine judgment. They summoned the children of Abraham back to the bloody covenant of circumcision. They promised that if the people would repent the judgment would dissipate, yet people denied that they needed to repent—all the while counting on God's blessing to continue. The prophets begged God to delay his wrath; meanwhile people continued worshiping golden calves in full view of the One who said, No idols. Prophets wept over the Israelites' inclination to offer sacrifices to stone-faced, lifeless Canaanite deities instead of to the Creator of life.

The role of the prophets, then, was prosecution. They sensed that the God of venomous snakes, fire and holes in the earth—by which thousands of disobedient perished in the wilderness—was preparing even worse forms of judgment for transgressors. They knew that human actions determine divine consequences.

Prophecy was also *persuasion*.[4] Though the jury's verdict had already been announced, the judge offered the opportunity of repentance until the last moment, when the guillotine of his wrath would fall on the necks of the disobedient. If the prosecutors could persuade people to change their ways, there would be an outpouring of God's loving blessing instead. With God there are always two options: wrath and love.

In the supernatural sense, wrath and love are not two different attributes but one and the same. For wrath is a function of love. It is also a function of holiness. But in the natural sense, a display of love is easily overwhelmed by a display of wrath. In the middle of a category 5 hurricane it is difficult to see God's love. And the weather report says that the hurricane of justice is presently headed for the shores of the disobedient. All residents need to move immediately to the higher ground of penitence. Meanwhile, far above the supernatural disasters on earth is a gentle, loving Father. His mercies are everlasting. His love is patient—to a point. Errant children dare not presume on his good graces forever. This Father's wrath is no less perfect than his love.

The question was—and is—can anyone or anything awaken people from their self-sufficiency and reorient their worldview in line with God's? "The task of prophetic ministry is to nurture, nourish, and evoke a consciousness and perception alternative to the consciousness and perception of the dominant culture around us."[5] In essence, the answers to life on this earth are not found on this earth. They must come from the One who sees and knows things from the eternal perspective. "Prophecy, then, may be described as *exegesis of existence from a divine perspective*."[6] But how to convince people of that? Much of the prophet's strategy was to preview God's fury on those who remained out of sync and God's faithfulness on those who would get in sync. In this sense prophecy was *prediction*, for it announced what God was going to do. Prediction's function was to make the prosecution and persuasion more convincing.[7]

The nature of prophecy, then, is threefold—in descending order of prominence—prosecution, persuasion and prediction (see figure 6.1).[8] When we add to the mix the rhetorical nature of prophetic language and the genre of poetry as the mode of expression, we begin to understand better the richness and power of prophecy.[9] But since prophecy is in part prediction, a question often comes up: to what extent did the pronouncements of the prophets reveal details about the future? While putting

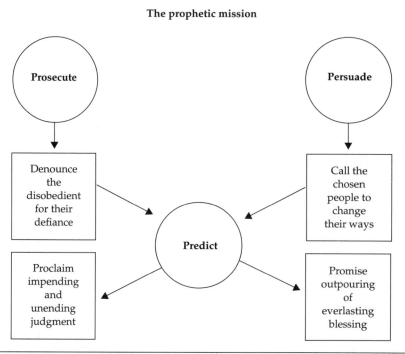

Figure 6.1. Role of the prophets

people on notice about God's character and intolerance of disobedience, while seeking to effect change in thinking and conduct, while speaking poetically with fertile images designed to impress concepts deep in the mind, were the prophets also revealing the specifics of future events? Does God intend for us to know particulars about the days and years ahead? Certainly the prophetic words of judgment are not empty words. Terrible events will occur—in some cases sooner, in some cases later. But are readers supposed to assemble detailed information about the future from the language of prophecy? When someone says, "I'm going to skin you alive," or "I'm going to punch your lights out," or "You're cruisin' for a bruisin'," is the intent to announce specific information about the future?

The nuance of this question has become important in modern society. Many readers assume that prophecy primarily predicts the future,[10] which raises a question. If the primary point of prophecy is that God's patience has a breaking point and his wrath has a beginning point, how much of prophecy is really predictive? Though the ferocity of God's wrath is incomprehensible, the prophets sketched ways in which the teeth of his wrath would take savage bites out of the disobedient. Since the intent of the sketches was striking prosecution rather than interesting information, perhaps the lead in prophets' pencils was too thick to spell out details about the future.

SPYING OUT THE FUTURE

A compelling urge in modern society is to take control. This urge may influence our understanding of prophecy. In order to have health, wealth and prosperity, we need control of the factors that determine health, wealth and prosperity. We ask, in effect, what can we do now that will guarantee things in the future? We want the best of everything, and to achieve it we need to manage all circumstances and aspects of life.

Take health. Physicians and researchers are seeking to make our future health more secure. The sale of vitamins and exercise machines skyrockets as people try harder to ensure a bright future for themselves. The worst loss of control is to be ill, not have an explanation and not to know what will make us well. That leaves us feeling powerless. We want assurance that the future will be under our control if we do this or that.

Another example is the weather. We have not learned how to control the weather, though meteorologists are seeking ways to do that too. Seeding clouds with chemicals has the potential of producing rain when we want it. But in the meantime, if we can at least know what the weather will bring, then we have gained a measure of control. Hence the daily weather report has become as essential as morning tea or coffee.

Control shows up in many places in our culture. One of the keys I touch most often on my PC keyboard is labeled "Ctrl." I am surprised that even my spellchecker recognizes the four-letter abbreviation.

Our ability to predetermine what the future will be will always be limited, so the urge to at least know what it will bring is powerful. Megatrend books, sci-fi movies and palm readers sell well. Consciously or not, everyone is caught up in the desire to know and control the future. Our investments, our health, our success are more within our control if we can anticipate the future.

Are Christians influenced in their approach to prophecy by this drive to know the future? Are we more excited by sermons concerning prophecy and the future or by sermons concerning providence and faithfulness? Are we likely to think of prophecy as prediction rather than prosecution? Combining our culture's thirst for knowledge about the future and the impression that biblical prophecy intends to reveal the details of the future, the pendulum of prophetic allure is swinging beyond its intended trajectory. We cannot tolerate a veil hanging between us and the grandfather clock of eternity, so we keep trying to peek. Any person or book that claims to predict the future gains a large audience.

Is a Christian's thirst for knowledge of the future a symptom of being squeezed into the mold of our culture (Rom 12:1-2)? Is the assumption correct that biblical prophecy can satisfy our curiosity about the future?

Any discussion of the predictive aspects of prophecy must proceed with caution, lest a thirst for information drive our interpretation. We must read the text in light of the author's intent, not in light of what we are searching for. We must allow the prophets' passion to be prosecution. We must examine carefully how pronouncements were given and how they were fulfilled. In sum, we must develop a careful hermeneutic for interpreting prophecy.

Fortunately, many of the pronouncements of prophecy have already come to pass. The sovereign *I will*s have already become *I did*s. This is good, because we can learn from the history of fulfillment. We ought to be able to understand better what prophecy reveals about things still future based on what it has revealed in the past. It makes sense that the fulfilled will guide us to the path of understanding the unfulfilled.

It will help if we set aside what we remember about biblical history and pretend for the moment that we do not know how prophecies were fulfilled. It is good practice to look at a pronouncement and postulate how we think it will be fulfilled. Then we can check our expected fulfillment with what the Bible reports actually happened. We may be surprised at the results. The practice should at least make us better interpreters of prophecy, both of prophecies that have been fulfilled and—even more to the point—of prophecies yet to be fulfilled.

Reading Prophecy Superficially

I performed an experiment with a class of undergraduate students in a course on the Old Testament. I distributed a list of selected prophecies in 1 and 2 Kings. It included statements like the following:

- The kingdom is going to be torn out of Solomon's hand (1 Kings 11:31).
- The whole kingdom will not be taken out of Solomon's hand (1 Kings 11:34).
- Solomon will rule the kingdom his whole life (1 Kings 11:34).
- David's descendants will be punished but not forever (1 Kings 11:39).
- The house of Jeroboam will burn like dung until it is all gone (1 Kings 14:10).
- The men belonging to Jeroboam who die in the city will be eaten by dogs, and those who die in the country will be food for the birds of the air (1 Kings 14:11).
- The dogs will lick up Ahab's blood, and they will devour Jezebel (1 Kings 21:23-24).

I then asked the students to discuss how they would expect these statements to be fulfilled. I quickly realized that they were unprepared to deal with the pronouncements of prophecy. Their tendency was to concentrate on the wording and miss the point. They struggled first with superficial issues. Did the burning of the *house* of Jeroboam refer to a fire in his *home?* If Solomon was king *all* the days of his life, what would it have been like to be ruling as a child? It did not take long, however, for the students to realize that such superficial readings would mean that, for example, Solomon held the kingdom in his hand, since it was taken out of his hand. Their tendency toward complete literalism underscores an important point: reading prophecy superficially may quickly lead to false conclusions about meaning.

Though the students' level of engagement improved, they still struggled with specific details, but with more valid questions. If the kingdom was torn out of Solomon's hand, was it taken away from him violently? Does the punishment of David's descendants refer to the exile still hundreds of years away? Were all of Jeroboam's family and friends eaten by either dogs or birds?[11]

When I noted that several announcements of judgment included threats about dogs and birds eating people, the students welcomed the possibility that those phrases may have been stereotypical statements of judgment.[12] So when they read that Ahab's blood would be licked up by dogs and that Jezebel would be eaten by dogs, there was a strong tendency to consider those phrases as fixed statements of judgment as well—until one student remembered that Jezebel was indeed eaten by dogs.

The experiment with these students raises important questions. Are we likely to understand prophecy correctly if we read it at only a surface level? Was the point of these pronouncements to tell the Israelites in advance what would happen in the future? What did the original hearers expect when they heard that the kingdom was going to be torn out of Solomon's hand, but also—later in the same prediction—that the whole kingdom would not be taken out of Solomon's hand and that he would rule the kingdom his whole life? In what sense would David's descendants be punished, but not forever?[13]

The pronouncements of the former prophets provide perspective on the pronouncements of the classical prophets. The people of Old Testament times would have had a growing sense of how the prophets spoke and what they could expect to see happen based on precedent—what previous prophets had said and what actually happened. Elijah's pronouncements would have shaped how Isaiah's pronouncements were understood. That is precisely what we should gain from analyzing the completed prophecies recorded in Scripture. We have centuries of pronouncements from numerous prophets, most of which have already been fulfilled. By reflecting on those that were fulfilled, we will be better prepared to interpret those awaiting completion.

READING PROPHECY IN REVERSE

Prophetic activity in the time of the Old Testament tended to come in spurts, and those spurts were usually associated with expressing God's judgment.[14] When disobedience flared up during the forty years in the wilderness, Moses functioned as a prophetic messenger of judgment. When disobedience flared up during the period of the judges, Samuel was both judge and prophet, announcing God's judgment on the sons of the priest Eli and later on the new king Saul. Elijah, Elisha, Ahijah and Huldah were part of a group of prophets referred to as former prophets, who called down judgment on kings when disobedience flared up in the period of the divided monarchy. Leading up to the fall of Samaria, the capital of the northern kingdom, prophets like Amos, Hosea and Micah were preaching judgment. Leading up to the fall of Jerusalem and the southern kingdom, prophets like Jeremiah and Ezekiel were preaching judgment.

The pronouncements of the former prophets are our special focus, because they have all been fulfilled, and the fulfillments allow us to reverse the prophetic process. Since we know what eventually happened, we can compare that with what the prophets said was going to happen. By reading prophecy in reverse we will see it from a different angle.

Indictment of Eli the priest (1 Sam 2:30-36; 3:11-14). An unidentified "man of God" went to the priest Eli and announced God's judgment:

> *I promised that your family and the family of your ancestor should go in and out before me forever. . . . See, a time is coming when I will cut off your strength and the strength of your ancestor's family, so that no one in your family will live to old age. . . . The only one of you whom I shall not cut off from my altar shall be spared to weep out his eyes and grieve his heart; all the members of your household will die by the sword.*[15] *. . . Your two sons . . . will die on the same day. I will raise up for myself a faithful priest, who shall do according to what is in my heart and in my mind. I will build him a sure house, and he shall go in and out before my anointed one forever. Everyone who is left in your family shall come to implore him for a piece of silver or a loaf of bread.* (1 Sam 2:30-36 NRSV)

A second version of judgment on the house of Eli is given to Samuel (1 Sam 3:11-14). The story of the young boy sleeping in the house of the Lord and hearing a voice during the night is well known. Three times Samuel thought the voice was the priest Eli calling him. The fourth time Samuel did as Eli instructed him, and when he heard the voice, he responded, "Speak, for your servant is listening." Surprisingly, God gave the young Samuel a message of judgment on the house of Eli:

> *I am about to do something in Israel that will make both ears of anyone who hears of it tingle. . . . I am about to punish his house forever for the iniquity that he knew, because his sons were blaspheming God. . . . The iniquity of Eli's house shall not be expiated by sacrifice or offering forever.* (1 Sam 3:11-14 NRSV)

The function of this language of judgment fits well with the surrounding context. The opening narratives of 1 Samuel set up a sharp contrast between the outgoing leadership of Eli and the incoming leadership of Samuel.[16] Eli's approval rating with the people and with God had been ruined by his two sons, who were also priests. They were abusing the sacrificial offerings as well as the women who served in the house of the Lord. As a father, Eli had failed. The whole situation was a tragedy.[17] But Samuel's story was a triumph. His parents did all the right things, as did Samuel. Trained as a priest but functioning as a judge and prophet, Samuel had God and the people's full approval.

To express the depths of God's despair with Eli and his sons, two versions of the decree of condemnation are preserved, one announced to Eli and one to the young Samuel. The language is extreme and emotional. There is no doubt about the severity of the judgment. If we were to attempt to determine, however, how God would judge, how would we fare? Would no descendant of Eli ever be a priest, save one? Was everyone in the family going to die by the sword? Would both sons die on the same day? Was no one going to live to a normal age? Was one descendant to be spared all this judgment, only to suffer a life of tears and sorrow? Would every descendant of Eli be under a perpetual curse? Would God deny forgiveness to all descendants of Eli? Who would replace Eli as priest and hold that office forever? These questions imply conclusions that would be logical based on the language of judgment.

Fulfillment. According to 1 Samuel 4:17-22, the Philistines captured the ark of God and killed the two sons of Eli. Upon hearing the news, ninety-eight-year-old Eli fell off his seat, broke his neck and died. The wife of one of Eli's sons died during childbirth, though her son, Ichabod, survived. Three descendants of Eli (Ahijah, Ahimelech and Abiathar) served as priests under Saul (1 Sam 14:3; 22:20; 2 Sam 8:17). When Saul killed the priests for siding with David, Abiathar escaped. He remained as priest for many years, during the reigns of David and Solomon, until Solomon deposed him for siding with Adonijah (1 Kings 2:22-27). The reference to a priest who would serve forever in place of Eli is nowhere explained in Scripture.

Were the pronouncements of condemnation on Eli's house fulfilled? While we can generally answer yes, we have questions. Why is it stated that no one would live to an old age? What about Abiathar? Why does the prophecy state that only one would not be cut off from the altar? What about Ahijah and Ahimelech? Why does it state that everyone would die by the sword? Who is the faithful priest appointed in Eli's place who served the Lord forever? When did the offspring of Eli go to the faithful priest for silver and bread? In what sense was the sin of Eli's family never forgiven?

The most transparent prediction in the language of judgment on Eli has to do with the death of his two sons. Much of the remaining language is more translucent than transparent (see figure 6.2). We could not have accurately anticipated the fulfillment of parts of the prophecy, and even after the fulfillment we are not sure what the fulfillment was for some parts of the prophecy.

Predictions of judgment

Transparent	**Translucent**
The *fact* of God's judgment on sinfulness is clear	Details about *how* judgment will occur may be unclear

Figure 6.2. Pattern of predictions

Indictment of King Solomon (1 Kings 11:11-13, 29-39). God spoke directly to Solomon about the judgment he deserved:

> I will most certainly tear the kingdom away from you and give it to one of your subordinates. . . . I will not do it during your lifetime. I will tear it out of the hand of your son. Yet I will not tear the whole kingdom from him, but will give him one tribe for the sake of David my servant and for the sake of Jerusalem. (1 Kings 11:11-13)

The prophet Ahijah gives a second version of the judgment. This time it is announced to Jeroboam, who had rebelled against Solomon. Ahijah tore the new robe he was wearing into twelve pieces, handed ten of the pieces to Jeroboam and spoke on the Lord's behalf:

> I am going to tear the kingdom out of Solomon's hand and give you ten tribes. . . . But . . . he will have one tribe. . . . I will not take the whole kingdom out of Solomon's hand; I have made him ruler all the days of his life. . . . I will take the kingdom from his son's hands and give you ten tribes. I will give one tribe to his son so that David my servant may always have a lamp before me in Jerusalem. . . . You will rule over all that your heart desires; you will be king over Israel. If you do whatever I command you . . . I will build you a dynasty as enduring as the one I built for David. . . . I will humble David's descendants . . . but not forever. (1 Kings 11:31-39)

These prophecies express the Lord's judgment on Solomon for instituting worship of pagan deities. For God it was a bitter disappointment to see the man self-destruct in whom he had invested so much. For Solomon it was a bitter disappointment to see the kingdom torn apart in which *he* had invested so much. The language of judgment is consequently very emotional. The prophecy is also an endorsement of Solomon's enemy Jeroboam as king over ten tribes. It includes a challenge for Jeroboam to follow the Lord's statutes and commands in order to achieve success as a ruler.

There is no doubt about the severity of the judgment. But if we were to attempt to determine the details of how God was going to judge Solomon, how would we fare? Was Jeroboam going to take over the kingdom violently, except for the one tribe? How far-ranging would his kingdom be, since God said Jeroboam could rule over all that his heart desired? How would David have a permanent presence in Jerusalem? How would David's descendants be humbled?

Fulfillment. According to 1 Kings 11:41—12:24 (cf. 2 Chron 10:1-19), Solomon remained king of the twelve tribes until his death. After his death, Rehoboam his son succeeded him. When the northern tribes requested that Rehoboam lighten the heavy yoke put on them by Solomon, he refused. So the ten tribes rebelled against Judah and made Jeroboam their king. Rehoboam remained in control of the tribes of Judah and Benjamin.

Were the pronouncements of condemnation on Solomon fulfilled? While answering generally yes, we have questions. Why do the pronouncements seem to indicate a violent takeover of Solomon's kingdom by saying it would be torn out of his hand? Why is the severity of the pronouncements lessened in the middle of the pronouncement, from tearing the kingdom from Solomon to taking it from his son to taking only ten of the tribes? Why are only ten tribes and one tribe referred to when there were twelve tribes? In what sense did David always have a lamp in Jerusalem? In what sense were David's descendants humbled?

The most transparent prediction in the language of judgment on Solomon has to do with the division of the kingdom in two parts, with Solomon's son ruling only one part. Much of the rest of the language is more translucent than transparent. We could not have accurately anticipated the fulfillment of parts of the prophecy, and even after the fulfillment we are not sure which events fulfilled which parts.

Note: Readers who need additional evidence of the translucence of predictions in the former prophets should continue reading the examples that follow. Other readers may skip ahead to the last example in this section, "Indictment of Judah" (p. 145).

Indictment of the altar at Bethel (1 Kings 13:1-3). Jeroboam incurred the wrath of God by setting up two golden calves, one in Bethel and the other in Dan. He instructed the people of the northern ten tribes to worship the golden calves rather than go to Jerusalem to worship. God was extremely angry.

An unnamed man of God came from Judah to Jeroboam as he was making an idolatrous offering at his new shrine at Bethel.

> *He cried out against the altar by the word of the LORD: "O altar, altar! This is what the LORD says: 'A son named Josiah will be born to the house of David. On you he will sacrifice the priests of the high places who now make offerings here, and human bones will be burned on you.'" That same day the man of God gave a sign: "This is the sign the LORD has declared: The altar will be split apart and the ashes on it will be poured out."* (1 Kings 13:1-3)

If we were to attempt to determine from these pronouncements how God was going to judge Jeroboam, how would we fare? Would we not expect a reformer by the name of Josiah to come from Judah to stop Jeroboam's pagan practices? Would we not expect the very priests sanctioned by Jeroboam to be offered as sacrifices on the pagan altars?

Fulfillment. According to 1 Kings 13:5, the altar split apart and the ashes poured out immediately after the prophecy. However, it was not until more than 250 years later (2 Kings 23:15-20) that Josiah demolished the high place and altar that Jeroboam had set up at Bethel. He removed bones from nearby tombs and burned them on the altar. The author of 2 Kings says that this was specifically done in fulfillment of the man of God's prophecy. Josiah also slaughtered the priests of the high places on the altars.

Were the pronouncements of condemnation on Jeroboam's altar fulfilled? The answer is yes. It was not in Jeroboam's lifetime as we would have expected, nor was it Jeroboam's priests that Josiah sacrificed as we would have expected, but the prophecy was fulfilled.

Indictment of King Jeroboam (1 Kings 14:10-16). Jeroboam's wife approached the prophet Ahijah on behalf of their sick son. Ahijah announced:

I am going to bring disaster on the house of Jeroboam. I will cut off from Jeroboam every last male in Israel—slave or free. I will burn up the house of Jeroboam as one burns dung, until it is all gone. Dogs will eat those belonging to Jeroboam who die in the city, and the birds of the air will feed on those who die in the country. . . . When you set foot in your city, the boy will die. All Israel will mourn for him and bury him. He is the only one belonging to Jeroboam who will be buried. . . .

The LORD *will raise up for himself a king over Israel who will cut off the family of Jeroboam. . . . And the Lord will strike Israel, so that it will be like a reed swaying in the water. He will uproot Israel from this good land that he gave to their forefathers and scatter them beyond the River.* (1 Kings 14:10-15)

Ahijah's prophecy to Jeroboam through his wife was an announcement of God's judgment on Jeroboam. It was clearly deserved, for Jeroboam had established pagan altars and appointed many priests for the high places. The author of 1 Kings comments that this was the sin of the house of Jeroboam that led to its downfall and its destruction from the face of the earth (1 Kings 13:34).

If we were to attempt to determine how God was going to judge Jeroboam based on this prophecy, how would we fare? In what sense would Jeroboam be separated from all the men of Israel? Was Jeroboam's family destined to die by fire? Was his son going to die the instant his wife entered the city? Were men who sided with Jeroboam destined to die and not be buried and to be eaten by dogs or birds? Were Jeroboam and his family going to be killed immediately? Was the Lord going to send Israel into dispersion at this point?

Fulfillment. According to 1 Kings 14:17-20, when Jeroboam's wife crossed the threshold of their house, her son died. The boy was buried and Israel mourned for him. Nadab, another son of Jeroboam, succeeded him, but only for two years until Baasha struck down Nadab and became king of Israel. Baasha killed Jeroboam's whole family, not leaving anyone who breathed. The author of 1 Kings says that this was done in fulfillment of Ahijah's prophecy (1 Kings 15:25-30).

Were the pronouncements of judgment on Jeroboam and his family fulfilled? Yes, but we would not have accurately anticipated how it would be fulfilled. What did the prophecy mean that every male in Israel would be cut off? Were the repeated statements that men would be eaten by dogs and birds stereotypical?[18] Why is it reported that Jeroboam's son died when his mother entered the house? Why was the rest of Jeroboam's family not killed immediately? In what sense did Israel become like a reed swaying in the water? Why was Israel not scattered beyond the river at this point? Much of the language of this prophecy is translucent rather than transparent.

Indictment of King Ahab (1 Kings 21:19-29; 22:17-28). Elijah announced judgment on Ahab:

> *In the place where dogs licked up Naboth's blood, dogs will lick up your blood—yes, yours! . . . I am going to bring disaster on you. I will consume your descendants and cut off from Ahab every last male in Israel—slave or free. I will make your house like that of Jeroboam son of Nebat and that of Baasha son of Ahijah. . . . Dogs will devour Jezebel by the wall of Jezreel. Dogs will eat those belonging to Ahab who die in the city, and the birds of the air will feed on those who die in the country.* (1 Kings 21:19-24)

Later Micaiah used a word picture and a vision to describe God's judgment of Ahab. He saw all of Israel scattered like sheep in the hills without a shepherd. The Lord said, "These people have no master. Let each one go home in peace" (1 Kings 22:17). Micaiah also saw a vision of the Lord on his throne and a lying spirit that spoke through the mouth of Ahab's prophets to entice him. The Lord decreed disaster for Ahab (1 Kings 22:17-23).

Fulfillment. Elijah and Micaiah's prophecies against Ahab revealed God's terrible wrath on Ahab. In response to Elijah, Ahab put on sackcloth and humbled himself. As a result, the Lord told Elijah that he would bring the disaster planned for Ahab on his son instead: "I will not bring this disaster in his day" (1 Kings 21:28-29). In response to Micaiah, Ahab had him thrown in prison to be kept there until Ahab returned from battle. Micaiah declared, "If you ever return safely, the LORD has not spoken through me" (1 Kings 22:28). Ahab was wounded in battle and died in his chariot. His blood that ran down on the floor of his chariot was washed out by a pool in Samaria, and dogs licked it up (1 Kings 22:29-38). "As the sun was setting, a cry spread through the army: 'Every man to his town; everyone to his land!'" (1 Kings 22:36).

After Ahab died, the fulfillment of the pronouncement about the destruction of his family was carried out by Jehu against Ahab's son Joram. Jehu killed Joram and left the corpse in a field that belonged to Naboth.

In addition, Jehu commanded that Jezebel be thrown to her death at Jezreel. Everything but her skull, hands and feet were eaten by dogs before she could be buried. Jehu also arranged for the killing of seventy sons of Ahab, and his chief men, close friends and priests (2 Kings 9:24-26, 30-37; 10:1-11).

Were the pronouncements of judgment on Ahab and his family fulfilled? Yes, but we would have had a difficult time figuring out how in advance. Though Elijah seems to give Ahab a reprieve, he dies in battle anyway. Furthermore, why was Ahab's blood not licked by the dogs whereas Naboth's was? Was the language about men being eaten by dogs and birds stereotypical? Why were the judgments against Ahab imposed instead on Joram? Much of the language of this prophecy is translucent rather than transparent.

Indictment of King Sennacherib (2 Kings 19:7, 21-34; cf. Is 37:21-38). The northern kingdom of Israel had ended in a moral and military disaster. Based on extreme licentiousness recorded in 2 Kings 17, God's patience had reached its limit. "So the LORD was very angry with Israel and removed them from his presence" (2 Kings 17:18). The instrument of God's wrath was the powerful armies of Assyria. These infamous conquerors deported the Israelites in mass to various places throughout the Assyrian kingdom, while repopulating the former territories of the northern tribes with Gentiles from a variety of foreign nations.

In sharp contrast to what happened in the north was the situation in the south. Instead of moral and military tragedy, it enjoyed moral and military victory. As the kingdom of Israel came to a sad end, the southern kingdom of Judah was experiencing a revival. King Hezekiah was actually doing what was right in the eyes of the Lord. Yet though he was disposing of the enemy within, Hezekiah was faced with a major threat from the enemy without. After the Assyrians conquered Samaria, it seemed that Jerusalem would be an easy target too. So a large army encamped against Jerusalem. By human standards, the people of Judah were doomed. But in response to Hezekiah's urgent pleas for deliverance, God sent Isaiah with a prophecy of assurance. Based on a report he would receive, Sennacherib would return to Assyria in defeat. He would fall by the sword.

> *Listen! I am going to put such a spirit in him that when he hears a certain report, he will return to his own country, and there I will have him cut down with the sword.*

> The Virgin Daughter of Zion
>   despises you and mocks you.
> The Daughter of Jerusalem
>   tosses her head as you flee. . . .
> I will put my hook in your nose
>   and my bit in your mouth,
> and I will make you return
>   by the way you came. . . .
> He will not enter this city
>   or shoot an arrow here.
> He will not come before it with shield
>   or build a siege ramp against it. (2 Kings 19:7, 21, 28, 32)

If we were to attempt to determine how God was going to deliver Hezekiah and Jerusalem, how would we fare? We would probably expect a report to come from somewhere within the Assyrian kingdom forcing Sennacherib to abandon the siege of Jerusalem. We might also expect Sennacherib to be killed upon his return to Nineveh.

Fulfillment. According to 2 Kings 19:35-37 (cf. 2 Chron 32:20-21; Is 37:36-38), the angel of the Lord put to death 185,000 men in the Assyrian camp in one night. Sennacherib was forced to withdraw and return to Nineveh. Sometime later, while he was worshiping in the temple of his god, his two sons assassinated him.

Were Isaiah's pronouncements of victory over Sennacherib fulfilled? The answer is yes, even though Isaiah's prophecy was more translucent than transparent.

Indictment of Judah (2 Kings 21:12-15). The Lord pronounced judgment on Judah through some unnamed prophets:

> I am going to bring such disaster on Jerusalem and Judah that the ears of everyone who hears of it will tingle. I will stretch out over Jerusalem the measuring line used against Samaria and the plumb line used against the house of Ahab. I will wipe out Jerusalem as one wipes a dish, wiping it and turning it upside down. I will forsake the remnant of my inheritance and hand them over to their enemies. They will be looted and plundered by all their foes, because they have done evil in my eyes and have provoked me to anger from the day their forefathers came out of Egypt until this day. (2 Kings 21:12-15)

A second indictment was given by a prophetess: God's anger would burn against this place and never be quenched. But because Josiah humbled himself before the Lord, he would die in peace. Josiah would not see the disaster to come on Judah (2 Kings 22:15-20).

Fulfillment. While these pronouncements of judgment were fulfilled when the Babylonians destroyed Jerusalem, the metaphorical language is noteworthy. Tingling ears, stretching a measuring line and plumb line over Jerusalem, wiping out Jerusalem and turning it upside down like a dish, forsaking the remnant, and God's anger burning forever are metaphors and hyperboles that make the prophecy translucent. Metaphoric language generally leaves us unsure of specifics before fulfillment.

But the pronouncement that Josiah would die in peace needs special attention. If we read the words on the surface, King Josiah was to be spared the judgment and die in peace. There was good reason for that, since he was an exception to the pattern of moral poverty among most of the kings of Judah. It surprises us, then, to read in 2 Kings 23:29 that Josiah was killed in battle with the Egyptian pharaoh Neco, thirty years before the destruction of Jerusalem.

Based on the language of the prophetess, we certainly would have expected Josiah's death to be peaceful instead of in the midst of battle. In retrospect, however, we can theorize that the point of the prophecy was to announce that he would not be present to see the destruction of Jerusalem. But we would not have anticipated that in advance. Also note that the prophetess's words that the Lord's anger would not be quenched were not intended to state that it would be eternal. This leaves us with further support for the thesis that prophecy can be more translucent than transparent.

WHAT DO FULFILLED PROPHECIES REVEAL REGARDING PROPHECY?

The pronouncements of judgment and their fulfillment in the former prophets provide key insight for interpreting prophecies yet to be fulfilled. The already fulfilled prophecies demonstrate a pattern of translucence rather than transparency. The intent was apparently not to give specific information about the future. Rather than predict with precision, the prophets sought to prosecute with power. In some cases pronouncements were fulfilled explicitly. But even then it had not been possible to know before fulfillment what would be fulfilled transparently.

In support of this conclusion, seven observations can be made about prophecy. These are based on the foregoing section, "Reading Prophecy in Reverse" (see figure 6.3).

Observations from analyzing prophecies already fulfilled

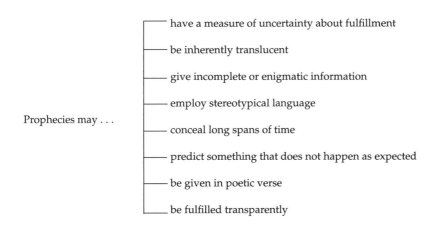

Prophecies may . . .

- have a measure of uncertainty about fulfillment
- be inherently translucent
- give incomplete or enigmatic information
- employ stereotypical language
- conceal long spans of time
- predict something that does not happen as expected
- be given in poetic verse
- be fulfilled transparently

Figure 6.3. Prophecy and prediction

1. Statements in a prophecy that are qualified by subsequent statements create *a measure of uncertainty about fulfillment.* The Lord first told Solomon that he was going to tear the kingdom away from him. Then he qualified this, saying that he would not tear it from him during his lifetime but would tear it out of the hand of his son. He further qualified it by saying he would not take the whole kingdom away but would allow him to keep one tribe. Ahijah's prophecy to Jeroboam included similar qualifications but with some variation. Eventually Ahijah stated that Solomon would rule the kingdom his whole life and that ten of the tribes would be taken from Solomon's son and given to Jeroboam (cf. 1 Kings 11:9-13). Elijah's prophecy to Ahab was qualified by subsequent statements as well. First he said, "I am going to bring disaster on you," but then he deferred the judgment to Ahab's son (1 Kings 21:21, 29). Evidently extenuating circumstances, people's response or special considerations can alter how a prophecy will be fulfilled.

2. Imagery and metaphor in prophecy are *inherently translucent.* Some-

times imagery supplemented the message that was expressed in words, and sometimes the imagery was the message. Ahijah tore his new cloak into twelve strips and gave ten of the strips to Jeroboam to graphically portray what he was saying. Ahijah said that David would have a lamp before the Lord in Jerusalem. Ahijah also said that the Lord would strike Israel so that it would be like a reed swaying in the water. Micaiah saw all of Israel like sheep in the hills without a shepherd. He also saw a vision of the Lord on his throne and a lying spirit that spoke through the mouth of Ahab's prophets to entice him. Isaiah said that the Lord was going to put a hook in Sennacherib's nose and a bit in his mouth. The Lord said that he was going to stretch a measuring line and a plumb line over Jerusalem and that he was going to wipe out Jerusalem as one wipes a dish.

Sometimes the significance of a metaphor is evident in the larger context of Scripture, but often we can only infer the meaning of the metaphor. The metaphor of David's lamp in Jerusalem may reflect the motif that light portrays a person's presence, as with the light of God's presence in the tabernacle. Thus David's light will remain in Jerusalem in the presence of his descendants. The metaphor of a reed swaying in water has a parallel in Jesus' reference to a reed swaying in the wind, but Jesus does not indicate the significance of the metaphor (Mt 11:7 = Lk 7:24). The metaphor of a measuring line and plumb line appears in other prophetic passages, though without explanation (e.g., Is 44:13; Zech 1:16).

3. Prophecies may be translucent because of *incomplete or enigmatic information.* Ahijah prophesied that ten tribes would be given to Jeroboam and that one tribe would remain separate; this left open the question of the twelfth tribe. Ahijah said that every male would be cut off from Jeroboam, whether slave or free. He also prophesied that David's descendants would be punished. The significance of the punishment of David's descendants probably reflects an interpretation of the events in the period of the divided monarchy. The prophecy may view Judah's loss of the ten tribes as punishment for the evil done by Solomon, but the intent of the term *punish* was not known until after it was fulfilled. In any event, until the time of fulfillment the meaning of some prophecies remains vague.

4. Prophecy may employ *stereotypical language of judgment,* leaving the fulfillment uncertain (see pp. 94-97). Denunciation and intimidation characterize such statements of judgment. Ahijah said that the kingdom would be torn out of Solomon's hand. The term *torn* graphically denotes a re-

moval of the kingdom from Solomon's hands as part of God's judgment. On one occasion Saul tore Samuel's robe, and Samuel responded with a prophecy that the Lord had already torn the kingdom away from Saul (1 Sam 15:27-28). Later the Lord told Solomon that he would punish him by tearing the kingdom away from him; he then qualified that to say that he would tear it away from his son (1 Kings 11:9-13). Ahijah's prophetic symbolism of tearing his own robe and then saying to Jeroboam that the kingdom was going to be torn out of Solomon's hand is an example of the language of judgment. In hindsight we understand that the kingdom was not taken from Solomon violently. But with foresight, a violent takeover of Solomon's kingdom may have been expected.

Ahijah said that Jeroboam's house would burn like dung, that every male in Israel would be cut off, that none of the people belonging to Jeroboam would be buried, that men in the city would be eaten by dogs, that men in the country would be eaten by birds, and that on the precise day the prophecy was being given the Lord had already raised up a new king who would cut off the family of Jeroboam. The Lord said that Baasha's house would be consumed like that of Jeroboam, that men in the city would be eaten by dogs and that men in the country would be eaten by birds. The Lord said that Ahab's house would be consumed like that of Jeroboam, that every male in Israel would be cut off, that men in the city would be eaten by dogs and that men in the country would be eaten by birds. The repetition of these phrases for three evil kings suggests that this is standard terminology for terrible judgment. In regard to Baasha, several elements of the announcements of judgment on Jeroboam and Ahab are omitted, yet the fulfillment for Baasha seems to be the same. It is common in announcements of judgment to use fixed expressions (e.g., 1 Sam 15:27-28). Furthermore, there is no evidence in the biblical text that these prophecies were carried out as stated. While that is an argument from silence, it has credibility in a context where validation of true prophets was important (Deut 18:21-22; 1 Kings 13:3, 5; 2 Kings 1:10-12; 7:1-20).

5. Prophecies may conceal *long spans of time* implicit within them. The Lord pronounced judgment on Jeroboam by means of Josiah. A normal reading would expect Josiah to come on the scene within Jeroboam's lifetime and deliver God's judgment. But these two individuals mentioned in the same prophecy were separated by hundreds of years. Ahijah predicted that the Lord would cut off the family of Jeroboam and that he would up-

root Israel and scatter them beyond the river. These events were separated by nearly two hundred years.

6. Prophecies may be translucent because they *appear to predict something that does not come about as expected*. Ahijah said that David would always have a lamp in Jerusalem, but there have been interruptions in the presence of the Davidic line in Jerusalem. Ahijah said that Jeroboam's sick son would die when Jeroboam's wife set foot inside the city, but her son died when she stepped over the threshold of their house. Elijah said that dogs would lick up Ahab's blood at the same place where they licked up Naboth's blood, but then God said that the judgment would instead go to Ahab's son, Joram. However, Joram's corpse was left in Naboth's field (not where Naboth died). Josiah was told that he would die in peace, but he was killed in a battle with Egypt.

This should not raise doubt about the authenticity of the prophetic word. It is not an issue of false prophecy but of intent. In hindsight we can see that Ahijah's statement about David's always having a lamp in Jerusalem assured the people that Judah would exist side by side with Israel and would not be replaced by Israel. In hindsight we can see that Josiah was promised a peaceful death in the sense that he would die before the fall of Jerusalem. The fact that his death was not "peaceful" as that word normally suggests does not negate the accuracy of the prophecy. The intent of Ahijah's statement about the death of the son was to announce that it would happen when his mother returned. The detail of whether that happened upon her entering the city or the house was insignificant to the fulfillment of the prophecy.

7. Prophecies that are given *in poetry* are likely to be translucent. Isaiah sent a poem to Hezekiah picturing the Assyrian army within sight of the walls of Jerusalem (2 Kings 19:21-28). He speaks as Sennacherib about his exploits: "With the soles of my feet I have dried up all the streams of Egypt." Isaiah speaks for the Lord about his power over Sennacherib: "I will put my hook in your nose and my bit in your mouth, and I will make you return by the way you came." He describes the response of Judah to Sennacherib's inability to attack Jerusalem as mockery from the walls of the city: "The Virgin Daughter of Zion despises you and mocks you. The Daughter of Jerusalem tosses her head as you flee." Figures of speech abound in the poetry of prophecy. That should suggest that correct understanding of prophetic poetry is often not possible until after the fulfillment.

This is not meant to suggest that prophecy cannot be fulfilled transparently. Jeroboam did become king over the northern ten tribes. Josiah was indeed born to the house of David. Josiah did burn bones on the pagan altars and sacrifice pagan priests on them. Jeroboam's pagan altar was indeed torn down, and the ashes were poured out. Ahab's blood was licked up by dogs. Sennacherib returned to his own country and fell by the sword.

But the nature of pronouncements in the former prophets suggests that transparent fulfillment is the exception rather than the rule. The prophets used prediction to enhance their prosecution and persuasion rather than to give details about the future.

IS TRANSLUCENCE A COMMON FEATURE OF PROPHECY?

The unlikelihood of knowing in advance whether the surface meaning of the words of predictions would be fulfilled precisely raises a question about other prophetic portions of Scripture. Is this characteristic of prophecy elsewhere as well? How have other prophecies been fulfilled?

Jeremiah 36:30. God announces judgment against Jehoiakim: he will not have a descendant to sit on the throne. But according to 2 Kings 24:6 (= 2 Chron 36:8), Jehoiachin succeeded his father. And Jeremiah gives an extensive portrayal of judgment on Jehoiachin as the next king after Jehoiakim (Jer 22:24-30). The reign of Jehoiachin was short-lived, however, lasting only three months, because he was deported to Babylon and replaced as king by his uncle. So in effect Jehoiakim's son did not succeed him, but this prophecy is translucent.

Jeremiah 22:30. God judged Jehoiachin with childlessness. But in 1 Chronicles 3:16-17 the genealogy of David is given, and one of his ancestors was Jehoiachin, who is reported to have had seven sons. Apparently the pronouncement of childlessness was a stereotypical way to express judgment. Another explanation may be that Jehoiachin was childless in the sense that his sons were all made eunuchs during the captivity.[19] In either case the prophecy is translucent.

Ezekiel 29:14. The Lord said that he would make Egypt so weak that it would never again rule over the nations. But as one of the Hellenistic kingdoms after Alexander the Great, Egypt gained control of more territory than ever before. Especially during the second century, the Ptolemies held dominion over many areas of the eastern Mediterranean, including

Cyrenaica, Cyprus, most of the Aegean Islands, parts of Asia Minor, and Palestine. Furthermore, "had Octavian not been successful against Antony and Cleopatra, Ptolemaic Egypt may have prevailed in the eastern Mediterranean."[20] So the language of judgment on Egypt is not transparent.

Joel 2:28-32. This oracle of blessing expresses God's mercy: "I will pour out my Spirit on all people. . . . I will show wonders in the heavens and on the earth, blood and fire and billows of smoke. The sun will be turned to darkness and the moon to blood." The unexpected fulfillment comes in Acts 2 on the Day of Pentecost. Peter says explicitly, "This is what was spoken by the prophet Joel" (Acts 2:16), and then he quotes Joel's words of cosmic significance (see pp. 167-68).[21]

Amos 9:1-4. This is one of many prophecies of judgment on the northern ten tribes. In addition to Amos, the prophets Isaiah, Hosea and Micah include descriptions of God's merciless wrath on Israel. The prophets made clear that Assyria would lay waste the northern kingdom, and whoever was not killed would be taken into captivity. The historian reports the judgment as follows: "So the LORD was very angry with Israel and removed them from his presence. Only the tribe of Judah was left. . . . So the people of Israel were taken from their homeland into exile in Assyria, and they are still there" (2 Kings 17:18, 23).

It surprises us to read later that when Josiah was repairing the temple, a collection was received from the people of Judah and Benjamin and from the inhabitants of Jerusalem, as well as from "the people of Manasseh, Ephraim and the entire remnant of Israel" (2 Chron 34:9). The destruction and deportation of the northern ten tribes was not as complete as we would have expected from the language used.

Haggai 2:6-9. The prophet encouraged the remnant that had returned to Jerusalem to rebuild the temple. God announced that this house would be filled with glory that would be greater than the former house of God. It would also be a place of peace. We would have expected those words to apply to the second temple. The Jews might have expected the same, while hoping that the Messiah would come into this temple in glory. But that did not happen.

Prophecies regarding the Messiah. The fulfillment of prophecy regarding God's Anointed One is often remarkably detailed *and* transparent.

- Isaiah 53 is probably the most detailed passage. But even in messianic prophecy there is translucence. "He will see his offspring and prolong his days. . . . He will divide the spoils with the strong" (Is 53:10, 12). In what sense was this fulfilled by Jesus? Would we have known in advance what parts of Isaiah 53 would be transparent and what parts would be translucent?

- Micah 5:2 mentions a ruler coming from Bethlehem. But the preceding verse refers to a ruler's being struck on the cheek with a rod, and the following verse refers to a woman in labor and his brothers' returning to join the Israelites. Though the Jewish leaders in Jesus' day identified Bethlehem as the place where the Messiah was to be born (Mt 2:4-6), the significance of the surrounding context would have been unclear.

- Zechariah 11:12 mentions thirty pieces of silver, and Matthew 27:9-10 says that the silver coins by which Jesus was betrayed were the fulfillment. But could anyone have anticipated such a fulfillment based on what Zechariah says?

- Zechariah 13:7 says, "Strike the shepherd, and the sheep will be scattered." According to Matthew 26:31, Jesus quoted this verse on the night of Peter's betrayal. But we would hardly have expected the prophecy to be fulfilled in that way.

- Malachi 4:5 states that Elijah will come before the day of the Lord. In the Gospels it is evident that the Jews were expecting Elijah to come back. In one instance Jesus says, "And if you are willing to accept it, he [John the Baptist] is the Elijah who was to come" (Mt 11:14). On another occasion Jesus says that Elijah has come (Mk 9:13). So we are left wondering whether Malachi's prophecy was completely fulfilled in John the Baptist.[22]

- In John 1:51, after calling Philip and Nathanael, Jesus announces, "You shall see heaven open, and the angels of God ascending and descending on the Son of Man." This image of angels ascending and descending between heaven and earth is an allusion to Jacob's ladder. But when did Philip and Nathanael or anyone else see that fulfilled as stated? Jesus may be using the image to convey the point that he would be in constant contact with heaven. What he would do and say could be explained only as coming from above, as if angels were continually bringing him instructions from his Father.

These examples of prophecies that are more translucent than transparent constitute a very incomplete list. There are many; in fact they are in the majority.[23] The point simply is that knowing in advance how prophecy would be fulfilled was generally impossible.

CONCLUSION

Were the original hearers of biblical prophecy able to anticipate its specific fulfillments? Probably not. Can we anticipate the specific fulfillments of biblical prophecy? Probably not. The bottom line is, if we grasp the intent of prophecy as primarily prosecution and persuasion, we will not expect it to reveal details of the future. The nature of the language of prophecy means it may be fulfilled with pinpoint accuracy or it may be fulfilled with similarity. It may be fulfilled immediately, or it may be fulfilled hundreds of years later. It is certain: what God has said will happen *will happen.* The intent of what God has said is clear: judgment will come. Prophecy is always accurate in what it intends to reveal. But exactly when and how things will happen is generally unclear. Biblical prophecies were not understood until after fulfillment. This was not because the hearers were inept. It was because prophecy is not primarily prediction.

Is prediction part of prophecy? Yes. After the fact, the fulfillment of predictions may be transparent. Before the fact, the fulfillment of predictions is generally translucent. But prediction is only one species of prophecy, and the prophets were prosecutors first and foremost.

7

HOW WILL PROPHECIES BE FULFILLED?

The twentieth century, particularly in America, saw a conflagration of prophetic speculation more than in any other century.[1] Fueled by premillennial dispensationalism, World Wars I and II, the return of Jews to Palestine, and popular Christian books and films, Christians were increasingly inflamed with the notion of living in the last days. The speculation continued as the millennium turned. To suggest that all of the last two thousand years have been the last days simply does not satisfy. *These* are the last days, and *these* current events are precisely what the Bible predicted will happen just before the Lord's return—or so it is claimed.[2] Even the return of Jesus is announced by some as occurring within a certain time period. Some said it would come within a generation of 1948 and the creation of the Jewish state, others in a certain year, and others in connection with Y2K. Perhaps these are extreme examples. Unfortunately they are well-publicized examples.

The truth is, the landscape of history is littered with burned-out Christian predictions, burning bushes that were claimed to be God-revealed details about the unfolding future. Most of them burn no longer. The piles of ashes raise serious questions. What do passersby think as they scan the landscape where trees of prophetic interpretation once stood tall? Books, articles and sermons claimed to identify the details of the future in the events of the present—who the Antichrist is, who the foe from the north is that will attack Israel, what nations are the ten toes of Daniel's statue. But the events that led to those identifications are no longer current. The climax of biblical prophecy did not come in the twentieth century.

Times have changed, yet the prognostications continue with whatever events are current. There is a good side to all of this: Christians need to live their lives as if they are living in the last days, which they are, and they have been, and they will continue to until the Lord returns. However, if the last days last through another millennium, we should not be surprised, since they have already lasted almost two thousand years beyond what anyone expected.

But there is a bad side to the sensationalism of some books on prophecy. The rush to claim fulfillment of prophecy in certain current events leaves dark questions hovering over the skeletons of failed forecasts. Outsiders may wonder whether Christians can be trusted to speak the truth, the whole truth and nothing but the truth. Outsiders may also wonder whether biblical prophecy itself is faulty. At the very least, outsiders may wonder whether biblical prophecy equivocates, given our inability to agree on how to understand it and our competing schools of eschatology. When outsiders fail to notice—or graciously overlook—these unintended deceptions, we are relieved. So is God.

The confusion about prophecy in the Christian community points to a crisis of interpretation.[3] Is something askew? Many well-intentioned Christians study the same Bible but come up with very different answers. And each of those different answers is often proclaimed to be true, unequivocally. Most cling to their eschatological edifice as if they would slide down a slippery slope into heresy if they let go.[4] But of all the views, only one can be correct, if any single one has a corner on the truth.

Regrettably, few seem to agonize over this crisis of interpretation. Fewer still attempt to do anything about it. For many the excitement of connecting events of the moment to biblical prophecy mutes the memory of failed predictions in previous sermons and books. But the church must be concerned. What are we teaching our faithful? Have we forgotten the caution of James 3:1 that teachers will be judged with greater strictness? And what are we teaching the unfaithful? Are we faithfully pointing the faithful and unfaithful to the Christ of prophecy?

FUTURESPEAK

Based on the foregoing chapters, it is time to sketch a framework for how prophecy should be interpreted. Perhaps we need a twenty-first-century approach to prophecy. Not because we are looking for a novel theory that ignores the original purpose of the biblical text; just the opposite. The foundation of our approach needs to be a careful reading of the Bible and its intended meaning.

I have attempted to assemble the building blocks throughout the chapters in this book. I can now summarize that evidence and begin erecting a structure for handling prophecy accurately. The point of referring to this as a twenty-first-century perspective on prophecy is to distinguish it from misdirected approaches of the past and to suggest that we *can* develop an approach that is more biblical. Hopefully, by moving beyond previous approaches—which in part were at odds with one another—we will actually find more on which to agree and less on which to disagree.

Prophecy and apocalyptic are distinctive literary forms. The human authors crafted the messages from God in genres that do not resemble anything else in Scripture. But they did not invent something completely new, for they adopted common literary forms from their own cultures and adapted them to the special needs of divine revelation. For example, the book of Revelation is sufficiently like Jewish apocalypses to be considered apocalyptic. But at the same time it is sufficiently different from Jewish apocalypses to be considered a special example of apocalyptic. For correct interpretation, no matter what genre in the Bible is being studied, we need to recognize the specific characteristics of that literary form.

In the case of prophecy and apocalyptic, the distinctives can be summed up in seven key features of the language of futurespeak (see figure 7.1).

1. Poetry

> *Instead of perfume there will be a stench;*
> *and instead of a sash, a rope;*
> *and instead of well-set hair, baldness;*
> *and instead of a rich robe, a binding of sackcloth;*
> *instead of beauty, shame. . . .*
> *And her gates shall lament and mourn;*
> *ravaged, she shall sit upon the ground.* (Is 3:24, 26 NRSV)

Arguably the most important feature of prophetic language is its poetry. Prophets did not communicate in the cut-and-dried terminology of law codes, land deeds and laundry lists or the flat language of rational, cerebral discourse. Instead they were communicating God's message in the

The language of futurespeak

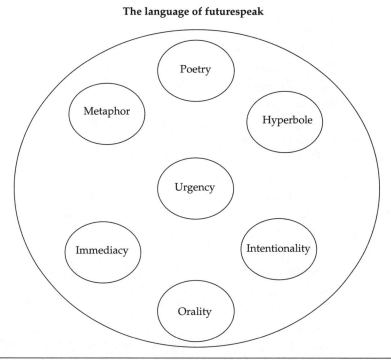

Figure 7.1. **Distinctives of prophecy and apocalyptic**

most convincing, emotive and memorable ways possible.[5] The prophets
were poets, not statisticians. They did not choose words with strict one-
to-one relationships between symbol and referent; they opted for colorful language. Using the parallelism of Hebrew poetry to great advantage, the prophets tended to be expansive, saying the same thing more
than once, but with different images and different emphases (e.g., Zeph
2:13-15). Simile, metaphor, allusion, hyperbole blend together in masterpieces of creative expression. "Since poetry is our best human model
of intricately rich communication, not only solemn, weighty, and forceful but also densely woven with intricate internal connections, meanings, and implications, it makes sense that divine speech should be
represented as poetry."[6] Because prophecy is poetic, it is inherently ambiguous and in some ways less precise. But because of the ambiguity it
is richer in meaning. Unfortunately "a lot of evangelicals are suspicious
of poetry."[7]

2. Metaphor

On this mountain the LORD of hosts will make for all peoples
a feast of rich food, a feast of well-aged wines,
of rich food filled with marrow, of well-aged wines strained clear.
And he will destroy on this mountain
the shroud that is cast over all peoples,
the sheet that is spread over all nations;
he will swallow up death forever.
Then the Lord GOD will wipe away the tears from all faces,
and the disgrace of his people he will take away from all the earth,
for the LORD has spoken. (Is 25:6-8 NRSV)

Common to communication from informal conversation to the highest level of writing is figurative language. Especially in the poetry of the prophets, metaphorical language is the lifeblood.[8] Words, phrases, sentences and even whole paragraphs may be metaphoric. The value of metaphor for the prophets is multifaceted. The most important function was to describe something that had never been experienced. Whether peering into heaven or into the future, the prophets used images known in their day to depict worlds that they and their hearers could know only in the broadest of terms. Thus images and metaphors are the norm rather than the exception. The language is visual, engaging, aesthetic and mysterious.

And with our distance from the language and culture of the ancient world, we are not good judges of what is literal and what is figurative. Perhaps the original hearers were not either. Perhaps even the author himself did not anticipate that some of his imagery might in God's providence be literally fulfilled. But that was the exception rather than the rule. As always, we see through a glass darkly. "Paradoxically, poetry (like music) can often be appreciated best when it is least perfectly understood."[9]

3. Hyperbole

The light of Israel will become a fire,
and his Holy One a flame;
and it will burn and devour
his thorns and briers in one day.
The glory of his forest and his fruitful land
the LORD will destroy, both soul and body,
and it will be as when an invalid wastes away.

> *The remnant of the trees of his forest will be so few*
>   *that a child can write them down.* (Is 10:17-19 NRSV)

When the prophets wanted to reveal the depths of God's wrath against sin or the depths of his love for those who repent, they often used hyperbole. In perfect wrath God will destroy everyone off the face of the earth. In perfect love he will cause all the deserts of the earth to blossom with roses.[10] Yet there are conditions inherent in God's judgment and blessing that were often not expressed. If the people repent, God will withhold judgment. If the people are disobedient, God will withhold blessing (Jer 18:7-10). The language of extremity is often in stylized forms that recur frequently to announce God's judgment and blessing. The city will become a wasteland. Or the reverse, the nations will stream to Jerusalem. In a variety of ways, the prophets used the rhetoric of extremity in order to make the greatest possible impact on their audience. "Such poetry is a kind of terrific verbal buttonholing of the listener."[11]

4. Orality

> *Now therefore hear this, you lovers of pleasures,*
>   *who sit securely,*
> *who say in your heart,*
>   *"I am, and there is no one besides me;*
> *I shall not sit as a widow*
>   *or know the loss of children"—*
> *both these things shall come upon you*
>   *in a moment, in one day:*
> *the loss of children and widowhood*
>   *shall come upon you in full measure,*
> *in spite of your many sorceries*
>   *and the great power of your enchantments.* (Is 47:8-9 NRSV)

Prophecy generally began as sermon rather than essay.[12] And the prophets preached powerful sermons, warning the people of impending judgment, pointing fingers of accusation at their sinfulness, urging repentance and promising God's faithfulness. In some cases prophets had preached for many years before they began to write (e.g., Jer 36:2).[13] When they or someone else compiled their prophecies, marks of orality remained: emotional appeal, rhetorical emphasis, repetition and so on. Even when prophetic sermons were put into writing, the written versions were still composed to be heard rather than read. For in the ancient world all reading was done out loud, and even more to the point, most people only heard the writings of the prophets read aloud or quoted from memory. So today hearing the prophets read by skilled readers brings their messages to life in remarkable ways.

5. Urgency

Your whole head is injured,
*   your whole heart afflicted.*
From the sole of your foot to the top of your head
*   there is no soundness—*
only wounds and welts
*   and open sores,*
not cleansed or bandaged
*   or soothed with oil.* (Is 1:5-6)

In other words, dial 911! The message of the prophets was charged with energy. In the context of establishing the covenant with his people, God promised wonderful rewards and warned of terrible consequences, all in the same breath. Warning signs in particular were written all over the front page of the covenant. Why? Because the sinfulness of the chosen people would test the terms of the covenant. To guard against that eventuality, God announced severe measures, both blessings for obedience and curses for disobedience. So when the prophets were called on to be covenant en-forcers, the pattern was already in place. And with the covenant tenuous at best because of the disobedience of the people, the prophets spoke with every bit of urgency possible. Words were chosen for shock value. This was code blue: God's chosen people were experiencing cardiac arrest, and life-saving measures were needed immediately.

6. Immediacy

On that day the LORD will whistle for the fly that is at the sources of the streams of Egypt, and for the bee that is in the land of Assyria. And they will all come and settle in the steep ravines, and in the clefts of the rocks, and on all the thornbushes, and on all the pastures.

On that day the Lord will shave with a razor hired beyond the River—with the king of Assyria—the head and the hair of the feet, and it will take off the beard as well. (Is 7:18-20 NRSV)

The occasion and focus of most prophecy were the immediate circumstances of the Israelites and the nations surrounding them. However, the language describing the crises the Israelites faced and the actions God would take for or against them is often so extreme that some interpreters conclude it must be eschatological. But the prophets could use end-of-the-world language for impending judgment.[14] For example, does the language of Isaiah 14 and Ezekiel 28 apply to the kings of Babylon and Tyre or to the fallen angel? With recognition of the freedom of prophetic language to be boldly metaphoric, a consensus is forming that the authors' intent had nothing to do with the fallen angel. So it is with most prophecy. There is limited evidence that the Old Testament prophets generally saw the distant future and predicted it. There is even less evidence that the immediate hearers had access to such a telescope.

7. Intentionality

When you stretch out your hands,
  I will hide my eyes from you;
even though you make many prayers,
  I will not listen;
  your hands are full of blood.
Wash yourselves; make yourselves clean;
  remove the evil of your doings
  from before my eyes;
cease to do evil,
  learn to do good;
seek justice,
  rescue the oppressed,
defend the orphan,
  plead for the widow. (Is 1:15-17 NRSV)

The function of language often transcends the surface meaning of the words. The intent of prophecy was to denounce godlessness among God's chosen people, to announce coming judgment and promised blessing, and to summon people to repentance. When we fail to understand the intentionality of prophecy, we easily misread it. "For prophecy is a sham unless it is experienced as a word of God swooping down on man and converting him into a prophet."[15]

This characterization of prophecy is foundational to correct interpretation of every prophetic statement in the Bible. It is essential to recognize that the meanings of prophecies are generally deeper than a simple surface reading of the text would suggest. That means that the critical issue is determining where the truth of the prophetic proclamation lies. Is the surface level of a given statement the intended truth, or are the words pointing to a truth that lies beyond the surface level?

A MANUAL FOR METAPHORS

Given the nature of prophecy, we should probably deduce that it offers panorama, not close-up details, and focus therefore on the big picture of prophecy's message. That is a significant shift away from attempting to determine the exact meaning of every word or verse. Many interpreters, however, will not be satisfied with only the panorama approach. Each piece of the puzzle will invite examination for its relevance to the larger scene.

Metaphors and validity of interpretation. Since metaphor is the most common feature of prophetic language, determining when a proclamation is metaphoric is critical, especially if we are seeking to decipher the significance of each dab of paint on the canvas. If a statement is thought to be a metaphor, then interpretation needs to seek out the underlying meaning of the metaphor. However, if the statement was not intended to be metaphoric, then the conclusion about the underlying meaning will be false. On the other hand, if a statement is thought *not* to be a metaphor, then interpretation will explore the normal meanings of the words. However, if the statement was metaphoric, then the conclusion about specific details of the statement will be false. Clearly, correct identification of metaphors will determine the validity of interpretation.

The more common error of the two, and the more dangerous, is missing a metaphor. If a teacher sends a book home with a child and says to devour it, and the child misses the metaphor and attempts to eat the book, the results will be problematic!

Assuming that no student of the Bible can tolerate false conclusions in his or her interpretations of Scripture, close study of Scripture requires a procedure to deal with metaphors. When determining what is metaphoric in prophecy, every interpreter must make a conscious effort to set aside prejudgments about eschatology. We must resist the inclination to be controlled by a previously adopted theology of prophecy. We must set aside our modern notions of what is or is not likely to be metaphoric. What is literal and what is not must not be determined simply by what could be literal or what could not be according to modern ways of thinking. We must construct a valid method for interpretation based on the original context and apply that method consistently before the implications for eschatology are considered—lest we get in the way of what we are trying to accomplish.

The hermeneutics of metaphor. Interpretation begins with identifying when a metaphor was used by an author. Chapter three attempted to provide a basic theory of language related to metaphor. But ultimately what is and what is not metaphoric depends on authorial intent.[16] Sometimes the intent may be obvious, based on context. When a speaker and hearer have a common language and culture, the chance of recognizing metaphors is much greater. But when an author's intent is not obvious, important questions must be raised.

Two examples will help illustrate this: "It turned out to be a blind alley," and "Wild animals shall live with hyenas in Babylon, and ostriches shall inhabit her" (Jer 50:39 NRSV). Are these metaphors? In the first example, the reference could be to walking or driving through a city and taking a wrong turn into an alley, presumably because one is lost. But the actual intent of the statement may have nothing to do with a city, or walking, or even an alley. In that case the meaning does not reside in dictionary definitions of the words but in metaphor. To nonnative English speakers who have not yet discovered the potential for metaphor in the statement, the words will be misleading. They will assume the meaning is on the surface, while the true meaning relates only distantly to the dictionary definitions of the words. Thus shared culture is determinant for correct identification of metaphors.

If "it turned out to be a blind alley" is recognized as a potential metaphor, numerous possibilities surface for what the statement may mean. The underlying thought may have to do with an unexpected turn of events; we thought we were headed in the right direction, but it turned out to be incorrect. We may have been investigating something, or exploring an idea, or shopping for something. The intended meaning of the statement may apply to almost limitless situations, though the basic idea will generally be present. In this case, context is determinant of the meaning of metaphors. There is usually some link in thought between the surface meaning and the metaphorical meaning, such as attempting something that did not materialize as expected, but the meaning is evident only if we understand the context.

In the second example, Jeremiah's statement about hyenas and ostriches could appear to be describing a menagerie of animals. Is it describing a city of zoos? Are some of the animals wild and others domesticated? More likely, is the statement saying that the city will be overrun with wild animals, perhaps in the absence of people? These notions are based on the assumption that the statement is not metaphoric. Given the limited degree of culture we share with the ancient world, we may not immediately recognize the potential for metaphor in a biblical statement, but we always need to be open to that possibility.

In the case of Jeremiah 50, if we are alert to the possibility that the hyenas and ostriches may be metaphoric, we may wonder whether the intent has anything to do with animals at all. The animals may denote something linked to the surface meaning, but apart from dictionary definitions. We might hypothesize that the wild animals are foreign invaders taking over the city. Or Jeremiah may be envisioning a period of upheaval in the city, with so much confusion that it would be like a madhouse of animals. Or it may be a way of stating that the city will be completely destroyed, with every person annihilated and only animals remaining. If we find that this phrase is used in language of judgment on other cities, we may conclude that it is stock language. Of course we must also ask whether the statement is designating the actual city of Babylon or whether that city represents another city.

The most important issue, once we allow for the potential of a metaphor, is the context of the statement. In the case of Jeremiah 50, the prophet speaks at length about God's judgment on Babylon. The text is full of poetic language: "Israel is a scattered flock that lions have chased away" (Jer 50:17). "I set a trap for you, O Babylon, and you were caught before you knew it. . . . The LORD has opened his arsenal and brought out the weapons of his wrath" (Jer 50:24-25). Note in particular:

> *Take up your positions around Babylon,*
> *all you who draw the bow.*
> *Shoot at her! Spare no arrows,*
> *for she has sinned against the LORD.*
> *Shout against her on every side!*
> *She surrenders, her towers fall,*
> *her walls are torn down.* (Jer 50:14-15)

From our present vantage point we see that the language was meta-phoric, because we know that Babylon was taken by the advancing Per-sian army without a siege. But based on a surface reading before the event, we probably would have expected something very different. Even with hindsight it may not be certain which statements in Jeremiah's prophecy were metaphoric and which not: "All who pass Babylon will be horrified and scoff because of all her wounds" (Jer 50:13).

Regarding the immediate context of the statement about hyenas and os-triches, the point is that Babylon will be destroyed. That is described in terms of complete destruction. "The sea will rise over Babylon; its roaring waves will cover her" (Jer 51:42). Babylon will never be inhabited again (Jer 50:39). These extreme statements seem to be stylized ways to empha-size the severity of destruction. To say that wild animals will inhabit it un-derscores God's radical judgment on Babylon.

Thus the reference to hyenas, ostriches and wild animals is apparently metaphoric, not predicting that these specific animals would inhabit Baby-lon. Similar to running into a blind alley, the metaphor goes beyond nor-mal dictionary definitions of words.

DIFFICULT METAPHORS

Some metaphoric language is particularly challenging and requires special consideration. In this case, experimenting with three approaches may help determine the significance of puzzling metaphors. Fundamentally, a meta-phor may be said "to stand proxy for something beyond itself."[17] In the case of the difficult metaphor "For you who revere my name the sun of right-eousness shall rise" (Mal 4:2 NRSV), the question is, for what is it proxy?

According to a substitution approach to metaphor, readers should de-termine what might be substituted in the sentence in place of "the sun of righteousness." The goal is to remove the unnecessary metaphor and make the meaning clear by an "it is" equation.

According to a comparison approach to metaphor, readers should de-termine what the sentence would say if it were a simile with *like* or *as* present.[18] Readers need to determine what associations are the point of the comparison and what associations are irrelevant.

However, the substitution and comparison views of metaphor are inad-equate for many metaphors. Most imply "it is as if" rather than a simple "it is."

If Malachi had said, "When the Lord comes you will recognize the sun of righteousness," the metaphor would be easier to decipher. Substitution would be evident in the immediate context, with "the sun of righteousness" referring to the Lord. Or using the comparison approach, *like* or *as* could be supplied, so that the statement would be "The Lord will come *like* the sun of righteousness."

But the complete sentence in Malachi is "For those who revere my name the sun of righteousness shall rise with healing in its wings." The text does not make it obvious who "the sun of righteousness" is, nor is it clear where to supply *like* or *as*. In this case neither simple substitution nor comparison is adequate to resolve the conundrum. Nor does the context of the paragraph—focusing on judgment of evildoers, who will be burned in an oven and will become ashes underfoot—provide obvious clues.

A third approach to metaphor, an interaction approach, may provide the solution. The comparison is still present, but the reader must now avoid looking for simple substitution and allow the parts of the sentence to interact with each other, the surrounding context and the author's culture.[19] "The terms cooperate and direct divergent meanings toward a new significance."[20]

With this approach, Malachi's statement makes good sense. In contrast to the terrible day of judgment that is coming on the unrighteous, a glorious day is coming for those who are obedient. The words *healing, wings, sunshine* and *righteousness* all work together to portray this wonderful event. Admittedly we do not know exactly what it will be, for the individual words *healing, wings, sunshine* and *righteousness* do not have specific referents. The referent for the whole sentence is general rather than specific. But it is very good news, and that may be the primary intent of the statement. The righteous can rest assured that the day of the Lord will bring extraordinary blessings. The next sentence in Malachi continues to underscore the excitement as well as the metaphoric images: "And you will go out and leap like calves released from the stall" (Mal 4:2).

Another example will help illustrate this point: "The sun shall be turned to darkness, and the moon to blood" (Joel 2:31). While it seems clear that this is metaphoric, it is not as clear what the metaphor is (see pp. 152, 176-77).[21] In the second statement, is *blood* a metaphor for red? That is, will the moon become red? Or is *moon* a metaphor for something above—will something red appear in the sky? Or is *blood* a metaphor for death—will there be mortal combat in the sky? Or is the phrase part of a description of cataclysmic events, having nothing to do with blood or even the color red, and nothing to do with the moon or even something in the sky?[22]

In English when we talk about throwing a monkey wrench into the works, are we saying anything about monkeys or wrenches? Because we have learned a referent for that phrase, which is unrelated to the words and their normal referents, we may not even think about a monkey wrench when we hear it mentioned. The metaphor expresses the thought "it is as if." Hence our interpretation of Joel 2:31 may conclude that the meaning of the metaphor is unrelated to the normal meanings of the individual parts of the metaphor. "The moon shall be turned to blood" designates a time of great upheaval, not necessarily any changes in the sky.

The juxtaposition of words with normal referents in a context where those referents no longer apply creates a tension that engages the reader in cognitive and emotive dissonance.[23] To express that idea another way, metaphoric language always has an air of mystery.[24] The ambiguity enriches the meaning. It is a message for the heart more than the head. In many cases this is where the reader should rest content. Attempts to resolve the tension may destroy the delicate balance and the emotive power of the metaphor.[25] The author may have intended for the audience to listen just as we watch a movie, enjoying the unfolding drama and not trying to discover meaning in every detail.[26]

MAPPING THE FUTURE

The earlier portions of this book sought to lay a groundwork for understanding the language of prophecy and apocalyptic. The final part will seek to point the way toward understanding what God wants us to know about the future. The Bible's prophecies that are yet to be fulfilled appear most clearly in the New Testament, and most frequently the genre of future expectation is apocalyptic. There was good reason. As Christians succumbed to increasing despair with their circumstances, they longed for hope. In response, New Testament authors found apocalyptic to be the ideal lens for looking at the immediate through the glass of the distant. Nearsightedness produces hopelessness, while farsightedness offers hope. Apocalypticism was a way of moving into another world and looking back on this world. When we stand aloof from the daily drudgery and see adversities from a heavenly perspective, hope is reborn.

What you see will *not* be what you get.

Apocalyptic gave Christians an answer to the dilemma of disenfranchisement. Though they were aliens in a foreign land, in this world yet not of this world, believing in the one true God yet accused of atheism, law-abiding citizens yet arraigned as criminals, their tendency toward gloom when they were at the mercy of pagan oppressors was mitigated by visions of a new day dawning. The sword of divine judgment will eventually cut off the hands of the persecutors. Every evil person and every evil aspect of this world will be destroyed—completely. At the same time the paths of divine blessing will be paved with gold for every overcomer. All the saints will soon be eating manna from heaven and fruit from the tree of life forever. With that hope on the horizon, Christians can manage the crises of the present. They can have confidence in something better, which will come sooner rather than later. We long expectantly for the ultimate new order and society, the kingdom of God in all its fullness.

In the Christian community, apocalypticism became a primary form of thought and expression. It shaped all future expectation. Appearing throughout the New Testament, it is especially evident in the Synoptic Gospels, 1 and 2 Thessalonians, 2 Peter, Jude and Revelation. The Lord will be revealed from heaven in blazing fire, with a crown of gold on his head and a sharp sickle in his hand; he will tread the winepress of the fury of the wrath of God Almighty (2 Thess 1:7; Rev 14:14; 19:15). But just how this totally new order and society will play out is hard to imagine given current experiences. In this case the freedom of apocalyptic to describe the future in imaginative language works perfectly.

Twelve themes of New Testament apocalyptic	
Striking presentation of the transcendent Lord	Horrors of animals
Unprecedented turmoil	Preservation of the remnant
Nearness of the end	New order and society
Terrifying judgment	Rewards for the righteous
Horrors in the heavens	Satanic adversaries
Horrors on earth	Backlash of evil

Figure 7.2. End-times imagery

In order to consider how unfulfilled prophecies will be fulfilled, I compiled and categorized the end-times imagery found in the New Testament. (For a complete list of the verses, see appendix C.) The goal of this analysis was to get behind the variety of expressions and identify the underlying themes of apocalyptic imagery. The result is twelve thematic features around which the imagery clusters (see figure 7.2). As it turns out, these themes are not limited to apocalyptic contexts. Even in the absence of specific apocalyptic form, New Testament writers express similar hope. An examination of each of the twelve clusters of end-times imagery will point to essential insights for understanding how prophecy will be fulfilled. Conclusions from previous chapters about the language of prophecy and apocalyptic will be applied to these prophecies not yet fulfilled.

THEME 1: STRIKING PRESENTATION OF THE TRANSCENDENT LORD

As noted in chapter four, Scripture always struggles to describe the Lord of glory in human terms. "I saw the Lord seated on a throne, high and exalted, and the train of his robe filled the temple" (Is 6:1). "Among the lampstands was someone 'like a son of man,' dressed in a robe reaching down to his feet and with a golden sash around his chest" (Rev 1:13). Whether Isaiah's or John's, human encounters with the divine are out-of-this-world experiences—barely describable. Comparisons in the biblical record of ways God appears suggest that there is no single way to describe God in human terms (see pp. 77-78).

In one sense, the inadequacy of language to depict deity may frustrate us. But in another sense, that inadequacy reveals the most important truth: God is transcendent. We simply cannot describe him. And if some think they can, they have minimized the splendor of Godness.

Attempts to describe the second coming are faced with similar challenges. How can the appearance of the Transcendent One be visualized? The solution is a variety of imagery accompanying the event: angels, clouds, a loud trumpet, a loud command, the voice of the archangel, blazing fire, thousands of his holy ones, a crown of gold, a sickle, a white horse, eyes of fire—imagery often associated with divine warfare.[27]

Representative verses for the presentation of the transcendent Lord include the following (for a complete list, see p. 224):

- The Son of Man will come on the clouds of the sky with power and great glory; he will send his angels with a loud trumpet call (Mt 24:30-31).
- The Lord will come down from heaven with a loud command, with the voice of the archangel, with the trumpet call of God (1 Thess 4:16).
- The Lord will be revealed from heaven in blazing fire (2 Thess 1:7).
- The Lord is coming with thousands upon thousands of his holy ones (Jude 14).
- There before me was a white cloud, and seated on the cloud was one "like a son of man" with a crown of gold on his head and a sharp sickle in his hand (Rev 14:14).
- There before me was a white horse, whose rider is called Faithful and True; with justice he judges and makes war; his eyes are like blazing fire (Rev 19:11).

The various images for the return of Jesus raise an important question. Are we to take a synoptic approach and seek to imagine an event encompassing all of the imagery? Does a complete picture of the parousia include all of the above accompanying details? Or is the function of these images to communicate that it will be startling, unique, wonderful—and beyond description? Should we judge the fulfillment of these prophecies by whether we see exactly what is described?

Trying to integrate the different images of the second coming into a complete picture is not easy. Will the loud sound be a command, the voice of the archangel or a trumpet—or all three? Will Jesus appear in blazing fire or on a white horse—or both? At his ascension, the disciples were told that Jesus would return the same way they had seen him go into heaven. The only thing that is reported in that context is that a cloud hid him from their sight as he ascended. Are the images associated with the second coming definite details that we will see, or is this apocalyptic language expressing a future event that is indescribable? The view that there are two aspects to the second coming, one to rapture the saints and another to return and set up the kingdom, does not solve the issue of the diversity of imagery.

It is probably vain to attempt a preconstruction of the precise details that will accompany the second coming. The point of the imagery is that the Lord's return will be the most dramatic divine visitation of earth ever to occur. Something that has never happened to this extent—a meeting of heaven and earth—is beyond human ability to conceptualize. To describe it in earthbound language is impossible. We can only assume that the images and metaphors used for the parousia are the best ways to express this futuristic event in current language.

THEME 2: UNPRECEDENTED TURMOIL

Apocalyptic announces a gloomy forecast for the whole world. Evil is escalating and it is affecting everything, from the sociopolitical realm to personal relationships. Any semblance of order in society is rapidly unraveling, and it will lead to a reign of fear and confusion. If we look back on the past, the coming evil will be equal to or worse than anything on record. If we look ahead to the future, the coming evil will exceed anything imaginable. The turmoil is pictured in grim ways. People will be hateful toward each other. They will be separated from one another. Family and friends will betray one another. They will be imprisoned. They will be executed. And anyone that survives all of that will resort to suicide. It would be better never to have been born.

Representative verses for unprecedented turmoil include the following (a more complete list is found on p. 225):

- "You will hear of wars and rumors of wars. . . . Nation will rise against nation, and kingdom against kingdom" (Mt 24:6-7).
- It will be dreadful for pregnant women and nursing mothers (Mt 24:16-21).
- Two will be in one bed—one will be taken, the other left (Lk 17:33-34).
- "Nations will be in anguish and perplexity at the roaring and tossing of the sea. Men will faint from terror" (Lk 21:25-26).
- The time will come when you will say, "Blessed are the barren . . . and the breasts that never nursed." As people flee they "will say to the mountains, 'Fall on us!'" (Lk 23:29-30).[28]
- "While people are saying, 'Peace and safety,' destruction will come on them suddenly, as labor pains on a pregnant woman, and they will not escape" (1 Thess 5:3).
- The beast and the ten horns will hate the prostitute, bring her to ruin, and leave her naked; they will eat her flesh and burn her with fire (Rev 17:16).

As is typical in apocalyptic, the coming terror is expressed in the worst ways possible and in as many ways as possible. Restricted to what they had experienced, apocalypticists did not have categories to depict future events in a futuristic language. Yet they wanted to paint vivid pictures of what was going to happen. The solution was to pile on a wide array of known images. It is much like Deuteronomy 28 and the Old Testament prophets. God's future judgment on disobedience was stated over and over in every conceivable form of adversity. Interpreters must allow for this dimension of prophecy. To describe the future in the language of the present, a diversity of specifics are given about what will happen, but those details may not be intended as exact predictions about what will happen. The point is the underlying theme of unprecedented turmoil.

It is not clear whether the turmoil being described characterizes the end or is a portent of the end. Much is in end-of-the-world language, but some statements point to disasters leading up to the end. "Such things must happen, but the end is still not come. . . . See, I have told you ahead of time. . . . Even so, when you see all these things, you know that it is near, right at the door" (Mt 24:6, 25, 33). "A time is coming, and has come, when you will be scattered, each to his own home" (Jn 16:32). The mixed signals about the timing of these disasters are not unusual for apocalyptic. It is common to have many more puzzle pieces than needed for the puzzle and still not have the specific pieces that we might want. Precisely what pieces fit where may not be clear before the prophecy is fulfilled.

THEME 3: NEARNESS OF THE END

Consistent in descriptions of the future is the expectation that whatever is going to happen will happen *soon*. The end of the ages has come. Now is the time for the kingdom to be ushered in. Though it is expected at any moment, it will be unexpected when it arrives.

Representative verses for nearness of the end include the following (pp. 225-27 contain more):

- "When you see all these things, you know that it is near, right at the door" (Mt 24:33).
- "No one knows about that day or hour, not even the angels in heaven, nor the Son, but only the Father" (Mt 24:36).
- "The Son of Man will come at an hour when you do not expect him" (Mt 24:44).
- "Be alert! You do not know when that time will come" (Mk 13:33).
- "When you see Jerusalem being surrounded by armies, you will know that its desolation is near" (Lk 21:20).

- "It is not for you to know the times or dates the Father has set by his own authority" (Acts 1:7).
- "About times and dates we do not need to write to you, for you know very well that the day of the Lord will come like a thief in the night" (1 Thess 5:1-2).
- "But you, brothers, are not in darkness so that this day should surprise you like a thief" (1 Thess 5:4).
- "He who is coming will come and will not delay" (Heb 10:37; cf. Hab 2:3).
- "The Judge is standing at the door!" (Jas 5:9).
- "The end of all things is near" (1 Pet 4:7).
- "The revelation of Jesus Christ . . . to show his servants what must soon take place" (Rev 1:1).
- "There will be no more delay!" (Rev 10:6).
- "I am coming soon!" (Rev 22:7; cf. Rev 22:12, 20).

Tension naturally exists between the notions that the faithful should be ready for the end and that they cannot be ready. The end is expected at any moment, but it will come at an unexpected moment. This dualism is due in part to the ethical dimension of apocalyptic. The call to purity is strengthened if the end will occur imminently, and it is strengthened if the end may catch us off guard. Because we expect it soon, we live accordingly. Because we cannot expect it precisely, we live accordingly. It is expected to be unexpected.

Presumably the second coming could have occurred in the first century—as many Christians expected—or in any century since. Was the Lord's return imminent across the span of two thousand years? What about the events in every generation that were identified as sure signs of his coming? To those who thought they had identified the sign that his coming would happen in their day, we express our condolences for their disappointment. But we also share in their embarrassment. Current events simply cannot be claimed as *the* sign of his coming, no matter how many wars and rumors of wars there are.

When current events are interpreted as signs of the Lord's imminent return, those conclusions are correct—in a sense. Many events occurring while Christians await the Lord's return may be signs of the times. But in another sense those conclusions are incorrect. To this point, no events have been the specific signs of the immediate arrival of the end times. Only when the last days arrive will we know what events actually occurred immediately before them. While it may be inconceivable for us at the beginning of the third millennium to think that the Lord's return could be delayed for another millennium, Jesus cautioned, "No one knows about that day or hour, not even the angels in heaven, nor the Son, but only the Father" (Mt 24:36).

So does the language of nearness misrepresent the timing of the end times? If the second coming does not appear in our lifetime, or in the lifetime of our children, or of their children, will we or they feel betrayed? The point that needs to be reinforced is that nearness may have a function not related to *time when*. The impact of language about judgment and blessing is increased when they are described as near (see pp. 101-2). The day of the Lord will be terrible, and its terribleness is worse the nearer it is.

THEME 4: TERRIFYING JUDGMENT

The language of judgment prominent in the Old Testament prophets continues in New Testament apocalyptic. God's punishment of the unrighteous will be merciless and eternal. The full measure of divine fury will be characterized by fire and separation, and there will be no opportunity for repentance. From the great winepress of God's wrath a long and deep river of blood will flow.

Representative verses for terrifying judgment include the following (with more listed on p. 227):

- Christ will burn "up the chaff with unquenchable fire" (Mt 3:12).
- "The subjects of the kingdom will be thrown outside, into the darkness, where there will be weeping and gnashing of teeth" (Mt 8:11).
- "It will be more bearable for Sodom on the day of judgment than for you" (Mt 11:24; cf. Lk 10:12, 14).
- "Depart from me, you who are cursed, into the eternal fire prepared for the devil and his angels" (Mt 25:41).
- "They will be punished with everlasting destruction and shut out from the presence of the Lord" (2 Thess 1:9).
- "Their condemnation has long been hanging over them, and their destruction has not been sleeping" (2 Pet 2:3).
- "I will cast her on a bed of suffering. . . . I will strike her children dead" (Rev 2:22-23).
- "The angel swung his sickle on the earth, gathered its grapes and

threw them into the great winepress of God's wrath. They were trampled in the winepress outside the city, and blood flowed out of the
press, rising as high as the horses' bridles for a distance of 1,600 sta-
dia" (Rev 14:19-20).

- "Come, gather together to eat the flesh of all people" (Rev 19:17-18).
- "If anyone's name was not found written in the book of life, he was
  thrown into the lake of fire, . . . the fiery lake of burning sulfur" (Rev
  20:15; 21:8).

Suffering and separation are constant features of judgment, but they are
expressed in different ways: thrown out into the darkness, weeping and
gnashing of teeth, eternal fire intended for the devil and his angels, down
to the depths, everlasting destruction, shut out from the presence of the
Lord, strike her children dead, spit you out of my mouth, drink the wine
of God's fury, eat the flesh of all people, a lake of fire, a lake of burning sulfur. From the variety of imagery, it is evident that a single way to describe
God's judgment in human language is inadequate. Each of the images
points to judgment in one way or another, describing it in bodily form,
though in many cases the judgment will be on spirits without bodies. The
graphic language describing God's judgment points to final separation
and severe suffering, but the exact form it will take is unclear.

THEME 5: HORRORS IN THE HEAVENS

The effect of the day of the Lord will be felt throughout the universe. Scrip-
tural depictions are stark. The sun and moon will turn to darkness and
blood. Stars will fall to the earth. The heavens—no longer "everlasting"—
will disappear. Fire will rain down on the earth. Everything that seems secure in the celestial world will be turned upside down.

Representative verses for horrors in the heavens include the following
(see p. 228 for more):

- "The sun will be darkened, and the moon will not give its light; the
  stars will fall from the sky, and the heavenly bodies will be shaken"
  (Mt 24:29; cf. Is 13:10; 34:4; Ezek 32:7; Joel 2:10, 31; 3:15).
- "Heaven and earth will pass away" (Mt 24:35).
- "The heavens will disappear with a roar; the elements will be de-
  stroyed by fire" (2 Pet 3:10).
- "The sun turned black like sackcloth made of goat hair, the whole
  moon turned blood red, and the stars in the sky fell to earth. . . . The

sky receded like a scroll" (Rev 6:12-14).

- "Hail and fire mixed with blood, and it was hurled down upon the earth" (Rev 8:7).
- "A great star, blazing like a torch, fell from the sky on a third of the rivers and on the springs of water—the name of the star is Wormwood" (Rev 8:10).
- "A third of the sun was struck, a third of the moon, and a third of the stars, so that a third of them turned dark. A third of the day was without light, and also a third of the night" (Rev 8:12).
- "The sun and sky were darkened by the smoke from the Abyss" (Rev 9:2).
- "There came flashes of lightning, rumblings, peals of thunder, an earthquake and a great hailstorm" (Rev 11:19).

If these images of changes in the sky are taken at face value, questions arise. Will only a third of the sun be darkened, or the whole sun? Will the moon be darkened, or will it turn to blood? Will the heavens above be destroyed by fire? It is more likely that these celestial horrors are metaphoric (see pp. 167-68). In the last days the impact of God's judgment will be felt everywhere. Everything will be topsy-turvy, and one way to suggest that is to describe the heavens as completely disoriented (cf. Acts 2:19-20).

THEME 6: HORRORS ON EARTH

The day of the Lord is described as having a drastic impact on everything on earth as well: earthquakes, fires, famines, plagues, violent seas, water that evaporates, becomes poisonous or turns to blood. A blazing star will fall from the sky and destroy much of the earth. Many people will die.

Representative verses for horrors on the earth include the following (pp. 228-29 list more):

- "There will be great earthquakes, famines and pestilences in various places and fearful events" (Lk 21:11).
- "Nations will be in anguish . . . at the roaring and tossing of the sea" (Lk 21:25).
- "The earth and everything in it will be laid bare" (2 Pet 3:10).
- Hail and fire mixed with blood was thrown on the earth, and a third of the earth and trees were burned up, and all the green grass (Rev 8:7).
- "A huge mountain, all ablaze, was thrown into the sea. A third of the sea turned into blood, a third of the living creatures in the sea died,

and a third of the ships were destroyed" (Rev 8:8-9).

- "A great star, blazing like a torch, fell from the sky on a third of the rivers and on the springs of water. . . . A third of the waters turned bitter, and many people died" (Rev 8:10-11).
- The sea "turned into blood like that of a dead man, and every living thing in the sea died" (Rev 16:3).
- The sun scorched people with fire, and they were "seared by the intense heat" (Rev 16:8).
- The great river Euphrates dried up (Rev 16:12).
- There was an earthquake more severe than any that has occurred on the earth; the great city split into three parts, and the cities of the nations collapsed (Rev 16:18-19).
- "Every island fled away and the mountains could not be found. . . . Huge hailstones of about one hundred pounds each fell upon men. . . . The plague was so terrible" (Rev 16:20-21).

The judgment on the earth is described in terms of what people fear most. The basic necessities of life will be unavailable. Because of famines and pestilences, there will be no food. There will be no water—it is variously described as drying up, becoming poisonous or turning to blood. The sun will scorch people instead of providing warmth. Earthquakes will destroy walls, leaving people without protection. Plagues will deprive people of good health. Trees and all green grass will be consumed by fire.

All of this fits well with the tendency of apocalyptic language to pile on image after image of destruction of things important to the hearers. This is the visualized language of prophecy (see pp. 90-97). Interpreters today may proclaim with boldness that the day of the Lord will be terrible beyond description. But they should beware of assuming that it will come in all the specific ways it is described.

THEME 7: HORRORS OF ANIMALS

The extremity of judgment on the earth is said to extend to animals. Locusts, horses and a red dragon—each a synthesis of grotesque features drawn from other animals—will wreak havoc on earth and even in the sky.

Here are representative verses for horrors of animals (with more listed on p. 229):

- There were locusts like horses ready for battle: they had crowns, faces like human faces, hair like women's hair, teeth like lions', breastplates of iron, tails and stings like scorpions'. The sound of their wings was like the thundering of many horses and chariots rushing into battle (Rev 9:7-10).

- The heads of the horses were like the heads of lions. Out of their mouths came fire, smoke and sulfur, and a third of humankind was killed. The power of the horses was in their mouths and in their tails; their tails were like snakes, and they could inflict injury with their heads (Rev 9:17-19).
- "An enormous red dragon [appeared] with seven heads and ten horns and seven crowns on his heads. His tail swept a third of the stars out of the sky and flung them to the earth" (Rev 12:3).

Common to apocalyptic literature are hideous creatures that are used as symbols of things in the spirit world. Since the spirit world is beyond human understanding, the apocalypticists looked for ways to imagine what it was like. In the agricultural world of the Bible, an invasion of locusts was greatly feared, so locusts matching the descriptions of Revelation 9 would have been a "holy terror." These horselike locusts apparently represent demons from the spirit world. They come up from the Abyss (Rev 9:1-2), their king is the ruler of the Abyss (Rev 9:11), and they attack people, not plant life (Rev 9:4). These descriptions of horrors of animals are another way to underscore the radical day of the Lord.

THEME 8: PRESERVATION OF THE REMNANT

Some people will be shown special mercy and will be spared the coming wrath of God's judgment. They are referred to as the elect, as God's holy people, as those who have been persecuted and as the 144,000.

Representative verses for preservation of the remnant include these (more can be found on p. 229):

- "He who stands firm to the end will be saved" (Mt 24:13).
- "They will gather his elect from the four winds, from one end of the heavens to the other" (Mt 24:31).
- "I saw under the altar the souls of those who had been slain" (Rev 6:9).
- There were 144,000 "sealed" from all the tribes of Israel; it "was a great multitude that no one could count . . . standing before the throne . . . wearing white robes and . . . holding palm branches in their hands" (Rev 7:4-9).

- "These are they who have come out of the great tribulation; they have washed their robes and made them white in the blood of the Lamb" (Rev 7:14).

Apocalyptic imagery focuses on the outpouring of God's wrath on the world. It will be real and relentless. For Christians that was welcome consolation, because it meant that the persecutors who were victimizing them would eventually become the victims—victims of the worst thing of all, the terrifying wrath of God. But there was even better news: Christians would be shielded from the judgment. How they will be spared is unclear. Their salvation is described in various ways: for their sake the days will be shortened, they will be rescued, they will be gathered to the Lord, they will be ushered into God's presence (as a result of persecution). The point is that God will protect the faithful.

THEME 9: NEW ORDER AND SOCIETY

As is true for all biblical prophecy, the language of blessing in New Testament apocalyptic is disproportionate to the language of judgment. Even so, there is no mistaking the glorious blessing awaiting the righteous. The Son will be enthroned in power and glory. Everything will be new. It will be a kingdom without end. The celebrations are described in language of feasting and drinking.

Representative verses for a new order and society include these (more are listed on pp. 229-30):

- "Then the righteous will shine like the sun in the kingdom of their Father" (Mt 13:43).
- "Come, you who are blessed by my Father; take your inheritance, the kingdom prepared for you since the creation of the world" (Mt 25:34).
- "Blessed is the man who will eat at the feast in the kingdom of God" (Lk 14:15).
- "You may eat and drink at my table in my kingdom" (Lk 22:30).
- "Then the end will come, when he hands over the kingdom to God the Father after he has destroyed all dominion, authority and power" (1 Cor 15:24).
- "You will receive a rich welcome into the eternal kingdom of our Lord and Savior Jesus Christ" (2 Pet 1:11).
- "We are looking forward to a new heaven and a new earth, the home

of righteousness" (2 Pet 3:13).

- "Then I saw a new heaven and a new earth, for the first heaven and the first earth had passed away" (Rev 21:1).

The primary designation of a future time of blessing is the "kingdom of God." Yet out of 160 occurrences of *kingdom* in the New Testament, the majority refer to the kingdom in the present sense. Only twenty-three occurrences include the idea of nearness or of a kingdom that is yet coming, while five other verses refer to the future restoration. Very few images of this future kingdom are actually given. The Son will rule it. All other kingdoms will have been destroyed. The righteous will be welcomed into it and will shine. Eating and drinking will have special significance. We know that the kingdom will be great, but its greatness is beyond our comprehension.

THEME 10: REWARDS FOR THE RIGHTEOUS

There is good news for those who have been followers, who have been righteous, who have worked hard, who have endured persecution and who are overcomers. Incredible rewards have been prepared: eternal life, sharing the Son's glory, and all the blessings and privileges of heaven.

These are some representative verses for rewards for the righteous (with more listed on pp. 230-31):

- "You who have followed me will also sit on twelve thrones, judging the twelve tribes of Israel" (Mt 19:28).
- "Come, you who are blessed by my Father; take your inheritance, the kingdom prepared for you since the creation of the world" (Mt 25:34).
- If we share in his sufferings we will also share in his glory (Rom 8:17).
- "There is in store for me the crown of righteousness, which the Lord, the righteous Judge, will award to me on that day" (2 Tim 4:8).
- "Blessed is the man who perseveres under trial, because . . . he will receive the crown of life" (Jas 1:12).
- "When the Chief Shepherd appears, you will receive the crown of glory" (1 Pet 5:4).
- "To him who overcomes, I will give the right to eat from the tree of life" (Rev 2:7).
- "To him who overcomes . . . I will give authority over the nations— 'He will rule them with an iron scepter; he will dash them to pieces

like pottery' [cf. Ps 2:9]. . . . I will also give him the morning star" (Rev 2:26-28).

- "To him who overcomes, I will give the right to sit with me on my throne" (Rev 3:21).
- "Blessed are those who are invited to the wedding supper of the Lamb!" (Rev 19:9).

Various images are used for heavenly rewards: an inheritance, crowns, the privilege to eat from the tree of life, some of the hidden manna, a white stone with a new name on it, the morning star, white clothing, a wedding feast. The rewards also include privileges: the recipients will sit with the Son on his throne; they will rule with authority over the nations; they will sit on twelve thrones judging the twelve tribes of Israel; God will make them pillars in his temple; he will write on them his name and the name of his city, the new Jerusalem (see pp. 28-31).

What these rewards will be—as well as when, where and how they will be given—is unclear. They may all be figurative expressions. The confluence of images suggests that the rewards will be wonderful beyond description.

THEME 11: SATANIC ADVERSARIES

Enemy forces seeking to undermine God's people and plans will perform counterfeit miracles, raise doubts, introduce heresy and slander heavenly things. Some of the most vindictive language in the New Testament is addressed to these forces of evil.

Representative verses for satanic adversaries include these (see pp. 231-32 for a more complete list):

- "The man of lawlessness is revealed. . . . He will oppose and will exalt himself over everything that is called God or is worshiped" (2 Thess 2:3-4).
- "The coming of the lawless one will be in accordance with the work of Satan displayed in all kinds of counterfeit miracles, signs and wonders, and in every sort of evil" (2 Thess 2:9-10).
- "Bold and arrogant, these men are not afraid to slander celestial beings. . . . They are like brute beasts, creatures of instinct, born only to be caught and destroyed. . . . These men are springs without water and mists driven by a storm" (2 Pet 2:10, 12, 17).
- "These dreamers pollute their own bodies, reject authority and slan-

der celestial beings. . . . They are clouds without rain, blown along by the wind. . . . They are . . . wandering stars, for whom blackest darkness has been reserved forever" (Jude 8, 12-13).

- "You tolerate that woman Jezebel. . . . By her teaching she misleads my servants" (Rev 2:20).
- A large red dragon appeared with seven heads and ten horns and seven crowns, and "his tail swept a third of the stars out of the sky and flung them to the earth" (Rev 12:3-4).
- "He has condemned the great prostitute who corrupted the earth by her adulteries" (Rev 19:2).
- An angel "seized the dragon, that ancient serpent, who is the devil, or Satan, and bound him for a thousand years" (Rev 20:2).

Satan's efforts to oppose God are described in various forms: false teachers, false prophets, the man of lawlessness, demons, dreamers, beasts, Jezebel, a red dragon, evil spirits that look like frogs, a prostitute (see pp. 120-27). Clear distinctions between the things these images refer to are not evident. The point is that the enemies of the faithful are God's enemies as well and that these enemies are terrible.

THEME 12: BACKLASH OF EVIL

In addition to the enemy's efforts to mislead people, the last days will be characterized by hatred, betrayal, dispersion, imprisonment, persecution, and martyrdom. As judgment comes upon evil people, they will turn against the saints and proceed to kill many.

Representative verses for backlash of evil include the following (and see p. 232):

- "Then you will be handed over to be persecuted and put to death, and you will be hated by all nations because of me" (Mt 24:9).
- "There will be . . . wrath against this people. They will fall by the sword and will be taken as prisoners to all the nations. Jerusalem will be trampled on by the Gentiles" (Lk 21:23-24).
- "The devil will put some of you in prison to test you, and you will suffer persecution for ten days" (Rev 2:10).
- "The woman was drunk with the blood of the saints, the blood of those who bore testimony to Jesus" (Rev 17:6).
- "I saw the souls of those who had been beheaded because of their testimony for Jesus" (Rev 20:4).

The day of the Lord will be a period of exhausting confusion for every-one. The unprecedented turmoil of human and natural disasters, the hor-rors in the heavens and on earth, the wine of God's fury being poured out on the unrighteous, the backlash from those under God's judgment against his followers—everyone will be faced with the worst distress and anguish ever experienced on this earth. Sinners will be brutalized under the wrath of a holy God. Saints will be brutalized under the boomerang of angry sinners. Unlike the sinners, with no basis for hope or escape, the saints are assured that God is in control and that the victory will be his. Though the faithful may be persecuted beyond measure, the vengeance being poured out against God's people will in the end be matched by an avenging of the blood of the martyrs (Rev 6:10; 18:6-7; 19:2).

WHAT IS THE FUNCTION OF PROPHECY?

This collection of excerpts from prophecies yet to be fulfilled highlights an important characteristic of prophecy and apocalyptic: it is a stained-glass window, not a crystal ball. Under divine inspiration, the sanctified imagi-nation of the biblical prophets communicated the themes of God's future judgment and blessing with vivid images. Look at the imagery and admire it, but do not attempt to see through the stained glass to what is off in the distance. The function of the prophets' language was to draw attention to basic ideas about the future, not to reveal precisely what will happen and when it will happen. Though the imagery may not adequately describe how the prophecy will be gloriously fulfilled, the pictures are painted as well as they can be in human terms. Underlying the imagery—and boldly portrayed by the imagery—are fundamental themes of the last days. This technique of sanctified imagination of the biblical prophets is similar to the method of apocalypticists in general. They freely created imagery or adapted imagery from other sources to give life to the ideas they wanted to communicate.

Many Christians may feel that if prophecy and apocalyptic are shown to be translucent rather than transparent, impressionistic rather than real-istic—a stained-glass window rather than a crystal ball—then prophecy has been stripped of precisely what they thought it was all about. So what *is* the role of prophecy? Prophecy always has been—and always will be—subject to misunderstanding until after it is fulfilled, if we simply look to it for details of the future. But the actual function of prophecy is not difficult to grasp. In chapter six, Old Testament prophecy was portrayed as prosecution, persuasion and prediction. In the New Testament, however, prosecution is much less prominent. The function of New Testament apocalyptic can be summarized as sevenfold (see figure 7.3).

Encouraging words from apocalyptic	
Divine disclosure	God understands our trials and will intervene to make things right.
Otherworldly perspective	The world as we know it is skewed; heaven's perspective is the right one.
Virtual reality	Apocalyptic transports us to another world where we can see behind the scenes of this world.
Worship	God is on the throne and will win the battle over evil once and for all.
Devotion	We must not be deceived by the things of this world; God alone is worthy of our loyalty.
Correction	If we have been yielding to temptation, the message of apocalyptic is a call to repentance.
Perseverance	We are temporarily in the grip of hostile powers; the challenge is to endure until the end.

Figure 7.3. Apocalyptic's message

1. *Divine disclosure.* The notion that humanity can have access to direct communication from God is basic to apocalypticism. It may come through angels, heavenly creatures, visions and journeys, but unmistakably it is supernatural revelation. Given the crisis the original hearers faced, divine messages expressed in unexpected ways functioned to assure them of God's awareness of their plight and his intention to intervene. For example:

- "The revelation of Jesus Christ . . . he made it known by sending his angel to his servant John" (Rev 1:1).
- Hearing the seven thunders, John was about to write, but he heard a voice from heaven say, "Seal up what the seven thunders have said and do not write it down" (Rev 10:4).
- "I took the little scroll from the angel's hand and ate it. . . . Then I was told, 'You must prophesy again about many peoples, nations, languages and kings'" (Rev 10:10-11).

2. *Otherworldly perspective.* New Testament apocalyptic seeks to change the way hearers think. The world is out of joint, at odds with anything or anyone connected to God and his heaven. There is temporal dualism (then and now), spatial dualism (here and there) and ontological dualism (us and them). In each case, heaven and earth could not be more opposite. In response, apocalyptic warns against being deceived by earthly perspectives and seeks to explain things heaven's way. *This* is the divine perspective. For example:

- "Let the reader understand" (Mt 24:15).
- "For this is the time of punishment in fulfillment of all that has been written" (Lk 21:22).
- "I will strike her children dead. Then all the churches will know that I am he who searches hearts and minds, and I will repay each of you according to your deeds" (Rev 2:23).
- "The angel said, 'Why are you astonished? I will explain to you the mystery of the woman and of the beast'" (Rev 17:7).

3. *Virtual reality.* The journey into another world and another time is described in detail so that hearers may experience secondhand what the author experienced firsthand. The intent was to give insight into the world inhabited by God and into the world of the future. Only then can misconceptions about what is presently happening on earth be corrected. For example:

- "On the Lord's Day I was in the Spirit" (Rev 1:10).
- "There before me was a door standing open in heaven. And the voice I had first heard speaking to me like a trumpet said, 'Come up here, and I will show you what must take place after this.' At once I was in the Spirit" (Rev 4:1-2).

Throughout the Apocalypse, John is in another world of heaven and the future, and variations on the formulas "I saw . . ." and "I heard . . ." appear frequently.

4. *Worship.* God's attributes are written in bold relief across the pages of futurespeak. His wrath against evil and his grace for the faithful will achieve their perfect balance in the events of the end. God's sovereignty may be embattled, but he ultimately will control the course of events. And when God makes himself known, as he will in the last days, everyone will worship him. Thus prophecy functions to summon people to worship him now, because ultimately they will. For example:

- "He comes to be glorified in his holy people and to be marveled at among all those who have believed" (2 Thess 1:10).
- "The twenty-four elders fall down before him . . . and worship him who lives for ever and ever" (Rev 4:10; cf. Rev 5:14).
- "Fear God and give him glory, because the hour of his judgment has come. Worship him who made the heavens, the earth, the sea and the springs of water" (Rev 14:7).

5. *Devotion.* The revelation of God's care for the elect and his grand plans for the future constitutes a call to be more fully devoted to him and to live in the light. And when God is understood better, the call to follow him is more convincing. For example:

- "Blessed are those who hear it and take to heart what is written in it" (Rev 1:3).
- "Wake up! Strengthen what remains and is about to die" (Rev 3:2).
- The dragon "went off to make war against . . . those who obey God's commandments and hold to the testimony of Jesus" (Rev 12:17).
- "Blessed is he who keeps the words of the prophecy in this book" (Rev 22:7).
- "Let him who does right continue to do right; and let him who is holy continue to be holy" (Rev 22:11).

6. *Correction.* If there was any doubt about God's displeasure over sin, the coming judgment will settle that question. Apocalyptic calls for repentance and announces stern warnings to any who might fall into sin. For example:

- "Remember the height from which you have fallen! Repent and do the things you did at first" (Rev 2:5).
- "Repent therefore! Otherwise, I will soon come to you and will fight against them with the sword of my mouth" (Rev 2:16).
- "Remember, therefore, what you have received and heard; obey it, and repent" (Rev 3:3).
- "Those whom I love I rebuke and discipline. So be earnest, and repent" (Rev 3:19).
- "These are those who did not defile themselves with women, for they kept themselves pure" (Rev 14:4).
- "Blessed are those who wash their robes" (Rev 22:14).

7. *Perseverance.* The difficulties of the present press the faithful almost beyond limit. Evil and suffering in this life have an explanation: we are

temporarily in the grip of hostile powers. Prophecy calls for endurance and perseverance, regardless of the circumstances. For example:

- "You have persevered and have endured hardships for my name, and have not grown weary" (Rev 2:3).
- "You remain true to my name. You did not renounce your faith in me" (Rev 2:13).
- "Hold on to what you have until I come" (Rev 2:25).
- "This calls for patient endurance and faithfulness on the part of the saints" (Rev 13:10; cf. 14:12).

CONCLUSION

How will prophecies be fulfilled? Are the detailed theories of the twentieth century (of premillennial dispensationalism in particular) valid interpretations of prophecy and apocalyptic? While many have assumed that prophecy reveals specific scenarios of future events, we may need to rethink those approaches. Futurespeak is rich in poetic imagery. Its function transcends the surface meaning of its words. Reading and hearing the words of prophecy and apocalyptic should thrill every faithful follower with a hope focused on the Christ of prophecy. But the compelling urge of modern people to know everything, including the future, must not lead us astray from the real purpose of prophecy.

What *does* God want us to know about the future? First, we know that Jesus will return. Though we do not know when, we should be prepared for the nearness of his coming, and at the same time we should be prepared for its distantness. It may happen at any moment, but it may not happen in our lifetime. Second, we know that Jesus will return in the most dramatic divine visitation of earth ever to occur. Precisely what circumstances will accompany his return are not clear, but we will certainly recognize it when it happens. Third, we know that the end times will be cataclysmic in every way. Purging the earth of sin and creating a new heaven and earth will mean everything being turned upside down. God's wrath against the godless will be merciless. Fourth, we know that God has wonderful plans in store for overcomers. We will shine like the sun in his kingdom! Fifth, we know that eventually God's name will be hallowed, his kingdom will come and his will will be done—by everyone, in every place, for all time.

Prophecy and apocalyptic, then, are not suitable for microscopes, so that we might scope out specific details of the future. But they are suitable for macroscopes, because they allow us to see the big picture of how God will bring to conclusion the present era and establish the kingdom of eternity.

*   *   *

Excursus: When Is It a Metaphor?

It would be advantageous for interpreting individual words and verses of prophecy if we could determine whether a statement of prophecy is metaphoric. Though that is often not possible, some criteria may be helpful. Since it is the details of prophecy that often mislead people because they fail to recognize the metaphors, it will be useful to flag representative prophecies to help identify when prophetic statements may be metaphoric. Recognizing metaphors is not simply a matter of common sense from a modern perspective, though in some cases metaphors are more obvious than others.

1. A metaphor may be identified and explained in the immediate context of the prophecy.

> So the LORD cut off from Israel head and tail,
>   palm branch and reed in one day—
> elders and dignitaries are the head,
>   and prophets who teach lies are the tail. (Is 9:14-15 NRSV)

Without the explanation provided by the prophet, we probably would not have understood his metaphors of head and tail and palm branch and reed, especially when these images have different referents in other contexts (cf. Deut 28:13; Is 19:15). In this case, however, Isaiah identifies the referents for the metaphors.

2. Metaphors may be recognized by the impossibility of two concepts linked together. "Circumcise yourselves to the LORD, remove the foreskin of your hearts" (Jer 4:4 NRSV). "Shower, O heavens, from above, and let the skies rain down righteousness" (Is 45:8 NRSV). As these examples demonstrate, many metaphors are obvious because they simply cannot be anything else.

3. The parallelism of Hebrew poetry often matches metaphor with referent.

Can a girl forget her ornaments,
   or a bride her attire?
Yet my people have forgotten me,
   days without number. (Jer 2:32 NRSV)

4. A simile may establish a figure of speech that is then carried on via metaphor.

Yet I planted you as a choice vine,
   from the purest stock.
How then did you turn degenerate
   and become a wild vine? (Jer 2:21 NRSV)

5. Numbers may be metaphoric, especially when there are carefully constructed numerical patterns.

The city that marched out a thousand
   shall have a hundred left,
and that which marched out a hundred
   shall have ten left. (Amos 5:3 NRSV)

6. When the prophets allude to the historical circumstances of the Israelites and make comparisons between their history and their current situation, they often use metaphors. For example, the exodus, the wilderness experience and Achan's sin in the valley of Achor become metaphors for what God will do (Is 4:5; Hos 2:15; 7:16; 8:13; 11:1, 5, 11; Hag 2:21-22).

They shall pass through the sea of distress,
   and the waves of the sea shall be struck down,
   and all the depths of the Nile dried up. (Zech 10:11 NRSV)

Zechariah is describing the return of Judah to the Promised Land, and he envisions a reoccurrence of the exodus through the Red Sea. In so doing he combines imagery from the sea and the Nile.

7. Metaphors are especially common when prophetic language is full of emotion.

The Lord will afflict with scabs
   the heads of the daughters of Zion,
   and the LORD will lay bare their secret parts. (Is 3:17 NRSV)

I will strip her naked
   and expose her as in the day she was born,

and make her like a wilderness,
  and turn her into a parched land,
  and kill her with thirst. . . .
I will lay waste her vines and her fig trees. (Hos 2:3, 12 NRSV; cf. Hos 2:18-19)

However, this criterion can result in circular reasoning, since the evidence for emotional language is primarily the extreme language of metaphor.

8. When a prophet uses an image that points to an underlying idea, the imagery is probably metaphoric. "When you pass through the waters, I will be with you; and through the rivers, they shall not overwhelm you" (Is 43:2 NRSV). The point is God's protection, not the specific trial his people will face. "I will bring your offspring from the east, and from the west I will gather you" (Is 43:5 NRSV). In this case the point is God's future blessing. References to the east and west are metaphoric for anywhere in the world the people are dispersed. It is also possible that the language of restoration is metaphoric for ways God will bless.

9. Metaphors in one part of the Old Testament may help identify metaphors in another part. The "Song of Moses," for example, describes God's care for Jacob in metaphoric language.

He set him atop the heights of the land,
  and fed him with produce of the field;
he nursed him with honey from the crags,
  with oil from flinty rock;
curds from the herd, and milk from the flock,
  with fat of lambs and rams;
Bashan bulls and goats,
  together with the choicest wheat—
  you drank fine wine from the blood of grapes. (Deut 32:13-14 NRSV)

Similar to these phrases, much of the language of God's care for his people in the prophets is metaphoric.

In that day I will restore
  David's fallen tent.
I will repair its broken places,
  restore its ruins,
  and build it as it used to be. (Amos 9:11)

An example that is less obviously metaphoric, but no less metaphoric, comes from the prophets Amos and Joel. In the words of Amos:

The time is surely coming, says the LORD,
  when the one who plows shall overtake the one who reaps,
  and the treader of the grapes the one who sows the seed;
the mountains shall drip sweet wine,
  and all the hills shall flow with it.
I will restore the fortunes of my people Israel,
  and they shall rebuild the ruined cities and inhabit them;
they shall plant vineyards and drink their wine,
  and they shall make gardens and eat their fruit.
I will plant them upon their land,
  and they shall never again be plucked up
  out of the land that I have given them,
    says the LORD your God. (Amos 9:13-15; cf. Joel 3:18 NRSV)

While parts of this language are almost surely metaphoric, there are several ways to understand the metaphors. The one who plows overtaking the one who reaps and the wine flowing all over the hills may be metaphors for agricultural prosperity. In an agricultural community, these words would have been welcome. The blessing of agricultural abundance would have fit well with restoration to the land. The restoration is depicted in rebuilding of cities, planting of vineyards and the like (see pp. 95-96). However, that description may be metaphoric for a future time of God's blessing. Clearly, then, every part of the prophetic corpus must be carefully examined for the presence of metaphoric language.

10. One of the prophets' techniques is to describe an idea in many different ways, using a diversity of poetic language. As image is added to image, the underlying point is highlighted repeatedly with a variety of metaphors.

He will stretch out his hand against the north
  and destroy Assyria,
leaving Nineveh utterly desolate
  and dry as a desert.
Flocks and herds will lie down there,
  creatures of every kind.
The desert owl and the screech owl
  will roost on her columns.

Their calls will echo through the windows,
  rubble will be in the doorways,
  the beams of cedar will be exposed. . . .
What a ruin she has become,
  a lair for wild beasts!
All who pass by her scoff
  and shake their fists. (Zeph 2:13-15)

Zephaniah is describing God's judgment on Assyria in the destruction of its capital, Nineveh. But for a poet it is not enough simply to state the fact. Zephaniah develops the point with a series of metaphors: lack of water replaces an abundance of water, animals replace people, the screech of owls replaces voices, rubble replaces finery, mockery replaces admiration. Metaphors are essential to the poetic development of basic concepts.

11. When prophecies seem to disagree with one another, the solution is usually the recognition of metaphoric language. For example, Amos makes it sound as if God has permanently turned his back on his people.

Then the LORD said to me,
"The end has come upon my people Israel;
  I will never again pass them by." (Amos 8:2 NRSV)

But that is not really the end of the story, for God still offers them hope.

I will restore the fortunes of my people Israel. . . .
I will plant them upon their land,
  and they shall never again be plucked up
  out of the land that I have given them,
    says the LORD your God. (Amos 9:14-15 NRSV)

12. Metaphors may appear in stylized language of judgment to depict the depths of divine wrath. Jeremiah's language about the destruction of Babylon (see pp. 164-66)—"Wild animals shall live with hyenas in Babylon, and ostriches shall inhabit her" (Jer 50:39 NRSV), and "All who pass Babylon will be horrified and scoff because of all her wounds" (Jer 50:13)—is similar to Zephaniah's language about Nineveh: "What a ruin she has become, a lair for wild beasts! All who pass by her scoff and shake their fists" (Zeph 2:15). When both prophets use similar language to describe God's judgment on two different cities, that suggests metaphors drawn from stock language.

These twelve criteria for identifying metaphors are not foolproof, but they may point in the right direction. However, as noted above, a lack of certainty in distinguishing between nonfigurative language and figurative language may not be the end of the world. Prophecy may be inherently and intentionally translucent.

CONCLUSION

W hen is the end of a journey the beginning? We have been on an extended journey and have followed the river of prophecy through diverse terrain. Some of it has been traveled before. Some parts are nearly virgin forests. Our objective was to discover the dynamic forces that make the river what it is. We also wanted to see where the river is headed.

Before beginning the exploration, I asked a variety of questions: How does the language of prophecy work? What was the role of the prophets, and how did they want their hearers to respond? What can we learn from prophecies that have already been fulfilled? What does God really want us to know about the future?

The first thing we did on our journey was to stand in awe of the whitewater of prophecy. Prophetic rhetoric describes God at the extreme limits of his attributes, humanity at the extreme limits of depravity, calamity at the extreme limits of catastrophe and prosperity at the extreme limits of divine approval. To describe God and his holiness in the language of earth and its fallenness, to describe impending manifestations of divine wrath and salvation in the language of the present, the prophets did unusual things with words. One example is the description of the rewards for overcomers in Revelation 2—3. The full range of colors of those rewards highlights the brilliance of the hope of humanity. The hope is being reunited with God for all eternity.

We did not get very far into our journey, however, before discovering seven problems coming at us from various directions. The very nature of prophetic language, which gives it power, makes it challenging. Prophecy is usually poetry, and it has all the features of Hebrew poetry. Rather than the straightforward language of propositions, it communicates in emotive, hyperbolic and figurative ways. Some prophecies are conditional, but we do not always know when. Some prophecies, if not most, were originally sermons, but we cannot always determine the context of the sermons. Some prophecies were fulfilled within the lifetime of the prophets and some await fulfillment, but we do not always know which is which. The biggest problem, of course, is not prophecy. Unless we enter into the world of prophecy and learn to think like prophets, the primary problem will be our ignorance.

Our exploration of prophecy began in earnest as we sought to understand the densely forested language of prophecy. In all communication, metaphors are more than mere ornamentation; they are the essence of perception and expression. Without metaphoric language, our thinking and communicating and relating would be much the poorer. Admittedly, metaphors introduce ambiguity, but that very ambiguity enriches meaning. With figurative language, surface meanings and dictionary definitions generally miss the point, so culture and context become determinative. Though metaphoric language appears throughout Scripture, the preponderance in poetic prophecy is notable. But given the mission of the prophets to awaken a cold and callused generation, that should not be surprising.

Our next foray was into two of the subgenres of prophecy, oracles of judgment and oracles of salvation. We saw first the inability of any one description of a theophany to capture a complete picture of deity. Similarly, expressions of God's wrath and love are full of diversity, because no single description is sufficient. We also noted the illocution of language and how words may function beyond what is obvious. We then sought to find the background for the language of destruction and blessing in the ancient Near East and in the Mosaic covenant. We found that God's judgment and salvation are visualized in diverse ways so that we may grasp their totality. That perspective was applied to major themes of destruction and blessing, and we found evidence of illocution, hyperbole and stereotypical language. Specific terms of judgment were used to express unspecified realities of judgment. Clearly the normal meanings of words will often not be the intended meanings of words.

The apocalyptic genre required special attention because of its distinctive characteristics. In addition to distinguishing between the prophetic and the apocalyptic, we paid close attention to the function of apocalyptic in the ink of inspired authors. But our primary focus in this chapter was the vision recorded in Daniel 8. Since it predicted events that have already come to pass, we were able to compare the language used for coming events with the outcomes of the predictions. We found that the predictions tended to be more allusive and symbolic than precise and explicit. Before the events were fulfilled, it seems unlikely that anyone could have anticipated how they would be fulfilled. We then fast-forwarded to the book of Revelation (chapters 12—13) in order to consider another example of an apocalyptic vision. Here too the imagery is allusive rather than specific, and the point of the vision is not in the detail but the overall effect. Apocalyptic is the impressionism of biblical literature.

At this point in our journey, our investigation became even more intense in a quest to understand the role of the prophets. If they were not predicting future events, what was their mission? We found that the purpose of the prophets was primarily prosecution and secondarily persuasion, with predictions of God's judgment and blessing functioning as part of prosecution and persuasion. However, given the thirst in modern culture to know the future, Christians are inclined to focus on the predictive elements in order to assuage their curiosity. Unfortunately that leads to much misunderstanding. The limitations of prophecy as a source of information for the future were demonstrated with examples from various prophetic parts of Scripture. It became evident that the predictive element of prophecy is more translucent than transparent. Prophecy is always accurate in what it intends to reveal, but rarely does it reveal information so that we may know the future in advance. Figures of speech function to describe not the details of what is going to happen but the seriousness of what is going to happen.

The last region of exploration was apocalyptic imagery in the New Testament. In order to interpret it correctly, I drew insights from earlier chapters to lay a foundation for a proper hermeneutic. The result is a *sine qua non* of any hermeneutic for prophecy: taking into account the nature of prophetic language as poetic, metaphoric, rhetorical, urgent, hyperbolic and fantastic. Careful consideration was also given to identifying and understanding metaphors in prophecy. On that basis, an examination of apocalyptic in the New Testament yielded twelve thematic features around which end-time images cluster. From the striking imagery to describe the presentation of the transcendent and glorious Lamb ("in blazing fire") to the terrifying imagery to describe his satanic adversaries ("brute beasts"), apocalyptic is a stained-glass window, not a crystal ball.

The scope of our exploration in these seven chapters was wide-ranging. In many areas we looked at representative data rather than at all the data. So the conclusions I have articulated are partly tentative. There are many questions that need to be addressed in more detail. But the exploration has discovered enough to suggest that rethinking the language of prophecy and apocalyptic is necessary. It is now time to consider some implications of this investigation and to recruit additional adventurers to continue the exploration. Though we are at the end of our journey, it is really the beginning.

A HERMENEUTIC FOR PROPHECY AND APOCALYPTIC

If the language of prophecy and apocalyptic is now better understood, our methodology for interpreting prophecy needs to be reshaped accordingly. Fundamentally, our objective must be to understand prophecy as it was originally intended. We need a hermeneutic of the heart; in most cases, prophecy is emotional as much as it is cerebral. We need a literary hermeneutic; prophecy uses remarkable literary techniques. We need a wide-angle hermeneutic; in most cases, individual objects do not make sense except as part of the larger picture. We need a 20-20 vision hermeneutic; if we are nearsighted we will fail to see clearly what prophecy describes afar off, and if we are farsighted we will be confused about what prophecy describes nearby. The following guidelines underscore the most important insights for interpreting prophecy accurately.

1. Since prophecy is powerful language designed for dramatic impact on its hearers, *listen to it with your heart, not just your head*. What did the author intend? Prophets amplified their messages with mega-wattage systems, powering tiny tweeters and huge subwoofers. We are supposed to feel every beat. And the most important vibration to be experienced is God. Savor the soaring language of the prophets' vivid images.

2. Since the prophets were prosecuting attorneys pronouncing God's wrath on guilty sinners, *look for evidence in the prophetic and historical books for the condition of the people at that time*. How did the catastrophes announced by the prophets relate to God's covenant with his people? What

were the people doing that called forth God's wrath? To interpret prophecy we must first see it through the lens of the lives of the original hearers. Then be prepared to be shaken to the very core as the words of the prophets encounter your own life. It will indeed be terrible to fall into the hands of an angry God.

3. Since prophecy promises incredible rewards for overcomers, *explore the full range of what heaven on earth will be like.* Reflect on Ezekiel's amazing imagery of the ideal temple with a river flowing from it (Ezek 40—47), on Joel's imagery of mountains dripping with new wine and flowing with milk (Joel 3:18), on John's imagery of the Holy City coming down out of heaven (Rev 21:10-27). How does future hope compensate for present helplessness? Note the function of apocalyptic language in calling the righteous to keep their robes pure and to endure patiently until they can join the 144,000.[1] Commit yourself to being cold or hot, but not lukewarm.

4. Since prophecy is poetic, *seek to understand what a prophet meant by what he said.* Take into account literary features like metaphors and hyperbole, rhetorical techniques, unexpressed conditions, stereotypical language, and rich symbolism. Beware of reading the words of the prophets superficially; instead look for indications of the function of the language. Biblical prophecies were generally not understood before they were fulfilled, so do not expect prophecy to provide a blueprint for the future.

5. Since prophecy may describe the same idea with a variety of images, *look for overarching themes.* If you do not understand the intent of a specific prophetic expression, it may be time to step back and take in the big picture. Not understanding some things does not imply not understanding *anything.*[2] Prophecy does reveal important things about the future, though many of its particulars may be present only to increase the visual impact of the primary point. Apocalyptic uses fantastic images to create a virtual-reality experience with an otherworldly perspective. The goal is to gain perspective about what is happening in this life by getting outside this life.

6. Since prophecy draws on present and earthy language to describe future and heavenly scenes, *expect the future reality to exceed your wildest imagination.*[3] Human words are simply inadequate for such faraway places and distant times. Look at prophecy as you would a stained-glass window: marvel at the skill of the artist and the beauty of the scenery. But do not suppose that we can see through the window and comprehend the fullness of majesty or the fullness of horror on the other side.

7. Since prophecy has been subjected to many different interpretations, *focus on what we can agree on.* Beyond that, be humble and considerate of other possibilities about how prophecy will be fulfilled. Prophecy is an arena not of arguments but of impressions.[4] The second coming is a defining doctrine of the Christian faith, but when peering off into the future to find out how events in the last days will unfold, we see through a glass darkly.

Though many other criteria for correct interpretation of prophecy have been developed throughout this book, these seven guidelines summarize the most important ideas. Additional perspectives on interpretation can be found in other discussions of prophecy.[5]

PLOWSHARES AND PRUNING HOOKS

The image of turning swords into plowshares and spears into pruning hooks appears in identical passages in Isaiah 2 and Micah 4. A reversal of the image appears in Joel 3. It is an appropriate image to demonstrate how the hermeneutical principles I have suggested may be applied to a text and its context. We begin first in the book of Psalms.

A common way the psalmists acclaim God's greatness is to speak of his rule over all nations, accompanied by the praise of all people: "God reigns over the nations; God is seated on his holy throne" (Ps 47:8). "All you have made will praise you, O LORD" (Ps 145:10). Recognizing that not all peoples acknowledge God's power and might, the poets expand that thought to say that sooner or later everyone *will* worship him:

> *All the ends of the earth*
> *will remember and turn to the LORD,*
> *and all the families of the nations*
> *will bow down before him.* (Ps 22:27)

> *So the name of the LORD will be declared in Zion*
> *and his praise in Jerusalem*
> *when the peoples and the kingdoms*
> *assemble to worship the LORD.* (Ps 102:21-22)

The psalmist's intent is to say that God is so great that he is worthy of universal praise.

Another form the psalmists' praise takes is to think of God as a mighty warrior, defeating enemies on every hand.[6] The imagery of snapping off bows, shattering spears and gathering shields for a bonfire is striking:

Come and see the works of the LORD,
   the desolations he has brought on the earth.
He makes wars cease to the ends of the earth;
   he breaks the bow and shatters the spear,
   he burns the shields with fire. (Ps 46:8-9)

In similar fashion Isaiah begins a section of prophecies regarding Judah and Jerusalem (Is 2:1) with a song of exaltation focusing on Zion. He describes a glorious temple on the highest of mountains, with people streaming to it from all over the globe. Everyone will come to learn God's ways and honor his laws; they will seek his justice to settle their disputes, and they will exchange their weapons for instruments of peace.

In the last days
the mountain of the LORD's temple will be established
   as chief among the mountains;
it will be raised above the hills,
   and all nations will stream to it.

Many peoples will come and say,
"Come, let us go up to the mountain of the LORD,
   to the house of the God of Jacob.
He will teach us his ways,
   so that we may walk in his paths."
The law will go out from Zion,
   the word of the LORD from Jerusalem.
He will judge between the nations
   and will settle disputes for many peoples.
They will beat their swords into plowshares
   and their spears into pruning hooks.
Nation will not take up sword against nation,
   nor will they train for war anymore.

Come, O house of Jacob,
   let us walk in the light of the LORD. (Is 2:2-5; cf. Mic 4:1-3)

Our first response should be to marvel at God's greatness. He is King of all kings and Lord of all nations, and every knee should bow before him. His law is perfect, and no education is complete without mastery of his statutes. His justice is righteous, and every disagreement should be settled in his courts. His peace passes all understanding, and every instrument of war should be melted in the fire of his furnaces. God is worthy of our worship.

Second, we should note the figures of speech. With hyperbole, the prophet describes the temple as being on a mountain higher than all others. Using stereotypical language, he describes nations streaming to it (cf. Jer 16:19). Using metaphor, he says that people will beat their swords into plowshares and their spears into pruning hooks (see pp. 39-40).

Third, we should look for the overarching theme of these verses. A common subject among the prophets is God's exaltation, often in the form of acclamation from people all over the earth. This is apparently Isaiah's intent in the passage at hand—it does not need to be a prediction regarding the last days. As seen above in the Psalms, one way to express God's praises is to picture everything he created bowing before him in worship. Examples abound in prophecy: "Therefore strong peoples will honor you; cities of ruthless nations will revere you" (Is 25:3). Even the people of Cush will come to Zion with gifts:

> At that time gifts will be brought to the LORD Almighty
> from a people tall and smooth-skinned,
>   from a people feared far and wide,
> an aggressive nation of strange speech,
>   whose land is divided by rivers—
> the gifts will be brought to Mount Zion, the place of the Name of the LORD Almighty.
> (Is 18:7)

Fourth, we must not overlook the function of these verses. Isaiah concludes with a summons to "walk in the light of the Lord." Based on the greatness of God—expressed in statements that his temple, his law, his justice and his peace excel all others—the chosen people are summoned to devotion. According to the accusations that Isaiah has already pronounced (Is 1:2-31), this call for change in their lives was sorely needed. Unfortunately, according to Isaiah's continued accusations (Is 2:6-11), these few verses focusing on God's preeminence among the nations had little effect.

Finally, we are ready to think about how Isaiah 2:2-5 may speak to our lives. This striking reminder of God's supremacy over all things great and small gives us ample reason to pause and worship him. We become participants with Isaiah in expressing praise to God. We too need to follow up our worship with walking in his glorious light.

Hence the phrase "plowshares and pruning hooks" is a significant image suggesting peace, as used by Isaiah, Micah and Joel. It has become one of the most recognized symbols from the Old Testament prophets. At the United Nations Headquarters in New York City, a bronze sculpture of a blacksmith pounding a sword into a plowshare has these words at the base: "We shall beat our swords into plowshares." Elsewhere in the UN building, Isaiah 2:4 is engraved on a wall. In Washington, D.C., thousands of handguns collected by the police department in efforts to reduce violence were welded onto a sixteen-by-nineteen-foot plowshare, with Isaiah 2:4 inscribed at the base. It stands in Judicatory Square. [7]

WHAT *DOES* PROPHECY PREDICT ABOUT THE FUTURE?

If biblical prophecy is not a crystal ball for looking into the future, what does God want us to know about the future?[8] Although interpreters must withhold judgment on many particulars of prophecy, unambiguous prophetic themes abound throughout Scripture, centering on the second coming of Jesus the Messiah. Even as there was a first advent, there will be a second one. It may be soon, or it may be far off, but it will happen.[9] Associated with Jesus' return will be a concentration of cataclysmic phenomena. And the ultimate purpose of Christ's return will be restoration: humanity's separation from God as a result of sin will be canceled by means of a final judgment on sin and a change of both people and their environment. Jesus will finally be Lord of all. God's triumph is certain!

We do not need to speculate about the color of the eyes of the Antichrist to know that he is evil and that the Lamb of God will be victorious over him. We do need to understand the nature and purpose of biblical prophecy, for prophecy is as vital to the purposes of Scripture as water is to the earth's atmosphere. We see this in several ways.

1. It is often *in retrospect or in the present* that biblical prophecies achieve their greatest importance. This in no way diminishes prophecy's value. Were it not for the messianic prophecies of the Old Testament fulfilled in Jesus, his followers might not have believed. On the night of Jesus' betrayal, he twice gave them an important perspective on all that he was saying to them: "I am telling you now before it happens, so that when it does happen you will believe that I am He" (Jn 13:19; cf. Jn 14:29; Mt 24—25). Much of the detail in biblical prophecy, then, is not intended to reveal the future as much as to confirm and explicate the past and illumine the present.

Ask any of Jesus' disciples whether they understood before Jesus' death the Old Testament prophecies about the Messiah. Ask, for example, the two on the road to Emmaus (Lk 24:13-35). It took a personal lesson from Jesus himself to help them understand how Jesus fulfilled those prophecies.

This was the experience of all who came in contact with Jesus. Even John the Baptist, who was given divine insight into who Jesus was, could not harmonize what he expected the Messiah to do with what Jesus was doing.[10] From prison John sent some of his disciples to ask Jesus whether he was the Messiah or whether they should look for someone else (Mt 11:2-3). If this gifted and Spirit-filled prophet failed to grasp the significance of the prophecies about the Messiah fulfilled before his very eyes, should not every follower of Christ be cautious about announcing in advance how prophecy will be fulfilled?

This is Peter's point about the Old Testament prophets and their prophecies of the coming salvation (1 Pet 1:10-12). The prophets wished to know when and how the Messiah would suffer and be glorified. However, they prophesied not to serve themselves but to confirm for future believers the authenticity of Christ's coming.

2. More than just a description of "the finish line," *prophecy puts the complete circuit of history into perspective.* It reveals God's agenda in the past and for the future. If we will spend eternity demonstrating our praise to the victorious Lamb, if in eternity the church will be united in one glorious body, if justice and righteousness will characterize eternity, then we have a clear sense of what God wants from us even now.

After describing the forthcoming disappearance of the heavens and the melting down of the earth, Peter asks the rhetorical question "What kind of people ought you to be?" He answers, "You ought to live holy and godly lives as you look forward to the day of God and speed its coming" (2 Pet 3:11-12). The promise that we will be like Jesus, although we do not fully understand what that means, gives a clear focus for how we should live until that time (1 Jn 3:2).[11]

3. While not the primary purpose, *prediction is an integral part of prophecy.* By the announcement of unexpected and striking events in the future, hearers are moved out of their immediate and troubled world into a future experience of otherworldly images and events. This is the essence of the apocalyptic genre. In the book of Revelation, the marvelous descriptions of vivid and figurative images are not intended to give us details about the

future but to encourage us with the news that heaven and the future are unlike anything on this earth. For Christians facing persecution, it is comforting to know that they can look forward to something far better than what this world has to offer.

4. Most important, *the central focus of prophecy is the Son of God*. Everything about the future is designed to make Jesus Christ preeminent. From the beginning of Genesis to the end of Revelation, from creation to the climax of history, everything revolves around Jesus as Messiah and victorious conqueror. Unfortunately, speculations about the course of future events have nearly eclipsed the Messiah as the central figure of prophecy.[12] But the real point of prophecy is to show how Christ will once again be the revelation of God in all his majesty and splendor.

Prophecy, then, focuses attention away from the present world to a new world where Christ will finally reign in power and glory. It will be the end of time. Jesus will restore this earth and his people to God's original design. Though it will be the end of the journey, it will really be the beginning.[13]

QUESTIONS FOR FUTURE EXPLORATION

While this study confirms things we can be sure of about prophecy and the future, it raises a number of questions as well. If we have clarified how to understand the language of prophecy and apocalyptic, then implications for theology and eschatology will need to be considered.

What is the message of the book of Revelation? This study of the language of prophecy and apocalyptic began with the goal of interpreting the Apocalypse correctly. While we have made significant progress in that direction, we are not there yet.[14] But we know enough not to stand too close to the impressionistic artwork and attempt to externalize a future event from elements that are internal to the apocalyptic description. Some explanations of Revelation have resulted from rushing headlong into interpretation without doing the necessary homework; I will resist that temptation. I can suggest, however, that some excellent commentaries on Revelation have appeared in recent years, though none have taken into full account the nature of the language of prophecy and apocalyptic.[15] Thus the conclusions of this book will be instructive for future studies of the last book of the Bible.

Is one view of eschatology more correct than another? In the study of last things, Christians have come to differing conclusions.[16] While Christians agree that Jesus will come again, attempts to understand the circumstances surrounding that event have led to positions known as amillennialism, premillennialism, postmillennialism, pretribulationalism, midtribulationalism, posttribulationalism and so on. Each is a *preconstruction;* that is, rather like attempting to *reconstruct* what happened in history based on sketchy details, eschatology is an attempt to preconstruct what will happen in the future based on supposed details that are also sketchy. As indicated in the preface, this book was not written to defend or dismantle any particular view. However, if my conclusions about the language of prophecy and apocalyptic are correct, all systems of eschatology are subject to reconsideration. The fundamental question is, does the language of prophecy intend to give us details from which we can preconstruct how the future will unfold?

Will there be a future restoration of the chosen people to Palestine? Central to amillennialism is the belief that many Old Testament prophecies regarding Israel will be fulfilled in the church. Central to premillennialism is the belief that many Old Testament prophecies will be fulfilled in a future nation of Israel. In both cases there may be a limited understanding of how prophecy speaks. When it seems improbable that Old Testament prophecies will be literally fulfilled in a future Israel, amillennialists assume that they were meant to be spiritualized and fulfilled in the church. When certain Old Testament prophecies seem not to have been literally fulfilled before the first advent, premillennialists assume that they will be fulfilled in a future Israel. For the chosen people, especially messianic Jews, descriptions of a regathering in Jerusalem are assumed to predict a great day when Jews everywhere will recognize their Messiah. However, in light of how the language of destruction and blessing works—illocution, visualization, conditionality, stereotypical features and the like (see pp. 83-97)—these viewpoints need to be reevaluated carefully.[17]

How are Old Testament prophecies quoted in the New Testament? A longstanding problem for scholars has been the correlations that New Testament authors make between Old Testament prophecies and New Testament fulfillments. The question is whether the prophet intended the meaning that the New Testament author finds in a prophetic statement. The starting point for these discussions needs to be what the Old Testament prophet meant in the original context. That cannot be determined without understanding the nature of prophetic language. Based on the investigations of this book, the intent of prophetic language can be analyzed more carefully.

While some people will surely think they already have clear-cut answers for these questions, hopefully they will be charitable in the positions of which they are convinced. "The hallmark of authentic Evangelicalism is not the uncritical repetition of old traditions but the willingness to submit every tradition, however ancient, to fresh biblical scrutiny and, if necessary, reform."[18] If a convincing consensus for a particular view of prophecy is not evident within the body of Christ, then that view should be considered a theory not a dogma.

UNLEASHING PROPHECY

One of C. S. Lewis's characters in *The Last Battle* makes a significant observation regarding Aslan: "Is it not said in all the old stories that He is not a Tame Lion?" Sadly, however, many people have inadvertently domesticated God. By allowing what we want God to be to influence what we think he is—to predecide what God we will accept and give allegiance to—we put him on a short leash, and the idea of fearing him becomes absurd. As someone has noted, God created humanity in his image, and humanity has been seeking to return the favor ever since! But we must not confine God to whatever we need at the moment and what we think we can understand on the spur of the moment. We must let God be God.

Sadly, people have also inadvertently domesticated prophecy. If every utterance can be analyzed and objectified and a futuristic significance extrapolated therefrom, we have tamed prophecy and forced it to be what we want it to be. True, modern Christians are held spellbound, but in the process we have muzzled the divine medium.[19] The intent of the prophets is to let the lion roar: the earth is going to be completely laid waste and totally plundered; it will dry up and wither (Is 24:3-4). Israel's wound is incurable (Jer 30:12). Earth's inhabitants will be burned up (Is 24:6). God's wrath will last forever (Jer 23:40). He will not hear prayers (Is 1:15).

The lion has roared—
  who will not fear?
The Sovereign Lord has spoken—
  who can but prophesy? (Amos 3:8)

Of course the lion occasionally purrs. Mountains and hills are going to burst into song, trees will clap their hands, desert and parched land will be glad, wilderness will rejoice and blossom (Is 55:12; 35:1). Instead of Israel's wound being incurable, God will heal all their wounds (Jer 30:17). Instead of the earth's inhabitants being completely annihilated, they will come from the ends of the earth to God's holy mountain (Is 27:13; 66:18). Instead of God's wrath lasting forever, it will last only a brief moment (Is 54:7).

An important question is, what will restore prophecy to its rightful place in the revelation of God's truth? In chapter one we stood in awe as the river of prophecy roared, crashing against boulders and canyon walls. We must return there again and again and listen to the river. But the river will not always roar and crash.

> Then the angel showed me the river of the water of life, as clear as crystal, flowing from the throne of God and of the Lamb down the middle of the great street of the city. On each side of the river stood the tree of life, bearing twelve crops of fruit, yielding its fruit every month. And the leaves of the tree are for the healing of the nations. . . . The Spirit and the bride say, "Come!" And let him who hears say, "Come!" Whoever is thirsty, let him come; and whoever wishes, let him take the free gift of the water of life. (Rev 22:1-2, 17)[20]

Listening to the river leaves no doubt about the glorious future for God's faithful followers. The sun never sets on this river. Trees on its golden banks offer abundant fruit and leaves of healing. Drinking its water gives eternal life. No matter how awful the dirge of our plight in this life, the song of eternity is sweeter.

This hope is the shared vision of the Christian community. It is a hope worth celebrating. It is worthy of poems and songs and sermons and books. It is the ultimate climax to our exploration of prophecy and apocalyptic.

A PARTING PLEA

Thanks for joining me on this journey. I realize that we did not all view prophecy through the same grid when we began, but hopefully we have gained insights that will result in fewer lines in our grids. Though not the raison d'être for this book, if improving our understanding of prophecy can help us be obedient to the Word of God, then something really valuable may be accomplished.

Unfortunately, we are heirs of a fractured Christianity. Theological posturing and pontificating about various issues—prophecy being near the top of the list—distracts us from a high calling. Jesus gave us the priority to promote and preserve unity. We are to be a community united on all fronts. My prayer is that we can achieve a sense of common hope and less division regarding prophecy. Though the goal of this study has been shedding light on prophecy, an equally important endeavor is summoning Christians to oneness.[21] We need an evangelical reunion.[22] Permit me to explain why I think this is important.

The *Grand* Commission, as I refer to it, was given in a prayer on the most important night of Jesus' earthly life. He is praying for his followers and specifically for all second and successive generations of believers. In this moment, the foremost thought on his mind is oneness, "that all of them may be one, Father, just as you are in me and I am in you" (Jn 17:21). This is not fleeting fancy, for Jesus continues, now linking oneness with the passing of the torch from deity to humanity: "I have given them the glory that you gave me, that they may be one as we are one" (Jn 17:22). It is an almost incomprehensible thought: the God of all glory divesting himself of glory and depositing it in all believers—first generation, second generation and all the way down the line to our generation. It is Shekinah glory.[23] And the measure of that glory is the degree of our unity.

But through the centuries the church has struggled with unity—even more so as time goes by. Yet Jesus prayed that it would be the other way around: "May they be brought to complete unity to let the world know that you sent me and have loved them even as you have loved me" (Jn 17:23). The first part of that divine request could be translated "that they may become completely one" (NRSV) or "all being perfected into one" (NLT). Thus it should be a primary goal of all Christians everywhere to achieve unity.

But Jesus also linked oneness with the *Great* Commission—"to let the world know" (cf. Mt 28:19-20). Unity is a means of making disciples of all nations.[24] It is a matter of obedience. At least the apostle Paul understood:

> *Make every effort to keep the unity of the Spirit through the bond of peace. There is one body and one Spirit—just as you were called to one hope when you were called—one Lord, one faith, one baptism; one God and Father over all, who is over all and through all and in all . . . until we all reach unity in the faith and in the knowledge of the Son of God and become mature, attaining to the whole measure of the fullness of Christ.* (Eph 4:3-5, 13)

So the mandate for the body of Christ is to make progress toward unity, including the subject of prophecy—*especially* the subject of prophecy. For our faith is linked closely with our hope: we cannot have one without the other. So it seems clear that we Christians ought to be emphasizing our common hope rather than our complicated eschatologies.[25] Unfortunately, from a human standpoint, unity on this subject may seem out of reach.[26] But Christ gave his life "to present her to himself as a radiant church, without stain or wrinkle or any other blemish, but holy and blameless" (Eph 5:27), and we should be willing to make equal sacrifice. Consequently our study of prophecy shall have extra benefit if it can help the body of Christ find common ground regarding eschatology. *If* we can move beyond the polarity and renew the theological center.[27]

The apostle Paul speaks of the wisdom that "God destined for our glory" and gives a fitting anticipation *and caution* for everyone Christian:

> *No eye has seen,*
>   *no ear has heard,*
> *no mind has conceived*
>   *what God has prepared for those who love him.* (1 Cor 2:9; cf. Is 64:4)

Appendix A

COMMON ENGLISH AND FRENCH METAPHORS

1. Common Metaphors in English

to twist your **arm**
to have an **ax** to grind
to have **bats** in the belfry
to **beat** a dead horse
to **beat** the band
to **bend** over backwards
to **bite** your head off
to **blow** your top
to **blow** your **brains out**
to go **bonkers** over something
to burst your **bubble**
to be a **bull** in a china shop
to grab the **bull** by the horn
to **bulldoze** your way in
to be a loose **cannon**
to **chew** you out
to **chill** out
to have a **chip** on your shoulder
to be left out in the **cold**
to throw **cold water** on someone
to blow your **cool**
to **cool** down
to **cross paths** with someone
to **crown** someone for a wrong done
to suffer a **crushing blow**
to throw you a **curve**
to **cut** the ground from under someone
to look **daggers** at someone
to be in the **dark** about something
to be a **dead duck**
to **deck** someone
to **dip** one's pen in venom

to live in a **dog-eat-dog** world
to speak with a **double-edged** tongue
to be **dragged** through the **mire**
to have **egg** on your face
to **fall** off the deep end
to be on the **firing line**
to blow your **fuse**
to have a short **fuse**
to take with a **grain of salt**
to get in each other's **hair**
to **hang** your head low
to barely **hang** in there
to learn a lesson of **hard knocks**
to feel **hemmed** in
to stir up a **hornet's** nest
to rule with an **iron hand**
to escape the **jaws** of death
to **jump** down your throat
to **lay** it on thick
to **lead** you by the nose
to keep you on a tight **leash**
to be on your last **leg**
to **lick** your wounds
to **lock** horns with someone
to put you through the **mill**
to hang a **millstone** around your neck
to be out of your **mind**
to **mop** up the floor with someone
to put your head in a **noose**
to cut off your **nose** to spite your face
to pay through the **nose**
to **poison** your mind

to **punch** your lights out

to **ring** off the hook

to rule the **roost**

to have a **screw** loose

to **shoot** yourself in the foot

to **shoot** someone for a wrong done

to **stick** to your guns

to take by **storm**

to talk **turkey**

to escape by the skin of your **teeth**

to be a **tempest** in a teapot

to be a **thorn** in your side

to walk **three feet** off the ground

to stick in your **throat**

to **tie** your hands behind your back

to be up**tight**

to **toot** your own horn

to fight **tooth and nail**

to **walk** all over someone

to be caught in a **web**

to crack the **whip**

to take the **wind** out of your sails

to throw someone to the **wolves**

to clip your **wings**

to pull the **wool** over your eyes

to be **wound** up

For more examples of metaphors, see Elyse Sommer and Dorrie Weiss, eds., *Metaphors Dictionary* (New York: Gale Research, 1995); P. R. Wilkinson, *Thesaurus of Traditional English Metaphors* (New York: Routledge, 1993); Laurence Urdang, *Picturesque Expressions: A Thematic Dictionary*, 2nd ed. (Detroit: Gale Research, 1985).

2. Common Metaphors in French

French	Literal translation	Meaning
il a une case de vide	he has an empty compartment	he is an airhead
il est tombé sur le crâne	he fell on his skull	he went off the deep end
il est casse-pieds	he is a foot-breaker	he is a pain in the . . .
il déraille	he is off the rails	he is off his rocker
ils ne tournent pas rond	they do not turn round	they are out to lunch
je *ne peux pas le sentir*	I can't smell him	he gets on my nerves
elle lui pose un lapin	she gave him a rabbit	she stood him up
il a le cafard	he has a cockroach	he is depressed
il lui a passé un savon	he gave her some soap	he told her off
ils se bouffent le nez	they eat each other's nose	they are at each other's throat
il est tombé dans les pommes	he fell into the apples	he passed out
il est un bouseux	he is cow dung	he is a hick
elle est une vieille bique	she is a old nanny-goat	she is an old hag
ça avait un effet boeuf	it had a meaty effect	it had a big impact
mon oeil!	my eye!	my foot!

c'est un zéro	he/she is a zero	he/she is a nothing
il a vu trente-six chandelles	he saw thirty-six candles	he saw stars
bête comme chou	as stupid as cabbage	that was off the wall
il a du sang de navet	he has the blood of a turnip	he is spineless
il en a gros sur la patate	he has it heavy on the potato	he has a heavy heart
quel oeuf!	what an egg!	what a blockhead!
c'est une soupe au lait	he's a milky soup	he has a short fuse
il bouffe à tous les râteliers	he eats from all dentures	he sponges off others
il est à ramasser à la petite cuillère	he could be scooped up with a spoon	he was a mess
il n'y est pas allé avec le dos de la cuillère	he didn't go with the back of the spoon	he laid it on thick
il a les chevilles enflées	he has swollen ankles	he has a big head

Appendix B

LANGUAGE OF BLESSINGS AND CURSES

Leviticus 26 and Deuteronomy 28 contain the highest concentration of the blessings and curses of the covenant, but many of those same blessings and curses appear throughout the Old Testament, especially in the prophets. To illustrate that and to show the nature of the language, I selected several themes of language and judgment and tracked them through the rest of the Old Testament. I attempted to be comprehensive, but I do not claim to be exhaustive.

For a partly similar compilation of the language of blessings and curses, see Douglas Stuart, *Hosea-Jonah*, Word Biblical Commentary 31 (Waco, Tex.: Word, 1987), pp. xxxiii-xlii.

1. Land and Productivity

Blessings

Gen 13:15	All the land that you see I will give to you and your offspring forever.
Gen 15:18	To your descendants I give this land, from the river of Egypt to the great river, the Euphrates.
Gen 17:8	The whole land of Canaan, where you are now an alien, I will give . . . to you and your descendants after you.
Gen 26:4	[I] will give them [your offspring] all these lands.
Gen 27:28	May God give you of heaven's dew and of earth's richness—and abundance of grain and new wine.
Ex 3:8	[I will] bring them up out of that land into a good and spacious land, a land flowing with milk and honey.
Ex 15:17	You will bring them in and plant them on the mountain of your inheritance.
Ex 23:31	I will establish your borders from the Red Sea to the Sea of the Philistines, and from the desert to the River.
Lev 26:4	The ground will yield its crops and the trees of the field their fruit.
Lev 26:10	You will still be eating last year's harvest when you will have to move it out to make room for the new.
Deut 6:10-11	The LORD your God brings you into a land he swore to your fathers . . . a land with large, flourishing cities you did not build, houses filled with all kinds of goods you did not provide, wells you did not dig, and vineyards and olive groves you did not plant.
Deut 7:13	[The LORD] will bless the fruit of your womb, . . . your grain, new wine and oil.
Deut 8:7	The LORD your God is bringing you into a good land . . . with streams and pools of water, with springs flowing in the valleys and hills.
Deut 8:8	[The LORD is bringing you into] a land with wheat and barley, vines and fig trees, pomegranates, olive oil and honey.
Deut 8:9	[The LORD is bringing you into] a land where the rocks are iron and you can dig copper out of the hills.
Deut 11:11-12	The land you are crossing the Jordan to take possession of is a land of mountains and valleys that drinks rain from heaven.
Deut 11:14	[The LORD] will send rain on your land in its season, both autumn and spring rains,

	so that you may gather in your grain, new wine and oil.
Deut 11:24	Every place where you set your foot will be yours: Your territory will extend from the desert to Lebanon, and from the Euphrates River to the western sea.
Deut 28:3	You will be blessed . . . in the country.
Deut 28:4	The crops of your land [shall be blessed].
Deut 28:8	The LORD will send a blessing on your barns.
Deut 28:11	The LORD will grant you abundant prosperity . . . the crops of your ground.
Deut 32:13	He made him ride on the heights of the land and fed him with the fruit of the fields. He nourished him with honey from the rock, and with oil from the flinty crag.
Deut 33:28	Israel will live in safety . . . in a land of grain and new wine, where the heavens drop dew.
Is 27:6	Jacob will take root, Israel will bud and blossom and fill all the world with fruit.
Is 30:23	In that day your cattle will graze in broad meadows.
Is 30:26	The moon will shine like the sun, and the sunlight will be seven times brighter, like the light of seven full days.
Is 32:15	The Spirit is poured upon us from on high, and the desert becomes a fertile field.
Is 32:20	Your cattle and donkeys [will] range free.
Is 35:1	The desert and the parched land will be glad; the wilderness will rejoice and blossom.
Is 41:18	I will make rivers flow on barren heights, and springs within the valleys. I will turn the desert into pools of water, and the parched ground into springs.
Is 41:19	I will put in the desert the cedar and the acacia, the myrtle and the olive. I will set pines in the wasteland.
Is 51:3	He will make her deserts like Eden, her wastelands like the garden of the LORD.

Curses

Gen 3:17-18	Cursed is the ground because of you; . . . thorns and thistles for you.
Gen 4:12	When you work the ground, it will no longer yield its crops for you.
Lev 26:16	You will plant seed in vain, because your enemies will eat it.
Lev 26:19	[I will] make the sky above you like iron and the ground beneath you like bronze.
Lev 26:20	Your soil will not yield its crops, nor will the trees of the land yield their fruit.
Lev 26:32	I will lay waste the land, so that your enemies who live there will be appalled.
Lev 26:33	Your land will be laid waste.
Deut 4:26	You will quickly perish from the land that you are crossing the Jordan to possess.
Deut 28:16	You will be cursed . . . in the country.
Deut 28:23	The sky over your head will be bronze, the ground beneath you iron.
Deut 28:30	You will plant a vineyard, but you will not even begin to enjoy its fruit.
Deut 28:33-34	A people that you do not know will eat what your land and labor produce. . . . The sights you see will drive you mad.
Deut 28:38	You will sow much seed in the field but you will harvest little, because locusts will devour it.
Deut 28:39	You will plant vineyards . . . but you will not drink the wine or gather the grapes, because the worms will eat them.
Deut 28:40	You will have olive trees throughout your country but you will not use the oil, because the olives will drop off.
Deut 28:42	Swarms of locusts will take over all your trees and the crops of your land.
Deut 28:50-51	A fierce-looking nation . . . will devour . . . the crops of your land until you are destroyed. They will leave you no grain, new wine or oil.
Deut 28:63	You will be uprooted from the land you are entering to possess.
Deut 29:22-23	[They] will see the calamities that have fallen on the land and the diseases with which the LORD has afflicted it. The whole land will be a burning waste of salt and sulfur—nothing planted, nothing sprouting, no vegetation growing on it.
Deut 30:18	I declare to you this day that you will certainly be destroyed. You will not live long in the land you are crossing the Jordan to enter and possess.

2 Kings 19:24	With the soles of my feet I have dried up all the streams of Egypt.
2 Kings 19:26	They are like plants in the field, like tender grass shoots, like grass sprouting on the roof, scorched before it grows up.
Is 19:5-6	The waters of the river will dry up, and the riverbed will be parched and dry. The canals will stink; the streams of Egypt will dwindle and dry up.
Is 42:15	I will lay waste the mountains and hills and dry up all their vegetation; I will turn rivers into islands and dry up the pools.
Jer 8:13	I will take away their harvest. . . . There will be no grapes on the vine. There will be no figs on the tree, and their leaves will wither.
Jer 12:13	They will sow wheat but reap thorns.
Jer 14:4-5	The ground is cracked because there is no rain in the land. . . . Even the doe in the field deserts her newborn fawn because there is no grass.
Jer 46:23	They will chop down her [Egypt's] forest, . . . dense though it be.
Jer 50:12	She will be the least of the nations—a wilderness, a dry land, a desert.
Jer 50:38	A drought on her waters! They will dry up.

2. Descendants
Blessings

Gen 1:28	Be fruitful and increase in number; fill the earth and subdue it.
Gen 9:1	Be fruitful and increase in number and fill the earth.
Gen 13:16	I will make your offspring like the dust of the earth, so that if anyone could count the dust, then your offspring could be counted.
Gen 15:5	Look up at heavens and count the stars. . . . So shall your offspring be.
Gen 17:5-6	I have made you a father of many nations. . . . I will make nations of you, and kings will come from you.
Gen 17:16	I will bless her so that she will be the mother of nations; kings of peoples will come from her.
Gen 22:17	I will surely bless you and make your descendants as numerous as the stars in the sky and as the sand on the seashore.
Gen 24:60	May you increase to thousands upon thousands.
Gen 26:4	I will make your descendants as numerous as the stars in the sky.
Gen 32:12	I will surely make you prosper and will make your descendants like the sand of the sea, which cannot be counted.
Ex 23:26	None will miscarry or be barren in your land.
Ex 32:13	I will make your descendants as numerous as the stars in the sky.
Lev 26:9	I will . . . make you fruitful and increase your numbers.
Deut 1:10-11	The LORD your God has increased your numbers so that today you are as many as the stars in the sky. May the LORD, the God of your fathers, increase you a thousand times
Deut 6:3	You may increase greatly in a land flowing with milk and honey.
Deut 7:13	[The LORD] will love you and bless you and increase your numbers. He will bless the fruit of your womb.
Deut 7:14	You will be blessed more than any other people; none of your men or women will be childless.
Deut 10:22	Now the LORD your God has made you as numerous as the stars in the sky.
Deut 28:11	The LORD will grant you abundant prosperity—in the fruit of your womb.
1 Chron 27:23	David did not take the number of the men twenty years old or less, because the LORD had promised to make Israel as numerous as the stars in the sky.
Neh 9:23	You made their sons as numerous as the stars in the sky.
Is 53:10	He will see his offspring and prolong his days.
Is 54:1	More are the children of the desolate woman than of her who has a husband.
Is 54:3	Your descendants will dispossess nations and settle in their desolate cities.
Jer 33:22	I will make the descendants of David my servant and the Levites who minister before me as countless as the stars of the sky and as measureless as the sand on the seashore.

Curses

Gen 3:16	I will greatly increase your pains in childbearing; with pain you will give birth to children.
Ex 22:24	Your wives will become widows and your children fatherless.
Lev 26:22	[Wild animals] will rob you of your children. . . . [They will] make you so few in number.
Lev 26:29	You will eat the flesh of your sons and the flesh of your daughters.
Deut 28:18	The fruit of your womb will be cursed.
Deut 28:30	You will be pledged to be married to a woman, but another will take her.
Deut 28:32	Your sons and daughters will be given to another nation, and you will wear out your eyes watching for them day after day, powerless to lift a hand.
Deut 28:41	You will have sons and daughters but you will not keep them, because they will go into captivity.
Deut 28:53	You will eat the fruit of womb, the flesh of the sons and daughters the LORD your God has given you.
Deut 28:54	Even the most gentle and sensitive man among you will . . . not give to one of them any of the flesh of his children that he is eating.
Deut 28:56-57	The most gentle and sensitive woman among you . . . will begrudge the husband she loves and her own son and daughter the afterbirth from her womb and the children she bears. For she intends to eat them secretly.
Deut 28:62	You who were as numerous as the stars in sky will be left few in number.
Josh 6:26	Cursed before the LORD is the man who undertakes to rebuild this city, Jericho: At the cost of his firstborn son will he lay its foundations; at the cost of his youngest will he set up its gates.
1 Sam 15:33	Your mother [will] be childless among women.
Is 48:18-19	If only you had paid attention to my commands, . . . [y]our descendants would have been like the sand, your children like its numberless grains.

3. Dispersion and Restoration

Dispersion

Gen 4:12	You will be a restless wanderer on the earth.
Gen 11:9	The LORD scattered them over the face of the whole earth.
Gen 49:7	I will scatter them in Jacob and disperse them in Israel.
Lev 26:33	I will scatter you among the nations.
Lev 26:34	All the time . . . you are in the country of your enemies.
Lev 26:36	[They will be full of fear] in the lands of their enemies.
Lev 26:38	You will perish among the nations; the land of your enemies will devour you.
Lev 26:39	Those of you who are left will waste away in the lands of their enemies.
Lev 26:41	I sent them into the land of their enemies.
Lev 26:44	They are in the land of their enemies.
Deut 4:27	The LORD will scatter you among the peoples, and only a few of you will survive among the nations.
Deut 28:36	The LORD will drive you and the king you set over you to a nation unknown.
Deut 28:37	[You will be scorned in] all the nations where the LORD will drive you.
Deut 28:41	Sons and daughters . . . will go into captivity.
Deut 28:63	You will be uprooted from the land.
Deut 28:6⁚	The LORD will scatter you among all nations, from one end of the earth to the other.
Deut 28:68	The LORD will send you back in ships to Egypt. . . . There you will offer yourselves for sale [as slaves].
Deut 29:28	The LORD uprooted them from their land and thrust them into another land.
Deut 30:4	[You have been] banished to the most distant land under the heavens.
Deut 32:26	I said I would scatter them.
Is 5:13	My people will go into exile.
Is 22:18	He will roll you up tightly like a ball and throw you into a large country.

Is 24:1	[The LORD] will ruin its face [the earth] and scatter its inhabitants.
Is 49:21	I was bereaved and barren; I was exiled and rejected.
Jer 9:16	I will scatter them among the nations . . . until I have destroyed them.
Jer 22:10	He will never return nor see his native land again.
Jer 30:16	All your enemies will go into exile.
Jer 48:7	You too will be taken captive, and Chemosh will go into exile.
Jer 48:46	The people of Chemosh are destroyed; your sons are taken into exile and your daughters into captivity.
Jer 50:17	Israel is a scattered flock that lions have chased away.

Restoration

Deut 4:30	In later days you will return to the LORD your God and obey him.
Deut 30:3	The LORD your God . . . [will] gather you again from all the nations where he scattered you.
Deut 30:3	Then the LORD your God will restore your fortunes.
Deut 30:4	From there the LORD your God will gather you and bring you back.
Deut 30:5	He will bring you to the land that belonged to your fathers, and you will take possession of it.
Deut 30:6	The LORD your God will circumcise your hearts and the hearts of your descendants, so that you may love him with all your heart.
Deut 30:9	Then the LORD your God will make you most prosperous.
Is 7:3	Your son [is named] Shear-Jashub ["A remnant will return"].
Is 10:21-22	A remnant will return . . . a remnant will return.
Is 11:11	The LORD will reach out his hand a second time to reclaim the remnant that is left of his people.
Is 11:16	There will be a highway for the remnant of his people.
Is 37:31-32	A remnant of the house of Judah will take root below and bear fruit above. . . . Out of Jerusalem will come a remnant, and out of Mount Zion a band of survivors.
Is 43:5-6	I will bring your children from the east and gather you from the west. I will say to the north, "Give them up!" and to the south, "Do not hold them back."
Is 51:11	The ransomed of the LORD will return.
Is 54:7	For a brief moment I abandoned you, but with deep compassion I will bring you back.
Is 58:12	Your people will rebuild the ancient ruins and will raise up the age-old foundations.
Is 61:4	They will renew the ruined cities that have been devastated for generations.
Jer 5:18	I will not destroy you completely.
Jer 23:3	I myself will gather the remnant of my flock out of all the countries where I have driven them.
Jer 29:14	I will gather you from all the nations and places where I have banished you.
Jer 30:11	Though I completely destroy all the nations . . . I will not completely destroy you.
Jer 30:18	The city will be rebuilt on her ruins.
Jer 31:8	I will . . . gather them from the ends of the earth.
Jer 33:7	I will bring Judah and Israel back from captivity and will rebuild them as they were before.
Jer 46:27	I will surely save you out of a distant place, your descendants from the land of their exile.
Jer 48:47	I will restore the fortunes of Moab in days to come.
Jer 50:5	They will ask the way to Zion and turn their faces toward it. They will come and bind themselves to the LORD in an everlasting covenant that will not be forgotten.

4. Desolation and Acclamation
Desolation

Lev 26:22	Your roads will be deserted.

Lev 26:31	I will turn your cities into ruins and lay waste your sanctuaries.
Lev 26:32	I will lay waste the land, so that your enemies who live there will be appalled.
Lev 26:33	Your land will be laid waste, and your cities will lie in ruins.
Lev 26:34	The land will enjoy its sabbath years all the time it lies desolate. . . . The land will rest and enjoy its sabbaths.
Lev 26:35	All the time that it lies desolate, the land will have the rest it did not have during the sabbaths you lived in it.
Lev 26:43	The land will be deserted by them and will enjoy its sabbaths while it lies desolate without them.
Deut 28:51	They will devour . . . the crops of your land.
Deut 28:51	They will leave you no grain, new wine or oil.
Deut 29:23	The whole land will be a burning waste of salt and sulfur.
Josh 6:26	Cursed before the LORD is the man who undertakes to rebuild this city, Jericho:
Judg 5:6	In the days of Jael, the roads were abandoned.
Is 13:12	I will make man scarcer than pure gold.
Is 13:20	She [Babylon] will never be inhabited or lived in through all generations.
Is 14:23	I will sweep her [Babylon] with the broom of destruction.
Is 17:1	Damascus will . . . become a heap of ruins.
Is 17:9	Their strong cities . . . will be like places abandoned to thickets and undergrowth. And all will be desolation.
Is 24:3	The earth will be completely laid waste and totally plundered.
Is 24:10	The ruined city [of the earth] lies desolate.
Is 25:2	You have made the city a heap of rubble, . . . it will never be rebuilt.
Is 27:10	The fortified city stands desolate, an abandoned settlement, forsaken like the desert.
Is 32:14	The fortress will be abandoned, . . . citadel and watchtower will become a wasteland forever.
Is 32:19	Hail flattens the forest and the city is leveled completely.
Is 34:2	The LORD is angry with all nations. . . . He will totally destroy them, he will give them over to slaughter.
Is 34:5	The people [of Edom] I have totally destroyed.
Is 34:13	She will become a haunt for jackals, a home for owls.
Is 41:2	He turns them to dust with his sword, to windblown chaff with his bow.
Is 51:8	For the moth will eat them up like a garment.
Is 64:10	Your sacred cities have become a desert; even Zion is a desert, Jerusalem a desolation.
Jer 4:7	Your towns will lie in ruins without inhabitant.
Jer 4:23	I looked at the earth, and it was formless and empty.
Jer 4:26	The fruitful land was a desert; all its towns lay in ruins.
Jer 4:29	All the towns are deserted; no one lives in them.
Jer 6:8	I will . . . make your land desolate so no one can live in it.
Jer 9:11	I will make Jerusalem a heap of ruins, a haunt of jackals.
Jer 11:8	I brought on them all the curses of the covenant.
Jer 11:22-23	Their young men will die by the sword, their sons and daughters by famine. Not even a remnant will be left to them.
Jer 12:11	It will be made a wasteland, . . . the whole land will be laid waste.
Jer 22:19	He will have the burial of a donkey.
Jer 25:9	I will completely destroy them and make them an object of horror and scorn.
Jer 25:12	[I will] make it [Babylon] desolate forever.
Jer 44:11-12	I am determined to bring disaster on you and to destroy all Judah. I will take away the remnant of Judah who were determined to go to Egypt to settle there. They will all perish in Egypt.
Jer 46:19	Memphis will be laid waste and lie in ruins without inhabitant.
Jer 46:28	I completely destroy all the nations among which I scatter you.

Jer 47:4	The day has come to destroy all the Philistines and to cut off all survivors.
Jer 48:9	Her towns will become desolate, with no one to live in them.
Jer 50:13	Because of the LORD's anger she will not be inhabited but will be completely desolate.
Jer 50:39	Desert creatures and hyenas will live there, and there the owl will dwell. It will never again be inhabited or lived in from generation to generation.
Jer 51:43	Her towns will be desolate, a dry and desert land, a land where no one lives, through which no man travels.
Jer 51:44	I will punish Bel in Babylon. . . . Nations will no longer stream to him.

Acclamation

Gen 27:29	May nations serve you and peoples bow down to you.
2 Sam 22:45-46	Foreigners come cringing to me; . . . they come trembling from their strongholds.
Is 2:2	The mountain of the LORD's temple will be established as chief among the mountains; . . . all nations will stream to it.
Is 5:26	Here they come [from the ends of the earth], swiftly and speedily!
Is 11:9	The earth will be full of the knowledge of the LORD.
Is 18:7	At that time gifts will be brought to the LORD Almighty.
Is 24:14	From the west they acclaim the LORD's majesty. . . . In the east give glory to the LORD.
Is 25:3	Strong peoples will honor you; cities of ruthless nations will revere you.
Is 25:6	On this mountain the LORD Almighty will prepare a feast of rich food for all peoples.
Is 27:13	Those who were perishing in Assyria and those who were exiled in Egypt will come and worship the LORD on the holy mountain in Jerusalem.
Is 42:4	In his law the islands will put their hope.
Is 42:10	Sing . . . from the ends of the earth, . . . you islands, and all who live in them.
Is 45:6	From the rising of the sun to the place of its setting men may know there is none besides me.
Is 45:20	Gather together and come; assemble, you fugitives from the nations.
Is 45:23	Before me every knee shall bow.
Is 49:1	Listen to me, you islands; hear this, you distant nations.
Is 49:7	Kings will see you and rise up, princes will see and bow down, because of the LORD, . . . who has chosen you.
Is 49:12	They will come from afar—some from the north, some from the west, some from the region of Aswan.
Is 51:4	My justice will become a light to the nations.
Is 51:5	The islands will look to me and wait in hope for my arm.
Is 52:10	All the ends of the earth will see the salvation of our God.
Is 56:7	These I will bring to my holy mountain.
Is 57:13	[He] will inherit the land and possess my holy mountain.
Is 59:19	From the west, men will fear the name of the LORD, and from the rising of the sun, they will revere his glory.
Is 60:3	Nations will come to your light, and kings to the brightness of your dawn.
Is 60:9	Surely the islands look to me; . . . bringing your sons from afar.
Is 62:2	The nations will see your righteousness, and all kings your glory.
Is 62:7	He establishes Jerusalem and makes her the praise of the earth.
Is 66:18	[I] am about to come and gather all nations and tongues, and they will come and see my glory.
Is 66:19	They will proclaim my glory among the nations.
Is 66:23	All mankind will come and bow down before me.

5. Roads and Highways
Blessings

Is 11:16	There will be a highway for the remnant of his people.
Is 19:23	In that day there will be a highway from Egypt to Assyria.
Is 26:7	You make the way of the righteous smooth.
Is 35:8	A highway will be there; it will be called the Way of Holiness.
Is 40:3	Make straight in the wilderness a highway for our God. . . . Every mountain and hill made low; the rough ground shall become level, the rugged places a plain.
Is 42:16	I will . . . make the rough places smooth.
Is 43:19	I am making a way in the desert and streams in the wasteland.
Is 45:13	I will make all his ways straight.
Is 49:11	I will turn all my mountains into roads, and my highways will be raised up.
Is 51:10	[It was you] who made a road in the depths of the sea.
Is 57:14	Build up, build up, prepare the road!

Curses

Lev 26:22	Your roads will be deserted.
Judg 5:6	In the days of Jael, the roads were abandoned.
Is 33:8	The highways are deserted, no travelers are on the roads.

6. Exposure

Deut 28:26	Your carcasses will be food for all the birds of the air and the beasts of the earth, and there will be no one to frighten them away.
1 Sam 17:44	Come here, . . . and I'll give your flesh to the birds of the air and the beasts of the field!
1 Sam 17:46	I will give the carcasses of the Philistine army to the birds of the air and the beasts of the earth.
1 King 14:11	Dogs will eat those belonging to Jeroboam who die in the city, and the birds of the air will feed on those who die in the country.
1 Kings 16:4	Dogs will eat those belonging to Baasha who die in the city, and the birds of the air will feed on those who die in the country.
1 Kings 21:19	In the place where dogs licked up Naboth's blood, dogs will lick up your blood.
1 Kings 21:23	Dogs will devour Jezebel by the wall of Jezreel.
1 Kings 21:24	Dogs will eat those belonging to Ahab who die in the city, and the birds of the air will feed on those who die in the country.
2 Kings 9:36	On the plot of ground at Jezreel dogs will devour Jezebel's flesh.
Jer 7:33	Then the carcasses of this people will become food for the birds of the air and the beasts of the earth, and there will be no one to frighten them away [Judah].
Jer 9:22	The dead bodies of men will lie like refuse on the open field, like cut grain behind the reaper, with no one to gather them [Zion].
Jer 15:3	I will send four kinds of destroyers against them, . . . the sword to kill and the dogs to drag away and the birds of the air and the beasts of the earth to devour and destroy [Jerusalem].
Jer 16:4	Their dead bodies will become food for the birds of the air and the beasts of the earth [Judah].
Jer 19:7	I will give their carcasses as food to the birds of the air and the beasts of the earth [Judah].
Jer 34:20	Their dead bodies will become food for the birds of the air and the beasts of the earth [Jerusalem].
Ezek 29:5	I will give you as food to the beasts of the earth and the birds of the air [Egypt].
Ezek 32:4	I will let all the birds of the air settle on you and all the beasts of the earth gorge themselves on you [Egypt].
Ezek 33:27	Those out in the country I will give to the wild animals to be devoured [Judah].
Ezek 39:4	I will give you as food to all kinds of carrion birds and to the wild animals [Gog].

Ezek 39:17-18	Call out to every kind of bird and all the wild animals: "Assemble and come together from all around to the sacrifice I am preparing for you, the great sacrifice on the mountains of Israel. There you will eat flesh and drink blood. You will eat the flesh of mighty men and drink the blood of the princes of the earth.

7. Forever

Num 24:20	Amalek was first among the nations, but he will come to ruin at last.
Deut 15:17	He will become your servant for life.
Deut 28:46	[These curses] will be a sign and a wonder to you and your descendants forever.
Josh 4:7	These stones are to be a memorial to the people of Israel forever.
1 Sam 1:22	After the boy is weaned, I will take him and present him before the LORD, and he will live there always.
1 Sam 20:23	The LORD is witness between you and me forever.
1 Kings 1:31	May my lord King David live forever!
1 Kings 9:3	I have consecrated this temple, . . . by putting my Name there forever.
1 Kings 12:7	They will always be your servants.
2 Kings 9:6	I anoint you king over the LORD's people Israel.
2 Kings 22:17	My anger will burn against this place and will not be quenched.
1 Chron 28:9	If you forsake [the LORD], he will reject you forever.
Ps 9:5	You . . . have destroyed the wicked; and you have blotted out their name for ever and ever.
Ps 21:4	[The king] asked you for life, and you gave it to him—length of days, for ever and ever.
Is 17:1	Damascus will no longer be a city but will become a heap of ruins.
Is 32:14	The fortress will be abandoned, . . . citadel and watchtower will become a wasteland forever [Jerusalem].
Is 32:17	The effect of righteousness will be quietness and confidence forever.
Is 34:10	[Edom] will not be quenched night and day; its smoke will rise forever.
Is 34:17	They will possess it forever and dwell there from generation to generation.
Is 45:17	Israel will be saved by the LORD with an everlasting salvation; you will never be put to shame or disgraced, to ages everlasting.
Is 59:21	As for me, this is my covenant with them, . . . My Spirit, who is on you, and my words that I have put in your mouth will not depart from your mouth, or from the mouths of your children, or from the mouths of their descendants from this time on and forever, says the LORD.
Jer 7:20	My anger and my wrath will be poured out on this place, . . . and it will burn and not be quenched [Judah].
Jer 15:14	For my anger will kindle a fire that will burn against you.
Jer 17:25	[Jerusalem] will be inhabited forever.
Jer 17:27	An unquenchable fire in the gates of Jerusalem . . . will consume her fortresses.
Jer 18:16	Their land will be laid waste, an object of lasting scorn.
Jer 23:40	I will bring upon you everlasting disgrace— everlasting shame that will not be forgotten [Judah].
Jer 32:40	I will make an everlasting covenant with them: I will never stop doing good to them [Judah].
Jer 35:19	Jonadab son of Recab will never fail to have a man to serve me.
Joel 3:20	Judah will be inhabited forever and Jerusalem through all generations.
Jon 2:6	I sank down; the earth beneath barred me in forever.

8. Shortness of Time

Is 9:14	The LORD will cut off from Israel both head and tail, . . . in a single day.
Is 10:17	In a single day it will burn and consume his thorns and his briers.
Is 32:10	In little more than a year you who feel secure will tremble; the grape harvest will fail.

Is 47:9	These will overtake you in a moment, on a single day: loss of children and widowhood.
Is 47:11	A catastrophe you cannot foresee will suddenly come upon you.
Is 54:7	For a brief moment I abandoned you, but with deep compassion I will bring you back.
Is 56:1	For my salvation is close at hand and my righteousness will soon be revealed.
Is 60:22	In its time I will do this swiftly.
Jer 4:20	In an instant my tents are destroyed, my shelter in a moment.
Jer 50:24	I set a trap for you, O Babylon, and you were caught before you knew it.
Jer 50:44	I will chase Babylon from its land in an instant.

Appendix C

END-TIMES IMAGERY
IN THE NEW TESTAMENT

It becomes evident, when analyzing the end-times imagery in the New Testament, that the imagery clusters around certain themes. Within each theme, various expressions were used to describe the same concept.

Notes regarding the collection of verses: I attempted to be comprehensive, but I do not claim to be exhaustive. By necessity there is some repetition of references because of multiple ideas in the same verse. Asterisks indicate references in the Gospels with synoptic parallels; I did not include citations to parallel passages.

1. Striking Presentation of the Transcendent Lord: *He will appear in blazing fire*

Mt 16:27	The Son of Man is going to come in his Father's glory with his angels.
Mt 24:30	The Son of Man [will be] coming on the clouds of the sky, with power and great glory.
Mt 24:31	He will send his angels with a loud trumpet call.
Mt 25:31	The Son of Man comes in his glory, and all [his] angels with him.
Mt 26:64*	In the future you will see the Son of Man sitting at the right hand of the Mighty One and coming on the clouds of heaven.
Acts 1:11	This same Jesus . . . will come back in the same way you have seen him go into heaven.
Eph 1:20-21	[Christ is seated at God's] right hand in the heavenly realms, far above all rule and authority, power and dominion, and every title that can be given, not only in the present age but also in the one to come.
1 Thess 4:16	The Lord himself will come down from heaven, with a loud command, with the voice of the archangel and with the trumpet call of God.
1 Thess 4:17	[We] will be caught up… in the clouds to meet the Lord in the air.
2 Thess 1:7	The Lord Jesus is revealed from heaven in blazing fire.
2 Thess 1:10	He comes to be glorified in his holy people and to be marveled at among all those who have believed.
2 Thess 2:8	The Lord Jesus will overthrow with the breath of his mouth and destroy by the splendor of his coming.
1 Pet 1:7	When Jesus Christ is revealed . . .
1 Pet 4:13	When [Christ's] glory is revealed . . .
Jude 14	The Lord is coming with thousands upon thousands of his holy ones.
Rev 1:7	He is coming with the clouds, and every eye will see him.
Rev 1:12-18	I saw seven golden lampstands, and among the lampstands was someone "like a son of man."
Rev 14:1	There before me was the Lamb, standing on Mount Zion, and with him 144,000 who had his name and his Father's name written on their foreheads.
Rev 14:14	There before me was a white cloud, and seated on the cloud was one "like a son of man" with a crown of gold on his head and a sharp sickle in his hand.
Rev 19:11-12	I saw heaven standing open and there before me was a white horse, whose rider is called Faithful and True. With justice he judges and makes war. His eyes are like blazing fire.

2. Unprecedented Turmoil: *Men will faint from terror*

Mt 24:6-7*	You will hear of wars and rumors of wars. . . . Nation will rise against nation, and kingdom against kingdom. There will be famines and earthquakes.
Mt 24:10-15*	Many will turn away from the faith and will betray and hate each other. . . . False prophets will appear. . . . Because of the increase of wickedness, the love of most will grow cold. . . . "The abomination that causes desolation" [will stand in the holy place].
Mt 24:16-21	Flee to the mountains. . . . Let no one . . . take anything out of the house. . . . How dreadful . . . for pregnant women and nursing mothers! Pray that your flight will not take place in winter or on the Sabbath. . . . There will be great distress, un-equaled from the beginning of the world . . . and never to be equaled again.
Mt 24:37	It was [the same] in the days of Noah.
Lk 17:22	The time is coming when you will long to see one of the days of the Son of Man, but you will not see it.
Lk 17:28	It was the same in the days of Lot.
Lk 17:33-34	Whoever tries to keep his life will lose it, and whoever loses his life will preserve it. . . . Two people will be in one bed; one will be taken and the other left. Two women will be grinding; . . . one will be taken and the other left.
Lk 21:16-17	You will be betrayed even by parents, brothers, relatives and friends, and they will put some of you to death. All men will hate you because of me.
Lk 21:23-26	There will be great distress in the land and wrath against this people. They will fall by the sword and will be taken as prisoners. . . . Jerusalem will be trampled on by the Gentiles, . . . nations will be in anguish and perplexity at the roaring and tossing of the sea. Men will faint from terror, apprehensive of what is coming on the world.
Lk 23:28-30	Weep for yourselves and for your children. For the time will come when you will say, "Blessed are the barren women, . . . and the breasts that never nursed!" . . . "They will say to the mountains, 'Fall on us!' "
Jn 9:4	Night is coming, when no one can work.
Rom 8:22-23	The whole creation has been groaning as in the pains of childbirth. . . . We ourselves, . . . groan inwardly as we wait eagerly for our adoption as sons.
1 Thess 2:16	They always heap up their sins to the limit. The wrath of God has come upon them at last.
1 Thess 5:3	While people are saying, "Peace and safety," destruction will come on them sud-denly, as labor pains on a pregnant woman, and they will not escape.
2 Tim 3:1	There will be terrible times in the last days.
Rev 6:4, 6	Its rider was given power to take peace from the earth and to make men slay each other.
Rev 6:15-17	Then the kings of the earth, princes, the generals, the rich, the mighty, and every slave and every free man hid in caves. . . . They called to the mountains and the rocks, "Fall on us and hide us from the face of him who sits on the throne and from the wrath of the Lamb!"
Rev 17:2	The kings of the earth committed adultery [with the great prostitute] and the inhab-itants of the earth were intoxicated with the wine of her adulteries.
Rev 17:16	The beast and the ten horns you saw will hate the prostitute. They will bring her to ruin and leave her naked; they will eat her flesh and burn her with fire.
Rev 18:5	Her sins [Babylon] are piled up to heaven, and God has remembered her crimes.
Rev 18:11	The merchants of the earth will weep and mourn over her [Babylon] because no one buys their cargoes any more.

3. Nearness of the End: *The beginning of birth pains*

Mt 3:2*	The kingdom of heaven is near [cf. Mt 4:17].
Mt 3:10*	The ax is already at the root of the trees.
Mt 16:3	You know how to interpret the appearance of the sky, but you cannot interpret the signs of the times.

Mt 24:6*	Such things must happen, but the end is still to come.
Mt 24:8*	These are the beginning of birth pains.
Mt 24:14	This gospel of the kingdom will be preached in the whole world . . . and then the end will come.
Mt 24:22*	For the sake of the elect those days will be shortened.
Mt 24:27	As lightning that comes from the east is visible even in the west, so will be the coming of the Son of Man.
Mt 24:28	Wherever there is a carcass, the vultures will gather.
Mt 24:34*	This generation will certainly not pass away until all these things have happened.
Mt 24:33*	When you see all these things, you know it is near, right at the door.
Mt 24:36	No one knows about that day or hour, not even the angels in heaven, nor the Son, but only the Father.
Mt 24:37-41	As it was in the days of Noah, . . . they knew nothing about what would happen until the flood came and took them all away. That is how it will be at the coming of the Son of Man. Two men will be in the field; one will be taken the other left. Two women will be grinding . . . one will be taken the other left.
Mt 24:43	If the owner of the house had known at what time of night the thief was coming, he would have kept watch.
Mt 24:44	The Son of Man will come at an hour when you do not expect him.
Mt 24:50*	The master of that servant will come on a day when he does not expect him and at an hour he is not aware of.
Mt 25:10	While they were on their way to buy the oil, the bridegroom arrived.
Mt 25:13	Keep watch, because you do not know the day or the hour.
Mk 13:33	Be alert! You do not know when that time will come.
Mk 13:35	You do not know when the owner of the house will come back—whether in the evening, or at midnight, or when the rooster crows, or at dawn.
Lk 12:56	You know how to interpret the appearance of the earth and the sky. How is it that you don't know how to interpret this present time?
Lk 21:20	When you see Jerusalem being surrounded by armies, you will know that its desolation is near.
Lk 21:24	Jerusalem will be trampled on by the Gentiles until the times of the Gentiles are fulfilled.
Jn 12:31	Now is the time for judgment on this world.
Acts 1:7	It is not for you to know the times or dates the Father has set by his own authority.
1 Cor 7:29	The time is short.
1 Thess 2:16	The wrath of God has come upon them at last.
1 Thess 5:1-2	About times and dates we do not need to write to you, for you know very well that the day of the Lord will come like a thief in the night.
1 Thess 5:4	But you, brothers, are not in darkness so that this day should surprise you like a thief.
2 Thess 2:7	The secret power of lawlessness is already at work;
Heb 10:37	He who is coming will come and will not delay [Hab 2:3].
Jas 5:9	The Judge is standing at the door!
1 Pet 4:5	[He] is ready to judge the living and the dead.
1 Pet 4:7	The end of all things is near.
1 Pet 4:17	It is time for judgment to begin.
2 Pet 3:10	The day of the Lord will come like a thief.
Rev 1:1	The revelation of Jesus Christ [is given] to show his servants what must soon take place.
Rev 1:3	The time is near.
Rev 3:3	I will come like a thief, and you will not know at what time I will come to you.
Rev 4:1	I will show you what must take place after this.
Rev 10:6	There will be no more delay!

Rev 14:7	The hour of his judgment has come.
Rev 16:15	I come like a thief! Blessed is he who stays awake and keeps his clothes with him.
Rev 22:7	I am coming soon! [cf. Rev 22:12, 20]
Rev 22:10	The time is near.

4. Terrifying Judgment: *The wine of God's fury*

Mt 3:7*	Who warned you to flee from the coming wrath?
Mt 3:12*	He will . . . burn up the chaff with unquenchable fire.
Mt 8:11	The subjects of the kingdom will be thrown outside, into the darkness, where there will be weeping and gnashing of teeth.
Mt 11:24	It will be more bearable for Sodom on the day of judgment than for you [cf. Lk 10:12, 14].
Mt 12:36	Men will have to give account on the day of judgment
Mt 25:30	Throw that worthless servant outside, into the darkness, where there will be weeping and gnashing of teeth.
Mt 25:41	Depart from me, you who are cursed, into the eternal fire prepared for the devil and his angels.
Mt 25:46	They will go away to eternal punishment.
Lk 10:15	You will go down to the depths.
Lk 11:31	The Queen of the South will rise at the judgment . . . of this generation and condemn them.
Lk 11:32	The men of Nineveh will stand up at the judgment with this generation and condemn it.
Lk 13:28	There will be weeping there, and gnashing of teeth.
Jn 5:28-29	A time is coming when all who are in their graves will hear his voice and come out. . . . Those who have done evil will rise to be condemned.
Jn 12:31	Now is the time for judgment on this world.
Acts 17:31	He will judge the world with justice.
1 Thess 2:16	The wrath of God has come upon them at last.
2 Thess 1:9	They will be punished with everlasting destruction and shut out from the presence of the Lord.
Heb 9:27	Man is destined to die once, and after that to face judgment.
Jas 5:9	The Judge is standing at the door!
1 Pet 4:5	[He] is ready to judge the living and the dead.
1 Pet 4:17	It is time for judgment to begin.
2 Pet 2:3	Their condemnation has long been hanging over them, and their destruction has not been sleeping.
2 Pet 2:9	Hold the unrighteous for the day of judgment.
Jude 7	[They suffer] the punishment of eternal fire.
Rev 2:22-23	I will cast her on a bed of suffering. . . . I will strike her children dead.
Rev 3:16	I am about to spit you out of my mouth.
Rev 6:16	[Hide us from] the wrath of the Lamb!
Rev 14:10	Drink of the wine of God's fury.
Rev 14:19-20	The angel swung his sickle on the earth, gathered its grapes and threw them into the great winepress of God's wrath. They were trampled in the winepress outside the city, and blood flowed out of the press, rising as high as the horses' bridles for a distance of 1,600 stadia.
Rev 19:15	Out of his mouth comes a sharp sword with which to strike down the nations. . . . He treads the winepress of the fury of the wrath of God Almighty.
Rev 19:17-18	Come, gather together . . . [to] eat the flesh of . . . all people.
Rev 20:11	I saw a great white throne.
Rev 20:15	If anyone's name was not found written in the book of life, he was thrown into the lake of fire.
Rev 21:8	Their place will be in the fiery lake of burning sulfur.

5. Horrors in the Heavens: *The name of the star is Wormwood*

Mt 24:29*	The sun will be darkened, and the moon will not give its light; the stars will fall from the sky, and the heavenly bodies will be shaken [cf. Is 13:10; 34:4; Ezek 32:7; Joel 2:10, 31; 3:15].
Mt 24:35*	Heaven and earth will pass away.
Lk 21:25	There will be signs in the sun, moon and stars.
Acts 2:19-20	I will show wonders in the heaven above. . . . The sun will be turned to darkness and the moon to blood [cf. Joel 2:30-31].
2 Pet 3:7	The present heavens and earth are reserved for fire.
2 Pet 3:10	The heavens will disappear with a roar; the elements will be destroyed by fire.
2 Pet 3:12	That day will bring about the destruction of the heavens by fire, and the elements will melt in the heat.
Rev 6:12-14	The sun turned black like sackcloth made of goat hair, the whole moon turned blood red, and the stars in the sky fell to earth. . . . The sky receded like a scroll.
Rev 8:5	There came peals of thunder, rumblings, [and] flashes of lightning.
Rev 8:7	Hail and fire mixed with blood, and it was hurled down upon the earth.
Rev 8:10-11	A great star, blazing like a torch, fell from the sky on a third of the rivers and on the springs of water—the name of the star is Wormwood.
Rev 8:12	A third of the sun was struck, a third of the moon, and a third of the stars, so that a third of them turned dark. A third of the day was without light, and also a third of the night.
Rev 9:2	The sun and sky were darkened by the smoke from the Abyss.
Rev 11:19	There came flashes of lightning, rumblings, peals of thunder, an earthquake and a great hailstorm.
Rev 13:13	[He caused] fire to come down from heaven to earth.
Rev 16:18	Then there came flashes of lightning, rumblings, [and] peals of thunder.
Rev 20:9	Fire came down from heaven and devoured them.

6. Horrors on Earth: *Huge hailstones of about one hundred pounds each*

Mt 24:2*	Not one stone here will be left on another.
Lk 21:11*	There will be great earthquakes, famines and pestilences in various places, and fearful events.
Luke 21:25	Nations will be in anguish . . . at the roaring and tossing of the sea.
Acts 2:19	I will show . . . signs on the earth below, blood and fire and billows of smoke [cf. Joel 2:30-31].
2 Pet 3:7	The present heavens and earth are reserved for fire, being kept for the day of judgment.
2 Pet 3:10	The earth and everything in it will be laid bare.
Rev 6:8	They were given power over a fourth of the earth to kill by sword, famine and plague.
Rev 6:14	Every mountain and island was removed from its place.
Rev 7:1-2	Four angels . . . [were] holding back the four winds of the earth to prevent any wind from blowing on the land or on the sea or on any tree.
Rev 8:5	The angel...hurled it [fire] on the earth; and there [was] . . . an earthquake.
Rev 8:7	Hail and fire mixed with blood [and] was hurled down upon the earth. A third of the earth was burned up, a third of the trees were burned up, and all the green grass.
Rev 8:8-9	A huge mountain, all ablaze, was thrown into the sea. A third of the sea turned into blood, a third of the living creatures in the sea died, and a third of all the ships were destroyed.
Rev 8:10-11	A great star, blazing like a torch, fell from the sky on a third of the rivers and on the springs of water. . . . A third of the waters turned bitter, and many people died.
Rev 11:6	These men have power to shut up the sky so that it will not rain, . . . power to turn the waters into blood and to strike the earth with every kind of plague.

Rev 11:13	There was a severe earthquake and a tenth of the city collapsed. Seven thousand people were killed.
Rev 16:2	Ugly and painful sores broke out on the people.
Rev 16:3	The sea . . . turned into blood like that of a dead man, and every living thing in the sea died.
Rev 16:4	The rivers and springs of water . . . became blood.
Rev 16:8	[The sun scorched the] people with fire. They were seared by the intense heat.
Rev 16:10-11	Men gnawed their tongues in agony. . . . because of their pains and their sores.
Rev 16:12	The great river Euphrates . . . dried up.
Rev 16:18-19	No earthquake like it has ever occurred. . . . The great city split into three parts, and the cities of the nations collapsed.
Rev 16:20-21	Every island fled away and the mountains could not be found. . . . Huge hailstones of about a hundred pounds each fell upon men, . . . the plague was so terrible.

7. Horrors of Animals: *Their tails were like snakes*

Rev 9:3	Out of the smoke locusts came down upon the earth and were given power like that of scorpions.
Rev 9:7-10	The locusts looked like horses prepared for battle. . . . They wore something like crowns of gold, and their faces resembled human faces. Their hair was like women's hair, and their teeth were like lions' teeth. They had breastplates like breastplates of iron, and the sound of their wings was like the thundering of many horses and chariots rushing into battle. They had tails and stings like scorpions.
Rev 9:17-19	The heads of the horses resembled the heads of lions, and out of their mouths came fire, smoke and sulfur. A third of mankind was killed. . . . The power of the horses was in their mouths and in their tails; for their tails were like snakes, having heads with which they inflict injury.
Rev 12:3	[The tail of] an enormous red dragon with seven heads and ten horns and seven crowns . . . swept a third of the stars out of the sky and flung them to the earth.
Rev 16:13	I saw three evil spirits that looked like frogs.

8. Preservation of the Remnant: *He will gather his elect from the four winds*

Mt 24:13*	He who stands firm to the end will be saved.
Mt 24:22*	For the sake of the elect those days will be shortened.
Mt 24:31*	They will gather his elect from the four winds, from one end of the heavens to the other.
1 Thess 1:10	[He] rescues us from the coming wrath.
1 Thess 5:9	God did not appoint us to suffer wrath but to receive salvation.
2 Thess 1:10	He comes to be glorified in his holy people.
2 Thess 2:1	[I write] concerning the coming of our Lord Jesus Christ and our being gathered to him.
Rev 6:9	I saw under the altar the souls of those who had been slain.
Rev 7:4-9	[Sealed were] 144,000 . . . from all the tribes of Israel. . . . [It] was a great multitude that no one could count, . . . standing before the throne . . . wearing white robes and . . . holding palm branches in their hands.
Rev 7:14	These are they who have come out of the great tribulation; they have washed their robes and made them white in the blood of the Lamb.
Rev 14:1	There before me was the Lamb; . . . with him [were] 144,000 who had his name and his Father's name written on their foreheads.

9. New Order and Society: *The righteous will shine like the sun in the kingdom*

Mt 3:2*	The kingdom of heaven is near [cf. Mt 4:17].
Mt 10:7	The kingdom of heaven is near.
Mt 13:43	Then the righteous will shine like the sun in the kingdom of their Father.
Mt 16:28*	They see the Son of Man coming in his kingdom.

Mt 19:28	At the renewal of all things, . . . the Son of Man sits on his glorious throne.
Mt 25:34	Come, you who are blessed by my Father; take your inheritance, the kingdom prepared for you since the creation of the world.
Mt 26:29*	I [will] drink it [this fruit of the vine] anew with you in my Father's kingdom.
Mk 11:10	Blessed is the coming kingdom of our father David!
Lk 1:33	His kingdom will never end.
Lk 13:28	You [will] see . . . all the prophets in the kingdom of God.
Lk 13:29	Feast in the kingdom of God.
Lk 14:15	Blessed is the man who will eat at the feast in the kingdom of God.
Lk 21:31	When you see these things happening, you know that the kingdom of God is near.
Lk 22:16	I will not eat it again until it finds fulfillment in the kingdom of God.
Lk 22:18	I will not drink again of the fruit of the vine until the kingdom of God comes.
Lk 22:30	You may eat and drink at my table in my kingdom.
Acts 1:6	Lord, are you at this time going to restore the kingdom to Israel?
1 Cor 15:24	Then the end will come, when he hands over the kingdom to God the Father after he has destroyed all dominion, authority and power.
Eph 1:10	The times will have reached their fulfillment—to bring all things in heaven and on earth together under one head, even Christ.
1 Thess 2:12	God . . . calls you into his kingdom and glory.
2 Tim 4:1	[He] will judge the living and the dead, and in view of his appearing and his kingdom.
2 Pet 1:11	You will receive a rich welcome into the eternal kingdom of our Lord and Savior Jesus Christ.
2 Pet 3:13	We are looking forward to a new heaven and a new earth, the home of righteousness.
Rev 11:15	The kingdom of the world has become the kingdom of our Lord and of his Christ, and he will reign forever and ever.
Rev 11:17	You have taken your great power and have begun to reign.
Rev 12:10	Now have come the salvation and the power and the kingdom of our God, and the authority of his Christ.
Rev 21:1	Then I saw a new heaven and a new earth, for the first heaven and the first earth had passed away.

10. Rewards for the Righteous: *We will reign with him*

Mt 5:11-12*	Blessed are you when people insult you, [or] persecute you. . . . Great is your reward in heaven.
Mt 16:27	The Son of Man is going to come in his Father's glory with his angels, and then he will reward each person according to what he has done.
Mt 19:28	You who have followed me will also sit on twelve thrones, judging the twelve tribes of Israel.
Mt 25:34	Come, you who are blessed by my Father; take your inheritance, the kingdom prepared for you since the creation of the world.
Mt 25:46	The righteous [go] to eternal life.
Rom 8:17	If indeed we share in his sufferings, . . . we may also share in his glory.
1 Cor 3:13-14	His work will be shown for what it is, because the Day will bring it to light. . . . If what he has built survives, he will receive his reward.
Eph 1:14	[The Spirit] is a deposit guaranteeing our inheritance until the redemption of those who are God's possession.
Eph 2:7	In the coming ages he [will] show the incomparable riches of his grace, expressed in his kindness to us.
Col 3:24	You will receive an inheritance from the Lord as a reward.
2 Tim 2:12	If we endure, we will also reign with him.
2 Tim 4:8	There is in store for me the crown of righteousness, which . . . the righteous Judge . . . will award to me on that day.

Jas 1:12	Blessed is the man who perseveres under trial. . . . He will receive the crown of life.
1 Pet 1:5	[You] are shielded by God's power until the coming of the salvation that is ready to be revealed in the last time.
1 Pet 5:4	When the Chief Shepherd appears, you will receive the crown of glory.
2 John 7-8	Many deceivers . . . have gone out into the world. . . . Watch out that you do not lose what you have worked for, but that you may be rewarded fully.
Rev 2:7	To him who overcomes, I will give the right to eat from the tree of life.
Rev 2:10	I will give you the crown of life.
Rev 2:17	To him who overcomes, I will give some of the hidden manna . . . [and] a white stone with a new name written on it.
Rev 2:26-28	To him who overcomes, . . . I will give authority over the nations—"He will rule them with an iron scepter; he will dash them to pieces like pottery" [Ps 2:9]. . . . I will also give him the morning star.
Rev 3:5	He who overcomes will . . . be dressed in white. I will never blot out his name from the book of life, but I will acknowledge his name before my Father and his angels.
Rev 3:12	Him who overcomes I will make a pillar in the temple of my God. . . . I will write on him the name of my God and the name of the city of my God, the new Jerusalem, . . . and I will also write on him my new name.
Rev 3:21	To him who overcomes, I will give the right to sit with me on my throne.
Rev 19:9	Blessed are those who are invited to the wedding supper of the Lamb!
Rev 20:4	I saw thrones on which were seated those who had been given authority to judge.
Rev 22:12	I am coming soon! My reward is with me, and I will give to everyone according to what he has done.

11. Satanic Adversaries: *The angels will seize the dragon*

Mt 24:11	Many false prophets will appear and deceive many.
Mt 24:24*	False Christs and false prophets will appear and perform great signs and miracles to deceive even the elect.
2 Thess 2:3-4	The man of lawlessness is revealed, . . . [and] will oppose and will exalt himself over everything that is called God or is worshiped.
2 Thess 2:7	The secret power of lawlessness is already at work.
2 Thess 2:9-10	The coming of the lawless one will be in accordance with the work of Satan displayed in all kinds of counterfeit miracles, signs and wonders, and in every sort of evil.
2 Pet 2:1-3	[False teachers] will secretly introduce destructive heresies, even denying the sovereign Lord. . . . These teachers will exploit you with stories they have made up.
2 Pet 2:10	Bold and arrogant, these men are not afraid to slander celestial beings.
2 Pet 2:12, 17	They are like brute beasts, creatures of instinct, born only to be caught and destroyed. . . . These men are springs without water and mists driven by a storm.
2 Pet 3:3-4	In the last days scoffers will come, scoffing and following their own evil desires. They will say, "Where is this 'coming' he promised?"
Jude 8, 12-13	These dreamers pollute their own bodies, reject authority and slander celestial beings. . . . They are clouds without rain, blown along by the wind; . . . wandering stars, for whom blackest darkness has been reserved forever.
Rev 2:9	I know the slander of those who say they are Jews and are not, but are a synagogue of Satan [cf. Rev 3:9].
Rev 2:14-15	You have people there who hold to the teaching of Balaam. . . . Likewise you also have those who hold to the teaching of the Nicolaitans.
Rev 2:20	You tolerate that woman Jezebel. . . . By her teaching she misleads my servants.
Rev 11:7	The beast that comes up from the Abyss will attack them, and overpower them and kill them.
Rev 12:3-4	Then another sign appeared in heaven: an enormous red dragon with seven heads and ten horns and seven crowns on his heads. His tail swept a third of the stars out of the sky and flung them to the earth.

Rev 13:1	I saw a beast coming out of the sea.
Rev 13:11	I saw another beast, coming out of the earth.
Rev 16:13-14	I saw three evil spirits that looked like frogs. . . . They are spirits of demons performing miraculous signs.
Rev 17:1	I will show you the punishment of the great prostitute, who sits on many waters.
Rev 19:2	He has condemned the great prostitute who corrupted the earth by her adulteries.
Rev 19:19-20	I saw the beast . . . make war against the rider on the horse. . . . But the beast was captured, and with him the false prophet.
Rev 20:2	He seized the dragon, that ancient serpent, who is the devil, or Satan, and bound him for a thousand years.
Rev 20:7	When the thousand years are over, Satan will be released from his prison.

12. Backlash of Evil: *Then you will be handed over to be persecuted*

Mt 24:9*	Then you will be handed over to be persecuted and put to death, and you will be hated by all nations because of me.
Mt 24:10	Many will turn away from the faith and will betray and hate each other.
Lk 21:23-24	There will be . . . wrath against this people. They will fall by the sword and will be taken as prisoners to all the nations. Jerusalem will be trampled on by the Gentiles.
Jn 16:31	A time is coming, and has come, when you will be scattered, each to his own home.
Rev 2:10	The devil will put some of you in prison to test you, and you will suffer persecution for ten days.
Rev 2:13	Antipas, my faithful witness, who was put to death in your city—where Satan lives.
Rev 13:7	He was given power to make war against the saints and to conquer them.
Rev 17:6	The woman was drunk with the blood of the saints, the blood of those who bore testimony to Jesus.
Rev 18:24	In her was found the blood of prophets and of the saints.
Rev 20:4	I saw the souls of those who had been beheaded because of their testimony for Jesus.

Notes

Preface
[1]C. Marvin Pate and Calvin B. Haines Jr., *Doomsday Delusions: What's Wrong with Predictions About the End of the World* (Downers Grove, Ill.: InterVarsity Press, 1995); Francis X. Gumerlock, *The Day and the Hour: A Chronicle of Christianity's Perennial Fascination with Predicting the End of the World* (Atlanta: American Vision, 2000).

[2]For example: Robert G. Clouse, Robert N. Hosack and Richard V. Pierard, *The New Millennium Manual: A Once and Future Guide* (Grand Rapids, Mich.: Baker, 1999); Richard Bauckham and Trevor Hart, *Hope Against Hope: Christian Eschatology at the Turn of the Millennium* (Grand Rapids, Mich.: Eerdmans, 1999); Daniel J. Lewis, *Three Crucial Questions About the Last Days* (Grand Rapids, Mich.: Baker, 1998); Richard Kyle, *The Last Days Are Here Again: A History of the End Times* (Grand Rapids, Mich.: Baker, 1998).

[3]On the theory of metaphor in chapter three, however, I am dependent on many who have preceded me.

[4]But cf. Rudolf Bultmann, "Is Exegesis Without Presuppositions Possible?" reprinted in *Existence and Faith: The Shorter Writings of R. Bultmann,* trans. S. Ogden (New York: Meridian, 1960), pp. 289-96.

[5]I was studying with James Charlesworth in 1974, while he was on the faculty at Duke University; his *Old Testament Pseudepigrapha* (Garden City, NY: Doubleday, 1983, 1985) was in preparation during that time.

[6]D. Brent Sandy and Ronald L. Giese Jr., eds., *Cracking Old Testament Codes: A Guide to Interpreting the Literary Genres of the Old Testament* (Nashville: Broadman & Holman, 1995).

[7]For the current status of the study of prophecy and apocalyptic, with excellent bibliography, see two chapters in *The Face of Old Testament Studies: A Survey of Contemporary Approaches*, ed. David W. Baker and Bill T. Arnold (Grand Rapids, Mich.: Baker, 1999): David W. Baker, "Israelite Prophets and Prophecy," pp. 266-94; and John N. Oswalt, "Recent Studies in Old Testament Apocalyptic," pp. 369-90.

[8]Daniel Taylor, *The Myth of Certainty: The Reflective Christian and the Risk of Commitment* (1986; reprint, Downers Grove, Ill.: InterVarsity Press, 1999).

[9]D. Brent Sandy, *The Production and Use of Vegetable Oils in Ptolemaic Egypt,* Bulletin of the American Society of Papyrologists Supplements 6 (Atlanta: Scholars Press, 1989).

Chapter 1: What Makes Prophecy Powerful?
[1]Gary V. Smith, *The Prophets as Preachers: An Introduction to the Hebrew Prophets* (Nashville: Broadman & Holman, 1994). For understanding the rhetoric of the prophets, see Martin Warner, ed., *The Bible as Rhetoric: Studies in Biblical Persuasion and Credibility* (London: Routledge, 1990); Phyllis Trible, *Rhetorical Criticism: Context, Method and the Book of Jonah*, Guides to Biblical Scholarship (Minneapolis: Fortress, 1994); and Dale Patrick, *The Rhetoric of Revelation in the Hebrew Bible,* Overtures to Biblical Theology (Minneapolis: Fortress, 1999).

[2]"The [prophets'] language is luminous and explosive, firm and contingent, harsh and compassionate, a fusion of contradictions." Abraham J. Heschel, *The Prophets*, 2 vols. in 1 (New York: HarperCollins, 1962), p. 7. See also: Walter Brueggemann, *Texts That Linger, Words That*

Explode: Listening to Prophetic Voices, ed. Patrick D. Miller (Minneapolis: Fortress, 2000);
Cyril Barrett, "The Language of Ecstasy and the Ecstasy of Language," in *The Bible as Rhetoric: Studies in Biblical Persuasion and Credibility,* ed. Martin Warner (London: Routledge, 1990), pp. 205-28.

[3]For explanation of the unique features of Hebrew thought and language, see J. C. L. Gibson, *Language and Imagery in the Old Testament* (Peabody, Mass.: Hendrickson, 1998); and G. B. Caird, *The Language and Imagery of the Bible* (London: Gerald Duckworth, 1980), reprinted with a new introduction by N. T. Wright (Grand Rapids, Mich.: Eerdmans, 1997), pp. 109-21. For the prophets the issue is largely poetic language; see Robert Alter, *The Art of Biblical Poetry* (New York: Basic Books, 1985), p. 139. Alter comments, "What essentially distinguishes prophetic verse from other kinds of biblical poetry is its powerfully vocative character." On poetry and other genres in the Bible, see, e.g., Leland Ryken, *Words of Delight: A Literary Introduction to the Bible,* 2nd ed. (Grand Rapids, Mich.: Baker, 1992).

[4]Many other examples could be cited, both in Isaiah and in other prophets: "The grave enlarges its appetite and opens its mouth without limit" (Is 5:14). "[They will be] driven before the wind like chaff on the hills, like tumbleweed before a gale" (Is 17:13). "The Lord gives you the bread of adversity and the water of affliction" (Is 30:20). "Death has climbed in through our windows and has entered our fortresses" (Jer 9:21). "I will make their widows more numerous than the sand of the sea" (Jer 15:8). "I will put hooks in your jaws and make the fish of your streams stick to your scales. . . . I will leave you in the desert, you and all the fish of your streams. . . . I will give you as food to the beasts of the earth and the birds of the air" (Ezek 29:4-5).

[5]Heschel, *Prophets,* p. 16.

[6]The question of the philosophy of language has been well traveled, from Plato to Augustine to postmodern deconstructionists. For a good overview, see Kevin Vanhoozer, "Language, Literature, Hermeneutics and Biblical Theology," in *A Guide to Old Testament Theology and Exegesis: The Introductory Articles from the "New International Dictionary of Old Testament Theology and Exegesis,"* ed. W. A. Vangemeren (Grand Rapids, Mich.: Zondervan, 1999), pp. 12-32.

[7]A seminal work on translation is George Steiner, *After Babel: Aspects of Language and Translation,* 3rd ed. (Oxford: Oxford University Press, 1998).

[8]Theologians have wrestled with this problem of the relation of language and theology since the twelfth century; for the view of Thomas Aquinas, see *Summa Theologica* 1a.13.2-7; for the view of Karl Barth, see Bruce McCormack, *Karl Barth's Critically Realistic Dialectical Theology: Its Genesis and Development, 1909-1936* (Oxford: Oxford University Press, 1995), pp. 269-73.

[9]Humans' communication with humans involves a surprising amount of ambiguity; Israel Scheffler, *Beyond the Letter: A Philosophical Inquiry into Ambiguity, Vagueness and Metaphor in Language* (London: Routledge & Kegan Paul, 1979). The Sapir-Whorf hypothesis argues that a particular language cannot be separated from the world of that language. Without shared context and values, meaning cannot be shared. See, e.g., Michael Agar, *Language Shock: Understanding the Culture of Conversation* (New York: William Morrow, 1994), pp. 66-68.

[10]George Steiner, *Real Presences: Is There Anything in What We Say?* (London: Faber & Faber, 1989), p. 20.

[11]Plato anticipated this problem when he said that earthly things are but pale imitations of eternal ideas. "Indeed the line that the theologians, or at least those of a more orthodox variety, want to walk is a most difficult and compelling one for, on the one hand, they must

8 {

acknowledge, with the literary critic, that the metaphors which concern them are allusive and embedded in particular traditions of interpretation and belief, and, on the other hand, they must argue that this affective element is not the whole, that somehow this language can claim to be descriptive of a God who cannot be named except in tropes and figures" (Janet Martin Soskice, *Metaphor and Religious Language* [Oxford: Clarendon, 1985], p. ix).

[12]Alter, *Art of Biblical Poetry*, p. 141.

[13]The letters are essentially oracles of judgment and blessing; David E. Aune, *Prophecy in Early Christianity and the Ancient Mediterranean World* (Grand Rapids, Mich.: Eerdmans, 1983), pp. 274-79.

[14]For an example of *of* as apposition in English, consider the phrase "the state of Texas." The genitive case could designate the same idea in Greek. Hence, for example, a "crown, which is life."

[15]At the Lord's command, some of the manna was placed in a jar for generations to come (Ex 16:33-35; cf. Heb 9:4, "This ark contained the gold jar of manna").

[16]I ask these questions tongue in cheek, though it is necessary to do so, because some readers may seek to understand the text at this level.

[17]C. J. Hemer, *The Letters to the Seven Churches of Asia in Their Local Setting* (Sheffield, U.K.: JSOT Press, 1986), pp. 96-97.

[18]Adele Berlin, "Introduction to Hebrew Poetry," in *New Interpreter's Bible* (Nashville: Abingdon, 1996), 4:311-12.

[19]G. K. Beale, *The Book of Revelation: A Commentary on the Greek Text* (Grand Rapids, Mich.: Eerdmans, 1999), pp. 173-74; on the eschatological presence of God in all its fullness in the whole of creation, see Jürgen Moltmann, *The Coming of God: Christian Eschatology*, trans. Margaret Kohl (Minneapolis: Fortress: 1996), e.g., p. 317.

[20]See Exodus 16; Deuteronomy 8:3; Psalm 78:23-25 ("men ate the bread of angels"); John 6:49-58 ("I am the living bread that came down from heaven").

[21]David E. Aune, *Revelation 1-5*, Word Biblical Commentary (Dallas: Word, 1997), 190, 95; Aune, however, does not connect the significance of the amulet with the theme of Revelation.

Chapter 2: What Makes Prophecy Problematic?

[1]Erwin Lutzer, *The Doctrines That Divide: A Fresh Look at the Historic Doctrines That Separate Christians* (Grand Rapids, Mich.: Kregel, 1989, reprint 1998); D. S. Russell, *Poles Apart: The Gospel in Creative Tension* (Louisville, Ky.: Westminster John Knox, 1991).

[2]For a helpful review of the history of the church structured around key events, see Mark A. Noll, *Turning Points: Decisive Moments in the History of Christianity* (Grand Rapids, Mich.: Baker, 1997).

[3]The issue took shape in the second century and became the subject of raging theological battles until the Council of Chalcedon in A.D. 451 (Gerald Bray, *Creeds, Councils and Christ* [Downers Grove, Ill.: InterVarsity Press, 1984]). For current issues regarding the deity of Christ, see Donald G. Bloesch, *Essentials of Evangelical Theology*, vol. 1, *God, Authority and Salvation* (1978; reprint, Peabody, Mass.: Prince, 1998), pp. 120-47.

[4]Though a defining doctrine, it is still being defined (Gilbert Bilezikian, "Hermeneutical Bungee-Jumping: Subordination in the Godhead," *Journal of Theological Studies* 40, no. 1 (March 1997): 57-68.

[5]For example, Stanley J. Grenz, *The Millennial Maze: Sorting Out Evangelical Options* (Downers Grove, Ill.: InterVarsity Press, 1992).

[6]The growing consensus on the hermeneutics of prophecy offers some hope; e.g., Gordon D. Fee and Douglas Stuart, *How to the Read the Bible for All Its Worth: A Guide to Understanding the Bible*, 2nd ed. (Grand Rapids, Mich.: Zondervan, 1993); Sidney Greidanus, *The Modern Preacher and the Ancient Text: Interpreting and Preaching Biblical Literature* (Grand Rapids, Mich.: Eerdmans, 1988); Grant R. Osborne, *The Hermeneutical Spiral: A Comprehensive Introduction to Biblical Interpretation* (Downers Grove, Ill.: InterVarsity Press, 1991).

[7]On biblical poetry, see Robert Alter, *The Art of Biblical Poetry* (New York: Basic Books, 1985); S. E. Gillingham, *The Poems and Psalms of the Hebrew Bible* (Oxford: Oxford University Press, 1994); David L. Petersen and Kent Harold Richards, *Interpreting Hebrew Poetry*, Guides to Biblical Scholarship (Minneapolis: Fortress, 1992); Leland Ryken, *Words of Delight: A Literary Introduction to the Bible*, 2nd ed. (Grand Rapids, Mich.: Baker, 1992); William W. Klein, Craig L. Blomberg and Robert L. Hubbard, *Introduction to Biblical Interpretation* (Dallas: Word, 1993), pp. 215-55.

[8]For various views see Ellen F. Davis, "Exploding the Limits: Form and Function in Psalm 22," *Journal for the Study of the Old Testament* 53 (March 1992): 93-105; James L. Mays, "Prayer and Christology: Psalm 22 as Perspective on the Passion," *Theology Today* 42 (October 1985): 322-31 [reprinted in *Psalms*, Interpretation (Louisville, Ky.: John Knox Press, 1994); Martin S. Rozenberg and Bernard M. Zlotowitz, *The Book of Psalms: A New Translation and Commentary* (Northvale, N.J.: Jason Aronson, 1999); Mark H. Heinemann, "An Exposition of Psalm 22," *Bibliotheca Sacra* 147 (July-September 1990): 286-308; John H. Reumann, "Psalm 22 at the Cross: Lament and Thanksgiving for Jesus Christ," *Interpretation* 28 (January 1974): 39-58.

[9]For example, Psalm 78:2 and Psalm 118:22-23. Tremper Longman argues that no psalm is exclusively messianic in a narrow sense (Tremper Longman III, *How to Read the Psalms* [Downers Grove, Ill.: InterVarsity Press, 1988], pp. 67-73).

[10]This point was first suggested to me by Richard Patterson; see, e.g., Claus Westermann, *The Living Psalms*, trans. J. R. Porter (Grand Rapids, Mich.: Eerdmans, 1989), p. 298.

[11]L. Paul Trudinger, "'Eli, Eli, Lama Sabachthani': A Cry of Dereliction or Victory?" *Journal of the Evangelical Theological Society* 17 (1974): 235-38.

[12]Admittedly, this reading follows the Septuagint; there is a thorny textual problem in the Hebrew.

[13]I have personally heard one preacher expound that the torment that Jesus suffered on the cross resulted in all of his bones becoming disjointed. So, is every statement in Psalm 22 literal? "It is in the failure to grasp the interplay between prose and poetry that doomsday prophets make a major mistake, overemphasizing the literal to the neglect of the symbolic" (C. Marvin Pate and Calvin B. Haines Jr., *Doomsday Delusions: What's Wrong with Predictions About the End of the World* [Downers Grove, Ill.: InterVarsity Press, 1995], p. 27).

[14]E.g., Matthew 16:22.

[15]Gillingham, "Poets, Poems and Performances," pp. 3-17.

[16]A pervasive metaphor in Scripture is the divine warrior; see Tremper Longman III and Daniel G. Reid, *God Is a Warrior*, Studies in Old Testament Biblical Theology (Grand Rapids, Mich.: Zondervan, 1995). Another common metaphor is human familial love, representing divine love; see Richard Patterson and Donald Fowler, "Human Familial Love as a Metaphor for Divine-Human Love," paper presented at the Evangelical Theological Society Annual Meeting, 2001.

[17]A full discussion of *literal* is in Kevin Vanhoozer, *Is There a Meaning in This Text? The Bible, the Reader and the Morality of Literary Knowledge* (Grand Rapids, Mich.: Zondervan, 1998), pp. 305-9.

[18]See Tremper Longman III, "What I Mean by Historical-Grammatical Exegesis—Why I Am Not a Literalist," *Grace Theological Journal* 11 (1990): 137-55; Vern S. Poythress, *Understanding Dispensationalists* (Grand Rapids, Mich.: Zondervan, 1987), pp. 78-96.

[19]Vanhoozer argues in favor of literal interpretations of Scripture but against *literalistic* interpretations of Scripture; *Is There a Meaning?* pp. 309-15.

[20]Janet Martin Soskice, *Metaphor and Religious Language* (Oxford: Clarendon, 1985).

[21]Abraham J. Heschel, *The Prophets*, 2 vols. in 1 (New York: HarperCollins, 1962), p. 14. See also Ryken, *Words of Delight*, p. 177; Klein, Blomberg and Hubbard, *Introduction to Biblical Interpretation*, p. 248.

[22]Unlike the other passages cited here, the context (Is 32:15) speaks of an end of what was just stated to be forever!

[23]Compare God's announcement when false prophets claimed to be speaking the oracle of the Lord: "Therefore, I will surely forget you and cast you out of my presence along with the city I gave to you and your fathers. I will bring upon you everlasting disgrace—everlasting shame that will not be forgotten" (Jer 23:39-40).

[24]Similar language of unending judgment is used in oracles against Babylon, Tyre and Edom; see pp. 99-101.

[25]The Hebrew describes the wounded soldiers as "pierced through."

[26]Walter Brueggemann, *The Land: Place as Gift, Promise and Challenge in Biblical Faith* (Philadelphia: Fortress, 1977); W. D. Davies, *The Gospel and the Land: Early Christianity and Jewish Territorial Doctrine* (Berkeley: University of California Press, 1974).

[27]John H. Walton, *Covenant: God's Purpose, God's Plan* (Grand Rapids, Mich.: Zondervan, 1994), pp. 108-21; Lyle Eslinger, *House of God or House of David: The Rhetoric of 2 Samuel 7*, Journal for the Study of the Old Testament Supplement Series 164 (Sheffield, U.K.: Sheffield Academic Press, 1994), pp. 90-94.

[28]G. B. Caird, *The Language and Imagery of the Bible* (London: Gerald Duckworth, 1980), reprint with introduction by N. T. Wright (Grand Rapids, Mich.: Eerdmans, 1997), pp. 112-13. The issue of God's changing his mind brings up the openness of God debate; here I make no attempt to take sides. See, e.g., Clark H. Pinnock, *Most Moved Mover: A Theology of God's Openness* (Grand Rapids, Mich.: Baker, 2001); and John Sanders, *The God Who Risks: A Theology of Providence* (Downers Grove, Ill.: InterVarsity Press, 1998).

[29]See, e.g., "Apocalyptic Visions of the Future," in *Dictionary of Biblical Imagery*, ed. Leland Ryken, J. C. Wilhoit and Tremper Longman III (Downers Grove, Ill.: InterVarsity Press, 1998), pp. 37-38.

[30]On the topic of orality, see Birger Gerhardsson, *Memory and Manuscript* (Grand Rapids, Mich: Eerdmans, 1998); Walter J. Ong, *Orality and Literacy: The Technologizing of the Word* (London: Methuen, 1982); Lou H. Silberman, ed., *Orality, Aurality and Biblical Narrative* (Decatur, Ga.: Scholars Press, 1987); S. Niditch, *Oral World and Written Word: Ancient Israelite Literature* (Louisville: Westminster John Knox, 1996); and John D. Harvey, *Listening to the Text: Oral Patterning in Paul's Letters* (Grand Rapids, Mich.: Baker, 1998).

[31]Personal communication from Dan Reid.

[32]Written versions of prophecy may be implied when Isaiah says to bind up the testimony (Is 8:16, 20); he also refers to a vision recorded on a scroll (Is 29:11-12) and to writing on a tablet (Is 30:8).

[33]See, e.g., J. A. Thompson, *The Book of Jeremiah* (Grand Rapids, Mich.: Eerdmans, 1980), pp. 27-49, 56-59.

[34]Emanuel Tov, *Textual Criticism of the Hebrew Bible*, 2nd ed. (Minneapolis: Fortress, 2000).

[35]José Faur, "God as Writer: Omnipresence and the Art of Dissimulation," *Religion and Intellectual Life* 6 (spring/summer 1989): 31-43.

[36]Raymond B. Dillard and Tremper Longman III, *An Introduction to the Old Testament* (Grand Rapids, Mich.: Zondervan, 1994), p. 294.

[37]Douglas R. Jones, *Jeremiah,* New Century Bible Commentary (Grand Rapids, Mich.: Eerdmans, 1992), p. 17.

[38]For an overview of the two views on the fulfillment of the restoration promises, see James M. Scott, "The Restoration of Israel," in *Dictionary of Paul and His Letters,* ed. Gerald F. Hawthorne, Ralph P. Martin and Daniel Reid (Downers Grove, Ill.: InterVarsity Press, 1993), pp. 796-805.

[39]N. T. Wright, *The New Testament and the People of God,* Christian Origins and the Question of God 1 (Minneapolis: Fortress, 1992), pp. 268-70; N. T. Wright, *Jesus and the Victory of God,* Christian Origins and the Question of God 2 (Minneapolis: Fortress, 1996), pp. xvii-xviii.

[40]It might be better not to think of wrath as an attribute of God, because if there were no sin, theoretically there would be no wrath. Alternatively, wrath might be considered a function of love. In any event, God's wrath must be taken just as seriously as his love. The modern tendency to focus primarily on God's love and to downplay his wrath is misleading.

[41]Paradox is related to the law of the excluded middle or dualism (perhaps an appropriate term would be "cognitive dualism"); Wright distinguishes ten types of duality but does not include this form (Wright, *New Testament and the People of God,* pp. 252-56).

[42]See, e.g., Caird, *Language and Imagery,* pp. 110-16; R. E. Clements, ed., *The World of Ancient Israel: Sociological, Anthropological and Political Perspectives* (Cambridge: Cambridge University Press, 1989); Jacob A. Loewen, *The Bible in Cross-Cultural Perspective* (Pasadena, Calif.: William Carey Library, 2000). "For the ancient peoples of the East, in order to express their ideas, did not always employ those forms or kinds of speech which we use today; but rather those used by the men of their time and centuries. What those exactly were, the commentator cannot determine, as it were, in advance, but only after a careful examination of the ancient literature of the East" (Pope Pius XII's encyclical *Divino Afflante Spiritu* on biblical studies, issued in 1943, par. 36).

[43]C. Marvin Pate and Calvin B. Haines Jr., *Doomsday Delusions: What's Wrong with Predictions About the End of the World* (Downers Grove, Ill.: InterVarsity Press, 1995), pp. 80-147.

[44]Vern S. Poythress, "Response to Paul S. Karleen's Paper 'Understanding Covenant Theologians,'" *Grace Theological Journal* 10, no. 2 (Fall 1989): 149, 154.

Chapter 3: How Does the Language of Prophecy Work?

[1]Wayne C. Booth, "Metaphor as Rhetoric," in *On Metaphor,* ed. Sheldon Sacks (Chicago: University of Chicago Press, 1979), p. 50; see Booth's helpful discussion of all that was transpiring in this use of metaphor.

[2]See in particular Aristotle *Rhetoric* 3 and *Poetics* 21-25; for a brief overview of the history of metaphor from Aristotle to Coleridge, see Terence Hawks, *Metaphor* (London: Methuen, 1972), pp. 6-56; for detailed analysis of Aristotle's views of metaphor, see Paul Ricoeur, *The Rule of Metaphor: Multi-disciplinary Studies of the Creation of Meaning in Language,* trans. Robert Czerny (Toronto: University of Toronto Press, 1977), pp. 9-43. An example of Aristotle's metaphors is "Patience is so like fortitude that she seems either her sister or her daughter."

[3]Aristotle commented, "Everything said metaphorically is obscure" (*Topica* 139b.34).

[4]Cicero *De Oratore;* Horace *Art of Poetry;* Longinus *On the Sublime;* Quintilian *Institutio Oratoria.*

[5]For a short review of the impact of various disciplines on the study of metaphor, see Hawks, *Metaphor*, pp. 57-89.

[6]For important insights on metaphors, see J. S. Mio and A. N. Katz, *Metaphor: Implications and Applications* (Mahwah, N.J.: Lawrence Erlbaum, 1996); within this collection, note especially, on the memorability of metaphors, Valerie F. Reyna, "Meaning, Memory and the Interpretation of Metaphors" (pp. 39-57); on simplifying profound ideas, Thompson says that metaphors "clothe the intangible, giving life to abstractions" (Seth Thompson, "Politics Without Metaphors Is Like a Fish Without Water," p. 188); on the ability of a metaphor to tell a story, Jeffery Scott Mio, "Metaphor, Politics and Persuasion" (p. 131).

[7]The seminal works that launched the modern study of metaphor were I. A. Richards, *The Philosophy of Rhetoric* (London: Oxford University Press, 1936); Max Black, "Metaphor," *Proceedings of the Aristotelian Society* 55 (1954): 273-94, reprinted as a chapter in *Models and Metaphors: Studies in Language and Philosophy* (Ithaca, N.Y.: Cornell University Press, 1962), pp. 25-47; Max Black, *The Labyrinth of Language* (New York: Frederick Praeger, 1968); Philip Wheelwright, *The Burning Fountain: A Study in the Language of Symbolism* (Bloomington: Indiana University Press, 1954); Philip Wheelwright, *Metaphor and Reality* (Bloomington: Indiana University Press, 1962). Especially during the 1970s and 1980s, the subject of metaphor drew the attention of many; for example, Ricoeur, *Rule of Metaphor*; J. David Sapir and J. Christopher Crocker, eds., *The Social Use of Metaphor: Essays on the Anthropology of Rhetoric* (Philadelphia: University of Pennsylvania Press, 1977); George Lakoff and Mark Johnson, *Metaphors We Live By* (Chicago: University of Chicago Press, 1980); Jerry H. Gill, *Wittgenstein and Metaphor* (Washington, D.C.: University Press of America, 1981). For more recent discussion of philosophy of language, see George Lakoff and Mark Johnson, *Philosophy in the Flesh: The Embodied Mind and Its Challenge to Western Thought* (New York: Basic-Books, 1999); Kevin J. Vanhoozer, "From Speech Acts to Scripture Acts: The Covenant of Discourse and the Discourse of Covenant," in *After Pentecost: Language and Biblical Interpretation*, The Scripture and Hermeneutics Series (Grand Rapids, Mich.: Zondervan, 2001), pp. 1-49; see other articles in this collection as well.

[8]See, e.g., the chapter "Life, Death and Time," in George Lakoff and Mark Turner, *More Than Cool Reason: A Field Guide to Poetic Metaphor* (Chicago: University of Chicago Press, 1989), pp. 1-51.

[9]Wheelwright, *Metaphor and Reality*, p. 111.

[10]This paragraph is based on one of the patterns of metaphors explored in Lakoff and Johnson, *Metaphors We Live By*, pp. 4-5.

[11]This is one of Aristotle's points about metaphor, which he discusses in his essays *Rhetoric* and *Poetics*.

[12]Donald Davidson, "What Metaphors Mean," in *On Metaphor*, ed. Sheldon Sacks (Chicago: University of Chicago Press, 1979), pp. 29-45.

[13]Monroe C. Beardsley, "The Metaphorical Twist," in *Essays on Metaphor*, ed. Warren Shibles (Whitewater, Wis.: Language, 1972), pp. 73-92.

[14]Lakoff and Johnson call these ontological metaphors, because they help us conceptualize a particular entity; *Metaphors We Live By*, pp. 25-32.

[15]Ted Cohen, "Metaphor and the Cultivation of Intimacy," in *On Metaphor*, ed. Sheldon Sacks (Chicago: University of Chicago Press, 1979), pp. 6-7; in the same volume, Don R. Swanson, "Afterthoughts," pp. 162-63; Israel Scheffler, *Beyond the Letter: A Philosophical Inquiry into Ambiguity, Vagueness and Metaphor in Language* (London: Routledge & Kegan Paul, 1979). People outside the community will be less able to understand the metaphors of the com-

munity; see, e.g., the representative list of French metaphors in appendix A.

[16]Elyse Sommer and Dorrie Weiss, eds., *Metaphors Dictionary* (New York: Gale Research, 1995; P. R. Wilkinson, *Thesaurus of Traditional English Metaphors* (New York: Routledge, 1993); A. P. Cowie, Ronald Mackin and I. R. McCaig, *Oxford Dictionary of Current Idiomatic English*, 2 vols. (Oxford: Oxford University Press, 1975-1983); Betty Kirkpatrick, *Dictionary of Clichés* (London: Bloomsbury, 1996); Laurence Urdang, *Picturesque Expressions: A Thematic Dictionary*, 2nd ed. (Detroit: Gale Research, 1985).

[17]E. W. Bullinger, *Figures of Speech Used in the Bible Explained and Illustrated* (1898; reprint, Grand Rapids, Mich.: Baker, 1968).

[18]Ibid., pp. v, xii.

[19]Some metaphors are lost or modified when translated into other languages. In Numbers 21:24, the KJV reads "smote him with the edge of the sword," while the Hebrew reads "with the mouth of the sword." The NIV and NRSV omit the metaphor and read "put him to the sword." In 1 Samuel 24:3 it is reported that Saul went into a cave to "cover his feet" in the Hebrew; the NIV and NRSV read "to relieve himself."

[20]Striking images simply for their own sake was not the intent of the biblical authors (Robert Alter, "Ancient Hebrew Poetry," in *The Literary Guide to the Bible*, ed. Robert Alter and Frank Kermode (Cambridge, Mass.: Harvard University Press, 1987), p. 617.

[21]Walter Brueggemann, *The Prophetic Imagination*, 2nd ed. (Minneapolis: Fortress, 2001), p. 45.

[22]John B. Gabel and Charles B. Wheeler, *The Bible as Literature: An Introduction* (Oxford: Oxford University Press, 1986), pp. 24-26.

[23]This point is explored in J. B. Russell, *A History of Heaven: The Singing Silence* (Princeton, N.J.: Princeton University Press, 1997).

[24]Brueggemann, *Prophetic Imagination*, p. 55.

[25]The starting point for consideration of metaphor is G. B. Caird, *The Language and Imagery of the Bible* (London: Gerald Duckworth, 1980), reprint with introduction by N. T. Wright (Grand Rapids, Mich.: Eerdmans, 1997); for more recent studies see Harold Fisch, *Poetry with a Purpose: Biblical Poetics and Interpretation* (Bloomington: Indiana University Press, 1988); James L. Kugel, *Poetry and Prophecy: The Beginnings of a Literary Tradition* (Ithaca, N.Y.: Cornell University Press, 1990); Adele Berlin, "On Reading Biblical Poetry: The Role of Metaphor," *Congress Volume, Cambridge 1995*, ed. J. A. Emmerton, Vetus Testamentum Supplements 66 (Leiden: Brill, 1997); for studies of specific metaphors see, e.g., Carol A. Newsom, "A Maker of Metaphors: Ezekiel's Oracles Against Tyre," *Interpretation* 38 (1984): 151-64, reprinted in *Interpreting the Prophets* (Philadelphia: Fortress, 1987), pp. 188-99, and in *"The Place Is Too Small for Us": The Israelite Prophet in Recent Scholarship*, ed. R. P. Gordon, Sources for Biblical and Theological Study (Winona Lake, Ind.: Eisenbrauns, 1995), pp. 191-204; J. Cheryl Exum, "Of Broken Pots, Fluttering Birds and Visions in the Night: Extended Simile and Poetic Technique in Isaiah," *Catholic Biblical Quarterly* 43, no. 3 (July 1981): 331-52, reprinted in *Beyond Form Criticism: Essays in Old Testament Literary Criticism*, ed. P. R. House, Sources for Biblical and Theological Study (Winona Lake, Ind.: Eisenbrauns, 1992); Kirsten Nielsen, *There Is Hope for a Tree: The Tree as Metaphor in Isaiah, Journal for the Study of the Old Testament* Supplement Series 65 (Sheffield, U.K.: Sheffield Academic Press, 1989).

[26]Stephen Geller, "Were the Prophets Poets?" *Prooftexts* 3 (1983): 211-21, reprinted in *"The Place Is Too Small for Us": The Israelite Prophet in Recent Scholarship*, ed. R. P. Gordon, Sources for Biblical and Theological Study (Winona Lake, Ind.: Eisenbrauns, 1995), pp. 50-73; Walter Brueggemann, *Finally Comes the Poet: Daring Speech for Proclamation* (Minneapolis: Fortress, 1989).

[27]See, for example, Caird, *Language and Imagery of the Bible,* pp. 131-43.

[28]Wheelwright, *Metaphor and Reality,* p. 93.

[29]Lakoff and Johnson, *Metaphors We Live By,* p. 36.

[30]Patricia A. Chantrill and Jeffery Scott Mio, "Metonymy in Political Discourse," in *Metaphor: Implications and Applications,* ed. J. S. Mio and A. N. Katz (Mahwah, N.J.: Lawrence Erlbaum, 1996), pp. 171-72.

[31]Lakoff and Johnson, *Metaphors We Live By,* p. 5.

Chapter 4: How Does the Language of Destruction and Blessing Work?

[1]For a basic introduction to the prophets, see Victor H. Matthews, *Social World of the Hebrew Prophets* (Peabody, Mass.: Hendrickson, 2001); Willem A. VanGemeren, *Interpreting the Prophetic Word* (Grand Rapids, Mich.: Zondervan, 1990); L. L. Grabbe, *Priests, Prophets, Diviners, Sages: A Socio-Historical Study of Religious Specialists in Ancient Israel* (Valley Forge, Penn.: Trinity, 1995); and Ben Witherington III, *Jesus the Seer: The Progress of Prophecy* (Peabody, Mass.: Hendrickson, 1999); a classic exploration of the phenomenon of prophecy is Abraham Heschel, *The Prophets,* 2 vols. in 1 (New York: HarperCollins, 1962).

[2]For discussion of different types of prophecy, see William W. Klein, Craig L. Blomberg and Robert L. Hubbard, *Introduction to Biblical Interpretation* (Dallas: Word, 1993), pp. 292-302.

[3]See the chapters "Language About God in the Old Testament" and "Images of God" in J. C. L. Gibson, *Language and Imagery in the Old Testament* (Peabody, Mass.: Hendrickson, 1998), pp. 22-33, 121-38; see the chapter "Anthropomorphism" in G. B. Caird, *The Language and Imagery of the Bible* (London: Gerald Duckworth, 1980), reprint with introduction by N. T. Wright (Grand Rapids, Mich.: Eerdmans, 1997), pp. 172-82.

[4]George Steiner, *Real Presences: Is There Anything in What We Say?* (London: Faber & Faber, 1989).

[5]Caird, *Language and Imagery of the Bible,* p. 174; cf. Herman Bavinck, *The Doctrine of God,* trans. William Hendriksen (Grand Rapids, Mich.: Eerdmans, 1951), p. 86.

[6]Tony Lane, "The Wrath of God as an Aspect of the Love of God," in *Nothing Greater, Nothing Better: Theological Essays on the Love of God,* ed. Kevin J. Vanhoozer (Grand Rapids, Mich.: Eerdmans, 2001).

[7]Gary V. Smith, *The Prophets as Preachers: An Introduction to the Hebrew Prophets* (Nashville: Broadman and Holman, 1994), pp. 5-45.

[8]See the chapter "The Rhetoric and Melodies of Hebrew Poetry," in Gibson, *Language and Imagery,* pp. 53-89.

[9]Michael Agar, *Language Shock: Understanding the Culture of Conversation* (New York: William Morrow, 1994) 140-63; John Austin, *How to Do Things with Words* (New York: Oxford University Press, 1965); John Searle, *Speech Acts: An Essay in the Philosophy of Language* (Cambridge: Cambridge University Press, 1969); John Searle, *Expression and Meaning: Studies in the Theory of Speech Acts* (Cambridge: Cambridge University Press, 1993).

[10]For discussion of intentionality and authority, see Kevin Vanhoozer, *Is There a Meaning in This Text? The Bible, the Reader and the Morality of Literary Knowledge* (Grand Rapids, Mich.: Zondervan, 1998), pp. 43-97.

[11]Caird, *Language and Imagery of the Bible,* pp. 20-25.

[12]Nico H. Frijda, Antony S. R. Manstead and Sacha Bern, *Emotions and Beliefs: How Feelings Influence Thoughts* (Cambridge: Cambridge University Press, 2000).

[13]Caird, *Language and Imagery of the Bible,* pp. 56-61.

[14]Peter C. Craigie, *The Book of Deuteronomy* (Grand Rapids, Mich.: Eerdmans, 1976), pp. 22-23,

334-53; Eugene Merrill, *Deuteronomy*, New American Commentary (Nashville: Broadman and Holman, 1994), pp. 339-72; cf. Bernard M. Levinson, *Deuteronomy and the Hermeneutic of Legal Innovation* (Oxford: Oxford University Press, 1997).

[15]These phrases with minor editing are taken from Joseph A. Fitzmyer, *The Aramaic Inscriptions of Sefire* (Biblica et Orientalia 19; Rome: Pontifical Biblical Institute, 1976); cf., Abraham Malamat, "Prophecy at Mari" in *Mari and the Early Israelite Experience* (Schweich Lectures 1984; Oxford University Press, 1989) 77-96; reprinted in *"The Place is too Small for Us": The Israelite Prophet in Recent Scholarship*, ed. R. P. Gordon, Sources for Biblical and Theological Study (Winona Lake, Ind.: Eisenbrauns, 1995) pp. 50-73; Timothy Gray Crawford, *Blessing and Curse in Syro-Palestinian Inscriptions of the Iron Age* (New York: Peter Lang, 1992); John G. Gager, ed., *Curse Tablets and Binding Spells from the Ancient World* (New York: Oxford University Press, 1992); Hans Ulrich Steymans, *Deuteronomium 28 und die ade zur Thronfolgeregelung Asarhaddons: Segen und Fluch im Alten Orient und in Israel* (Göttingen: Vandenhoeck & Ruprecht, 1995).

[16]These phrases with minor editing are taken from Donald J. Wiseman, "The Vassal Treaties of Esarhaddon," *IRAQ* 20, pt. 1 (London: British School of Archaeology in Iraq, 1958); cf. F. Charles Fensham, "Common Trends in Curses of the Near Eastern Treaties and *KUDUR-RU*-Inscriptions Compared with Maledictions of Amos and Isaiah," *ZAW* 75:2 (1963): 155-75.

[17]Patrick D. Miller, *Deuteronomy*, Interpretation (Louisville: John Knox Press, 1990), p. 194.

[18]Doug Stuart organizes the types of curses and blessings differently and ends up with twenty-seven types of curses and ten types of restoration blessings; Douglas Stuart, *Hosea-Jonah*, Word Biblical Commentary 31 (Waco, Tex.: Word, 1987), pp. xxxii-xlii.

[19]See especially G. B. Caird, *The Language and Imagery of the Bible* (1980; reprint, Grand Rapids, Mich.: Eerdmans, 1997), pp. 109-16; Brueggemann says that prophetic language is characterized by "outrageous and extreme figures;" *Theology of the Old Testament*, p. 625; I. H. Eybers, "Some Examples of Hyperbole in Biblical Hebrew," *Semitics* 1 (1970): 38-49.

[20]Richard L. Schultz, *The Search for Quotation: Verbal Parallels in the Prophets*, Journal for the Study of the Old Testament Supplement Series 180 (Sheffield, U.K.: Sheffield Academic Press, 1999).

[21]Heschel, *Prophets*, p. 2.

[22]Cf. the use of cosmic imagery as metaphor for restoration; M. A. Sweeney, *Isaiah 1-39 with an Introduction to Prophetic Literature*, Forms of Old Testament Literature (Grand Rapids, Mich.: Eerdmans, 1996), p. 314.

[23]Homer Heater Jr., "Do the Prophets Teach That Babylonia Will Be Rebuilt in the *Eschaton*?" *JETS* 41, no. 1 (March 1998): 23-43.

[24]Sweeney, *Isaiah 1-39*, p. 314.

[25]Heater, "Do the Babylonians Teach," pp. 31-36. For the prophecies regarding Tyre see Dean Ulrich, "Dissonant Prophecy in Ezekiel 26 and 29," *Bulletin for Biblical Research* 10, no. 1 (2000): 121-41; Thomas Renz, "Proclaiming the Future: History and Theology in the Prophecies Against Tyre," *Tyndale Bulletin* 51, no. 1 (2000): 17-58.

[26]Or we might say to someone whom we have not seen for a long time, "I have not seen you forever."

[27]Tremper Longman notes in a personal communication, "I think that the two lovers who say 'I will love you forever' is not simply an intensifier but is saying 'my forever.'"

[28]Daniel J. Lewis, *Three Crucial Questions About the Last Days* (Grand Rapids, Mich.: Baker, 1998), pp. 19-23.

Chapter 5: How Does the Language of Apocalyptic Work?

[1]Compare the views, e.g., of Louis F. Hartman and Alexander A. Di Lella, *The Book of Daniel,* Anchor Bible (Garden City, N.Y.: Doubleday, 1978), pp. 9-18, and J. G. Baldwin, *Daniel: An Introduction and Commentary,* Tyndale Old Testament Commentaries (Downers Grove, Ill.: InterVarsity Press, 1978), pp. 13-59; also Tremper Longman III, *Daniel,* NIV Application Commentary (Grand Rapids, Mich.: Zondervan, 1999), pp. 21-24.

[2]Prediction written after the fact is referred to as *ex eventu;* see, e.g., J. E. Goldingay, *Daniel,* Word Biblical Commentary (Dallas: Word, 1989), p. xxxix; Baldwin, *Daniel,* pp. 35-59; cf. J. G. Baldwin, "Is There Pseudonymity in the Old Testament?" *Themelios* 4 (1978): 6-12.

[3]Diodorus Siculus 16.85-86. For full discussion of how Macedon rose to power and gained supremacy over Greece, see J. B. Bury, S. A. Cook and F. E. Adcock, eds., *Cambridge Ancient History,* vol. 6, *Macedon* (Cambridge: Cambridge University Press, 1964); Ulrich Wilcken, *Alexander the Great,* trans. G. C. Richards (New York: W. W. Norton, 1967); N. G. L. Hammond, G. T. Griffith and F. W. Walbank, *A History of Macedonia,* 3 vols. (Oxford: Oxford University Press, 1972-1988); and N. G. L. Hammond, *The Macedonian State: Origins, Institutions and History* (Oxford: Clarendon, 1989).

[4]The title was *strategon autokratora* (Diodorus Siculus 16.89, 17.4). Welles translates the title "president and general plenipotentiary" (C. B. Welles, *Alexander and the Hellenistic World* [Toronto: A. M. Hakkert, 1970], p. 18). The title may have been created, however, by Diodorus (A. B. Bosworth, *Conquest and Empire: The Reign of Alexander the Great* [Cambridge: Cambridge University Press, 1988], p. 190 n. 5).

[5]Ernst Badian, "The Death of Philip II," *Phoenix* 17 (1963): 244-50; J. R. Ellis, "The Assassination of Philip II," in *Ancient Macedonian Studies in Honor of Charles Edson,* ed. H. J. Dell (Thessaloniki, Greece: Institute for Balkan Studies, 1981), pp. 99-137; A. B. Bosworth, "The Death of Alexander the Great: Rumours and Propaganda," *Classical Quarterly* 21 (1971): 112-30.

[6]E. A. Fredricksmeyer, "On the Final Aims of Philip II," in *Philip II, Alexander the Great and the Macedonian Heritage,* ed. W. L. Adams and E. N. Borza (Lanham, Md.: University Press of America, 1982), pp. 85-98; the most complete (though secondhand) accounts from antiquity of Alexander's campaign against Persia—from the battle at the Granicus River to Alexander's victory celebrations in Babylon—are given in Diodorus 17.17-118 and Arrian, *Anabasis of Alexander;* for discussion of the sources for Alexander, see Bosworth, *Conquest and Empire,* pp. 295-300. For accounts of Alexander's campaigns, see N. G. L. Hammond, *Alexander the Great: King, Commander and Statesman* (Park Ridge, N.J.: Noyes, 1980), and Peter Green, *Alexander of Macedon, 356-323 B.C.: A Historical Biography* (Berkeley: University of California Press, 1991).

[7]E. N. Borza, *The Impact of Alexander the Great: Civilizer or Destroyer?* (Hinsdale, Ill.: Dryden, 1974). Welles, *Alexander the Great,* pp. 47-48: "In the spring of 323, Alexander came down into Mesopotamia and proceeded slowly toward Babylon. He planned . . . to undertake a campaign into Arabia. . . . Alexander lived only for fighting and adventure. . . . War and exploration were his passion, and he would go on as long as he could." For an example of Alexander's failure as an administrator, see Arrian 6.27.3-5 and the discussion by Ernst Badian, "Harpalus," *Journal of Hellenic Studies* 81 (1961): 16-43.

[8]For detailed treatments of the successors of Alexander and the developments of the Hellenistic period, see F. W. Wallbank et al., eds., *Cambridge Ancient History,* 2nd ed., vol. 7, pt. 1: *The Hellenistic World* (Cambridge: Cambridge University Press, 1984); Peter Green, *Alexander to Actium: The Historical Evolution of the Hellenistic Age* (Berkeley: University of California Press, 1990); and the classic and still valuable Michael Rostovtzeff, *Social and*

PLOWSHARES & PRUNING HOOKS

Economic History of the Hellenistic World, 3 vols. (Oxford: Clarendon, 1941).

[9]The governors and their satrapies were Peucestas in Persia, Peithon in Media, Ptolemy in Egypt, Lysimachus in Thrace, Antigonus in Phrygia, Leonnatus in Hellespontine Phrygia, Laomedon in Syria, Eumenes in Cappadocia, Stasanor in Bactria, Philotas in Cilicia, Asander in Lycia and Menander in Lydia (Welles, *Alexander the Great,* pp. 51-52).

[10]See, for example, Rostovtzeff, *Social and Economic History,* 2:551-602.

[11]Ronald L. Giese, "Literary Forms of the Old Testament," in *Cracking Old Testament Codes: A Guide to Interpreting the Literary Genres of the Old Testament,* ed. D. B. Sandy and R. L. Giese (Nashville: Broadman & Holman, 1995), pp. 17-23.

[12]See Richard Patterson, "Old Testament Prophecy," in *A Complete Literary Guide to the Bible,* ed. Leland Ryken and Tremper Longman III (Grand Rapids, Mich.: Zondervan, 1993), pp. 296-309.

[13]Figure 5.1 and the list of characteristics on pp. 108-9 appeared previously in the chapter on apocalyptic I coauthored in *Cracking Old Testament Codes,* pp. 178-86.

[14]There are many discussions of the characteristics of apocalyptic; e.g., M. E. Stone, "Apocalyptic Literature," in *Jewish Writings of the Second Temple Period,* Compendia Rerum Iudaicarum ad Novum Testamentum, ed. M. E. Stone (Philadelphia: Fortress, 1984), pp. 392-94; N. T. Wright, *The New Testament and the People of God* (Minneapolis: Fortress, 1992), pp. 280-338; in general see John J. Collins, ed., *The Encyclopedia of Apocalypticism,* 3 vols. (New York: Continuum, 1998).

[15]In this list of characteristics of apocalyptic, there is one notable omission: most apocalypses in the ancient world were pseudonymous (see above, p. 103).

[16]For English translations of apocalyptic texts in the pseudepigrapha related to the Old Testament, see James H. Charlesworth, ed., *The Old Testament Pseudepigrapha,* vol. 1, *Apocalyptic Literature and Testaments* (Garden City, N.Y.: Doubleday, 1983).

[17]Much has been written on the definition of the apocalyptic genre; for a helpful review, see Dave Mathewson, "Revelation in Recent Genre Criticism: Some Implications for Interpretation," *Trinity Journal* 13 n.s. 2 (fall 1992): 193-204; John J. Collins, "Introduction: Towards the Morphology of a Genre," *Apocalypse: The Morphology of a Genre, Semeia* 14 (1979): 5-8.

[18]Leland Ryken, *Words of Life: A Literary Introduction to the New Testament* (Grand Rapids, Mich.: Baker, 1987), p. 23; though Ryken's statement is referring to biblical literature in general, it is especially fitting for apocalyptic.

[19]While the identification of Daniel 7—12 as apocalyptic is widely accepted, it is possible to argue that Daniel's visions are merely a form of kingdom oracles that introduce the final era. As such they approximate the apocalyptic genre but "are considerably removed from apocalyptic" (Patterson, "Old Testament Prophecy," 303). But see a discussion of the development of the apocalyptic form: John J. Collins, *The Apocalyptic Imagination: An Introduction to the Jewish Matrix of Christianity* (New York: Crossroad, 1984), p. 3.

[20]Polybius 29.21.1-6.

[21]Goldingay's comment underscores the nonreferential nature of this motif: "The two horns on the single ram then suggest Media and Persia, here recognized to be one yet distinguishable" (*Daniel,* p. 208). For the nature of the Medo-Persian empire, see Edwin Yamauchi, *Persia and the Bible* (Grand Rapids, Mich.: Baker, 1990), p. 57.

[22]Cf. Daniel 7:17. J. A. Montgomery, *A Critical and Exegetical Commentary on the Book of Daniel,* International Critical Commentary (Edinburgh: T & T Clark, 1927), p. 348.

[23]Some commentaries assume wrongly, since Daniel does not mention the ram charging eastward, that Persia was the most eastern part of the empire; for example, H. C. Leupold, *Ex-*

position of Daniel (Grand Rapids, Mich.: Baker, 1969), pp. 337-38. Lacocque suggests that since Persia lay to the east of Palestine, conquests farther east would be insignificant (André Lacocque, *The Book of Daniel*, trans. D. Pellauer [Atlanta: John Knox Press, 1979], p. 160). Though the Masoretic Text lacks "east," Papyrus 967, 4QDan^a and the LXX of Daniel 8:4 include a reference to the expansion of the Persian empire to the east.

[24]Calvin uses the phrase in Daniel 8:4, "as it pleased," to suggest that the Persians simply chose not to conquer all the kingdoms they attempted to (John Calvin, *Commentaries on the Book of the Prophet Daniel*, ed. Thomas Myers [Grand Rapids, Mich.: Eerdmans, 1948], 2:87).

[25]*Hēgemōn* occurs more than forty times in the Septuagint, translating five different Hebrew words, with meanings ranging from chief, captain and governor to ruler and prince, but never king.

[26]Porteous is one of few commentators to acknowledge that Alexander was not the first: "the Macedonian dynasty that preceded him being ignored" (N. W. Porteous, *Daniel: A Commentary* [Philadelphia: Westminster Press, 1965], p. 122).

[27]Alexander's defeat of Darius at the battle of Issus in 333 B.C. was a very important victory for the Greeks. It was a complete rout of the Persians. Arrian (2.14) records a letter that Alexander reportedly sent to Darius in which Alexander lays claim to the title of king of Asia because of his victory at Issus. Had not Alexander marched to Egypt, giving Darius two years to regroup, the battle of Issus would likely have been the ultimate defeat of the Persians.

[28]*Jerome's Commentary on Daniel*, trans. Gleason L. Archer (Grand Rapids, Mich.: Baker, 1958), p. 85.

[29]Leupold rewrites history in order to match Daniel's prophecy when he says that the entire area conquered by Alexander "ultimately came under the dominion of four rulers who practically quartered the territory among themselves" (*Exposition of Daniel*, p. 344).

[30]Montgomery, *Critical and Exegetical Commentary on the Book of Daniel*, p. 332. Hartman admits, "Although it is historically true that, at the death of Alexander, his empire was divided up among four of his generals . . . our author may not have had this division primarily in mind, for the boundaries and rulers of these regions soon shifted" (*Book of Daniel*, p. 235).

[31]J. W. Swain, "The Theory of Four Monarchies; Opposition History Under the Roman Empire," *Classical Philology* 35 (1940): 1-21; David Flusser, "The Four Empires in the Fourth Sibyl and in the Book of Daniel," *Israel Oriental Studies* 2 (1967): 148-175; Martin Noth, "The Understanding of History in Old Testament Apocalyptic," in *The Laws in the Pentateuch and Other Studies* trans. D. R. Ap-Thomas (Philadelphia: Fortress, 1967), pp. 194-214; and G. F. Hasel, "The Four World Empires of Daniel 2 Against Its Near Eastern Environment," *Journal for the Study of the Old Testament* 12 (1979): 17-30.

[32]Collins, *Apocalyptic Imagination*, pp. 74-80.

[33]Historically, Elam suffered severe destruction; about 645 B.C. Ashurbanipal destroyed Elam. Less than fifty years later Nebuchadnezzar attacked. And finally under Cyrus II, Elam became part of the Persian empire, appearing second in the list of satrapies (after Media).

[34]For example, see Michael Kalafian, *The Prophecy of the Seventy Weeks of the Book of Daniel: A Critical Review of the Prophecy As Viewed by Three Major Theological Interpretations and the Impact of the Book of Daniel on Christology* (Lanham, Md.: University Press of America, 1991).

[35]Tremper Longman III, *Literary Approaches to Biblical Interpretation*, Foundations of Contemporary Interpretation 3 (Grand Rapids, Mich.: Zondervan, 1987), p. 131.

[36]E. W. Bullinger, *Figures of Speech Used in the Bible: Explained and Illustrated* (1898; reprint,

Grand Rapids, Mich.: Baker, 1968), pp. 769-71.

[37]See, e.g., E. C. Lucas, *Decoding Daniel: Reclaiming the Visions of Daniel 7—11*, Grove Biblical Series 18 (Cambridge: Cambridge University Press, 2000).

[38]Robert H. Mounce, *The Book of Revelation*, rev. ed., New International Commentary on the New Testament (Grand Rapids, Mich.: Eerdmans, 1998), p. 230.

[39]For analysis of the imagery of these chapters, see Richard Bauckham, *The Climax of Prophecy: Studies on the Book of Revelation* (Edinburgh: T & T Clark, 1993), pp. 174-98; Richard Bauckham, *The Theology of the Book of Revelation*, New Testament Theology (Cambridge: Cambridge University Press, 1993), pp. 88-94; G. B. Caird, *The Revelation of St. John the Divine* (London: Adam & Charles Black, 1971), pp. 147-77; Adela Yarbro Collins, *The Combat Myth in the Book of Revelation* (Missoula, Mont.: Scholars Press, 1976); David E. Aune, *Revelation 6-16*, Word Biblical Commentary 52b (Nashville, Tenn.: 1998), pp. 660-695, 725-740; G. K. Beale, *The Book of Revelation*, New International Greek Testament Commentary (Grand Rapids, Mich.: Eerdmans, 1999), pp. 621-730.

[40]Bryan Chapell, *Christ-Centered Preaching: Redeeming the Expository Sermon* (Grand Rapids, Mich.: Baker, 1994), pp. 40-43.

[41]Leonard L. Thompson, "Mooring the Revelation in the Mediterranean World," *Society of Biblical Literature Seminar Papers* (Atlanta: Scholars Press, 1992), p. 651.

[42]Adela Yarbro Collins, *Crisis and Catharsis: the Power of the Apocalypse* (Philadelphia: Westminster Press, 1984), p. 144.

[43]Paul S. Minear, *New Testament Apocalyptic*, Interpreting Biblical Texts (Nashville: Abingdon), p. 93.

[44]Collins, *Apocalyptic Imagination*, p. 14. The vision of Daniel 8 is less cryptic and allusive, however, than the vision of Daniel 7 (Goldingay, *Daniel*, p. 201). For many scholars the material in apocalyptic is more for graphic effect than for predictive significance; e.g., Rowland, *Open Heaven*, p. 237.

[45]David L. Barr, "The Apocalypse of John as Oral Enactment," *Interpretation* 40, no. 3 (July 1986): 243-56; David L. Barr, "The Reader of/in the Apocalypse: Exploring a Method," *Eastern Great Lakes and Midwest Biblical Society Proceedings* 10 (1990): 79-91.

Chapter 6: How Have Prophecies Been Fulfilled?

[1]For discussion of the prophets and their roles, see, e.g., Lester L. Grabbe, *Priests, Prophets, Diviners, Sages: A Socio-historical Study of Religious Specialists in Ancient Israel* (Valley Forge, Penn.: Trinity Press International, 1995); Willem A. VanGemeren, *Interpreting the Prophetic Word* (Grand Rapids, Mich.: Zondervan, 1990); for an overview of the history of interpretation of the prophets, see Ronald E. Clements, *Old Testament Prophecy: From Oracles to Canon* (Louisville, Ky.: John Knox Press, 1996), pp. 1-20.

[2]Carol J. Dempsey, *Hope amid the Ruins: The Ethics of Israel's Prophets* (St. Louis: Chalice, 2000).

[3]The more common way to refer to the primary role of the prophets is *proclamation*; e.g., Gene M. Tucker, "Prophecy and Prophetic Literature," *The Hebrew Bible and Its Modern Interpreters*, ed. Douglas A. Knight and G. M. Tucker (Chico, Calif.: Scholars Press, 1985), p. 339. Prophets can also be referred to as "covenant enforcement mediators" (Gordon D. Fee and Douglas Stuart, *How to Read the Bible for All Its Worth: A Guide to Understanding the Bible*, 2nd ed. [Grand Rapids, Mich.: Zondervan, 1993], p. 167).

[4]See Yehoshua Gitay, *Prophecy and Persuasion: A Study of Isaiah 40—48* (Bonn, Germany: Linguistica Biblical, 1981); Yehoshua Gitay, *Isaiah and His Audience: The Structure and Meaning of Isaiah 1—12*, Studia Semitica Neerlandica (Assen, Netherlands: Van Gorcum, 1991).

[5]Walter Brueggemann, *The Prophetic Imagination,* 2nd ed. (Minneapolis: Fortress, 2001), p. 3.

[6]Abraham J. Heschel, *The Prophets,* 2 vols. in 1 (New York: HarperCollins, 1962), p. xii.

[7]As Gary Smith notes, "Before a prophet can communicate God's way to live, God must reveal knowledge about His plans for a group of people and send a prophet to deliver that message" (Gary V. Smith, *The Prophets as Preachers: An Introduction to the Hebrew Prophets* [Nashville: Broadman and Holman, 1994], p. 14).

[8]As Robert Alter notes, "What are the principal modes of prophetic poetry? The overarching purpose is reproof (and not, I would contend, prediction), and this general aim is realized through three related poetic strategies: (1) direct accusation; (2) satire; (3) the monitory evocation of impending disaster" (Robert Alter, *The Art of Biblical Poetry* [New York: Basic Books, 1985], p. 141).

[9]Rhetorical criticism is an important discipline related to prophecy; see, e.g., Dale Patrick, *The Rhetoric of Revelation in the Hebrew Bible,* Overtures to Biblical Theology (Minneapolis: Fortress, 1999).

[10]"Through much of Christian history, the prophetic books have been read primarily as sources of predictions of the coming Christ, and of the eschaton" (Donald E. Gowan, *Theology of the Prophetic Books: The Death and Resurrection of Israel* [Louisville, Ky.: Westminster John Knox, 1998], p. 2; note Gowan's survey of various scholarly assessments of the prophets).

[11]Another question could be asked: Were the men who were cut off from Ahab simply separated from him? First Kings 21:21 says that every male in Israel, whether slave or free, would be cut off from Ahab.

[12]For example: The men belonging to Baasha who die in the city will be eaten by dogs, and those who die in the country will be food for the birds of the air (1 Kings 16:4).

[13]Based on 1 Kings 14:15 and the pronouncement that the Lord would strike Israel so that it would be left like a reed swaying in the water, and that he would uproot Israel and scatter them beyond the River, we could also ask what the people expected from that statement.

[14]Gowan, *Theology of the Prophetic Books,* pp. 8-9; Smith, *Prophets as Preachers,* p. 14.

[15]The reading "die by the sword" is in the LXX and the Qumran manuscript 4QSam[a]; the Hebrew has "die like mortals."

[16]This passage also highlights the change in priestly leadership to the priesthood of Zadok (Walter Brueggemann, *First and Second Samuel,* Interpretation [Louisville, Ky.: Westminster John Knox, 1990], pp. 23-24).

[17]Both 1 and 2 Samuel contain numerous examples of personal tragedies (John Goldingay, *Men Behaving Badly* [Carlisle, U.K.: Paternoster, 2000]).

[18]In the prophet Jehu's indictment of King Baasha, the same language of judgment appears, leaving us with similar questions: "I am about to consume Baasha and his house, and I will make your house like that of Jeroboam son of Nebat. Dogs will eat those belonging to Baasha who die in the city, and the birds of the air will feed on those who die in the country" (1 Kings 16:3-4).

[19]Walter Kaiser et al., *Hard Sayings of the Bible* (Downers Grove, Ill.: InterVarsity Press, 1996), p. 310.

[20]D. B. Sandy, "Ptolemies," in *Dictionary of New Testament Background,* ed. C. A. Evans and S. E. Porter (Downers Grove, Ill.: InterVarsity Press, 2000), p. 870.

[21]Some argue that only part of Joel's prophecy was fulfilled on Pentecost, but that is begging the question.

[22]For a list of Old Testament prophecies that are not fulfilled literally in the New Testament,

see Louis Berkhof, *The Kingdom of God: The Development of the Idea of Kingdom, Especially Since the Eighteenth Century* (Grand Rapids, Mich.: Eerdmans, 1951), p. 165.

[23]Genesis 2:17 is a case in point: God warns the man that he must not eat from the tree of the knowledge of good and evil, "for in the day that you eat of it you shall die" (NRSV). Was God's pronouncement of judgment fulfilled? Yes, but not as we might have expected based on the language. The fulfillment was not according to the normal meanings of the words. Though we hardly notice the translucent nature of the statement, the point of the pronouncement was apparently not to declare the specifics of how judgment would fall.

Chapter 7: How Will Prophecies Be Fulfilled?

[1]Robert G. Clouse, Robert N. Hosack and Richard V. Pierard, *The New Millennium Manual: A Once and Future Guide* (Grand Rapids, Mich.: Baker, 1999); Paul Boyer, *When Time Shall Be No More: Prophecy Belief in Modern American Culture* (Cambridge, Mass.: Harvard University Press, 1992).

[2]Richard Kyle, *The Last Days Are Here Again: A History of the End Times* (Grand Rapids, Mich.: Baker, 1998).

[3]"In our estimation, the basic flaw of the doomsday prophet is hermeneutical" (C. Marvin Pate and Calvin B. Haines Jr., *Doomsday Delusions: What's Wrong with Predictions About the End of the World* [Downers Grove, Ill.: InterVarsity Press, 1995], p. 22).

[4]"This is not to say that eschatology is dispensable, but that no scheme of eschatology should stand at the center of one's faith. There is a center, but it is the cross and resurrection of Jesus, not a speculative calendar about the end of the world" (Daniel J. Lewis, *Three Crucial Questions About the Last Days* [Grand Rapids, Mich.: Baker, 1998], p. 17).

[5]David L. Petersen and Kent H. Richards, *Interpreting Hebrew Poetry* (Minneapolis: Fortress, 1992), pp. 8-9.

[6]Robert Alter, *The Art of Biblical Poetry* (New York: Basic Books, 1985), p. 141.

[7]Louis A. Markos, "Poetry-Phobic: Why Evangelicals Should Love Language That Is Slippery," *Christianity Today* (October 1, 2001): p. 66; cf. W. B. Stanford, *Enemies of Poetry* (London: Routledge & Kegan Paul, 1980).

[8]"The prophetic employment of images stands out as extreme in its art with more vivid form and stronger meanings than any other biblical poetry" (Donald K. Berry, *An Introduction to Wisdom and Poetry* [Nashville: Broadman and Holman, 1995], p. 337); cf. C. E. Armerding, "Images for Today: Word from the Prophets," *Studies in Old Testament Theology*, ed. R. L. Hubbard (Dallas: Word, 1992).

[9]S. E. Gillingham, *The Poems and Psalms of the Hebrew Bible* (Oxford: Oxford University Press, 1994), p. 16.

[10]G. B. Caird comments, "Prophecy deals more often than not in absolutes" (*The Language and Imagery of the Bible* [London: Gerald Duckworth, 1980]; reprinted with introduction by N. T. Wright [Grand Rapids, Mich.: Eerdmans, 1997], p. 112).

[11]Alter, *Art of Biblical Poetry*, p. 141.

[12]Walther Zimmerli, "From Prophetic Word to Prophetic Book," in *The Place Is Too Small for Us: The Israelite Prophets in Recent Scholarship*, trans. Andreas Köstenberger, ed. R. P. Gordon, Sources for Biblical and Theological Study 5 (Winona Lake, Ind.: Eisenbrauns, 1995), pp. 419-42.

[13]Prophets may have sung their oracles (Berry, *Introduction to Wisdom and Poetry*, p. 175).

[14]Caird, *Language and Imagery*, pp. xxii, 256-59.

[15]Abraham Heschel, *The Prophets*, 2 vols. in 1 (New York: HarperCollins, 1962), p. xii.

[16]See the chapter "On How to Identify a Metaphor" in J. J. A. Mooij, *A Study of Metaphor: On the Nature of Metaphorical Expressions, with Special Reference to Their Reference*, North-Holland Linguistic Series 27 (Amsterdam: North-Holland, 1976), pp. 18-28; Albert N. Katz, "On Interpreting Statements as Metaphor and Irony: Contextual Heuristics and Cognitive Consequences," in *Metaphor: Implications and Applications*, ed. J. S. Mio and A. N. Katz (Mahwah, N.J.: Lawrence Erlbaum, 1996), pp. 1-2.

[17]Philip Wheelwright, *Metaphor and Reality* (Bloomington: Indiana University Press, 1962), p. 29.

[18]The substitution, comparison and interaction views of metaphor are discussed in detail in Max Black, "Metaphor," *Proceedings of the Aristotelian Society* 55 (1954): 273-94, reprinted as a chapter in *Models and Metaphors: Studies in Language and Philosophy* (Ithaca, N.Y.: Cornell University Press, 1962), pp. 30-44.

[19]For the interactions of the terms of a metaphor, see I. A. Richards, *The Philosophy of Rhetoric* (London: Oxford University Press, 1936), chaps. 5-6, and Black, *Models and Metaphors*, pp. 38-44; for critique of the interaction view, see George Lakoff and Mark Turner, *More Than Cool Reason: A Field Guide to Poetic Metaphor* (Chicago: University of Chicago Press, 1989), pp. 131-35.

[20]Carl Hausman, *Metaphor and Art: Interactionism and Reference in the Verbal and Nonverbal Arts* (Cambridge: Cambridge University Press, 1989), p. 7.

[21]Metaphors can be divided into nominal, predicative and sentential (Valerie F. Reyna, "Meaning, Metaphor and the Interpretation of Metaphors," in *Metaphor: Implications and Applications*, ed. J. S. Mio and A. N. Katz [Mahwah, N.J.: Lawrence Erlbaum, 1996], pp. 39-40).

[22]"The reference of the metaphorical statement [is] the power to redescribe reality" (Paul Ricoeur, *The Rule of Metaphor: Multi-disciplinary Studies of the Creation of Meaning in Language*, trans. Robert Czerny [Toronto: University of Toronto Press, 1977], p. 6).

[23]On the tensive nature of metaphor, see Philip Wheelwright, *The Burning Fountain: A Study in the Language of Symbolism* (Bloomington: Indiana University Press, 1954), pp. 101-22; Wheelwright, *Metaphor and Reality*.

[24]Though metaphors are conceptually unclear, they nourish thought; Kevin Vanhoozer, *Is There a Meaning in This Text? The Bible, the Reader, and the Morality of Literary Knowledge* (Grand Rapids, Mich.: Zondervan, 1998), p. 133; Carl Hausman, *Metaphor and Art*, p. 5.

[25]Paul Ricoeur, "The Metaphorical Process," in *On Metaphor*, ed. Sheldon Sacks (Chicago: University of Chicago Press, 1979), pp. 152-53.

[26]See, e.g., Susan Niditch, *Oral and Written Word: Ancient Israelite Literature* (Louisville, Ky.: Westminster John Knox, 1996).

[27]Tremper Longman III and Daniel G. Reid, *God Is a Warrior*, Studies in Old Testament Biblical Theology (Grand Rapids, Mich.: Zondervan, 1995); Harold Wayne Ballard, *The Divine Warrior Motif in the Psalms* (North Richland Hills, Tex.: BIBAL, 1999).

[28]N. T. Wright, among others, understands the imagery of the Sermon on the Mount to refer to the destruction of Jerusalem in A.D. 70 (Wright, *Jesus and the Victory of God*, Christian Origins and the Question of God 2 [Minneapolis: Fortress, 1996], pp. 329-36).

Conclusion

[1]I am assuming that the 144,000 is symbolic for saints, many of whom were martyred.

[2]"It is a logical mistake to confuse the impossibility of certainty in understanding with the impossibility of understanding" (E. D. Hirsch Jr., *Validity in Interpretation* [New Haven, Conn.: Yale University Press, 1967], p. 17).

[3]Trevor Hart, "Imagination for the Kingdom of God? Hope, Promise, and the Transformative Power of an Imagined Future," in *God Will Be All in All: The Eschatology of Jürgen Moltmann*, ed. Richard Bauckham (Edinburgh: T & T Clark, 1999): pp. 49-85.

[4]Note the chapter "A Hermeneutics of Humility and Conviction," in Kevin Vanhoozer, *Is There a Meaning in This Text? The Bible, the Reader and the Morality of Literary Knowledge* (Grand Rapids, Mich.: Zondervan, 1998), pp. 455-68.

[5]Willem A. VanGemeren, "Oracles of Salvation," Trent C. Butler, "Announcements of Judgment," and D. Brent Sandy and Martin C. Abegg, "Apocalyptic," in *Cracking Old Testament Codes: A Guide to Interpreting the Literary Genres of the Old Testament*, ed. D. B. Sandy and R. L. Giese (Nashville: Broadman, 1995), pp. 146-52, 166-68, 187-90; Walter C. Kaiser Jr. and Moisés Silva, *An Introduction to Biblical Hermeneutics: The Search for Meaning* (Grand Rapids, Mich.: Zondervan, 1994), pp. 148-58; Gordon D. Fee and Douglas Stuart, *How to Read the Bible for All Its Worth: A Guide to Understanding the Bible*, 2nd ed. (Grand Rapids, Mich.: Zondervan, 1993), pp. 165-86; William W. Klein, Craig L. Blomberg and Robert L. Hubbard Jr., *Introduction to Biblical Interpretation* (Dallas: Word, 1993), pp. 302-12; Grant R. Osborne, *The Hermeneutical Spiral: A Comprehensive Introduction to Biblical Interpretation* (Downers Grove, Ill.: InterVarsity Press, 1991), pp. 216-20, 227-32.

[6]Tremper Longman III and Daniel G. Reid, *God Is a Warrior*, Studies in Old Testament Biblical Theology (Grand Rapids, Mich.: Zondervan, 1995); Harold Wayne Ballard, *The Divine Warrior Motif in the Psalms* (North Richland Hills, Tex.: BIBAL, 1999).

[7]For more information on these images and numerous other contemporary examples, see James Limburg, "Swords to Plowshares: Texts and Contexts," in *Writing and Reading the Scroll of Isaiah: Studies of an Interpretive Tradition*, ed. C. C. Broyles and C. A. Evans, Vetus Testamentum Supplements 52, no. 1 (Leiden, Netherlands: Brill, 1997), pp. 279-93; Piper Lowell, "A .38-Caliber Plowshare," *Christianity Today*, October 2, 1995, pp. 38-39.

[8]For a reasoned discussion of the end-times from a pre-millennial, post-tribulational perspective, see Brent Kinman, *History, Design, and the End of Time: God's Plan for the World* (Nashville: Broadman & Holman, 2000).

[9]On the tension between imminence and delay, see Charles L. Holman, *Till Jesus Comes: Origins of Christian Apocalyptic Expectation* (Peabody, Mass.: Hendrickson, 1996).

[10]D. Brent Sandy, "John the Baptist's 'Lamb of God' Affirmation in Its Canonical and Apocalyptic Milieu," *Journal of the Evangelical Theological Society* 34, no. 4 (1991): 447-59.

[11]For a probing reflection on how Christian hope for the future influences Christian life in the present, see Rowan A. Greer, *Christian Hope and Christian Life: Raids on the Inarticulate* (New York: Crossroad, 2001).

[12]Adrio König, *The Eclipse of Christ in Eschatology: Toward a Christ-Centered Approach* (Grand Rapids, Mich.: Eerdmans, 1989).

[13]An earlier version of this section ("What Does Prophecy Predict About the Future?") appeared in D. Brent Sandy, "Did Daniel See Mussolini? The Limits of Reading Current Events into Biblical Prophecy," *Christianity Today*, February 8, 1993, p. 36.

[14]For a summary of principal viewpoints, see C. Marvin Pate, ed., *Four Views on the Book of Revelation* (Grand Rapids, Mich.: Zondervan, 1998). A correct understanding of the book probably includes aspects of several of the views: some parts of Revelation seem to address issues that Christians were facing in the first century; some parts are underscoring the ongoing conflict between good and evil; other parts seem to be broadly eschatological, looking forward to God's final victory. For an example of the future exploration necessary to interpret the Apocalypse, see Alan Garrow, "Revelation's Assembly Instructions," in *Escha-*

tology in Bible and Theology: Evangelical Essays at the Dawn of a New Millennium, ed. K. E. Brower and M. W. Elliott (Downers Grove, Ill.: InterVarsity Press, 1997), pp. 187-98.

[15]David E. Aune, *Revelation,* 3 vols., Word Biblical Commentary 52a-c (Nashville, Tenn.: Thomas Nelson, 1997-1999); G. K. Beale, *The Book of Revelation,* New International Greek Testament Commentary (Grand Rapids, Mich.: Eerdmans, 1999).

[16]See, for example, Robert G. Clouse, Robert N. Hosack and Richard V. Pierard, *The New Millennium Manual: A Once and Future Guide* (Grand Rapids, Mich.: Baker, 1999); Millard J. Erickson, *A Basic Guide to Eschatology: Making Sense of the Millennium* (Grand Rapids, Mich.: Baker, 1998). Eschatology as a discipline of theology has been a prominent topic in recent decades: e.g., Stephen Williams, "Thirty Years of Hope: A Generation of Writing on Eschatology," in *Eschatology in Bible and Theology: Evangelical Essays at the Dawn of the New Millennium,* ed. K. E. Brower and M. W. Elliott (Downers Grove, Ill.: InterVarsity Press, 1997), pp. 243-62 (see other essays in this collection as well); Hans Schwarz, *Eschatology* (Grand Rapids, Mich.: Eerdmans, 2000).

[17]See, e.g., Jacques Doukhan, *Israel and the Church* (Peabody, Mass.: Hendrickson, 2002).

[18]John Stott in an interview; Roy McCloughry, "Basic Stott: Candid Comments on Justice, Gender, and Judgment," *Christianity Today,* January 8, 1996, p. 28.

[19]"No paraphrase, neither commentary or systematic theology, can ever exhaust the riches of the metaphor" (Vanhoozer, *Is There a Meaning in This Text?* p. 133).

[20]For another description of this eschatological river, see Ezekiel 47:1-12; cf., e.g., Psalm 46:4.

[21]John M. Frame, *Evangelical Reunion: Denominations and the Body of Christ* (Grand Rapids, Mich.: Baker, 1991); cf. Richard G. Hutcheson Jr. and Peggy Shriver, *The Divided Church: Moving Liberals and Conservatives from Diatribe to Dialogue* (Downers Grove, Ill.: InterVarsity Press, 1999).

[22]John Stott, *Evangelical Truth: A Personal Plea for Unity* (Downers Grove, Ill.: InterVarsity Press, 1999).

[23]On the Shekinah glory, see Jürgen Moltmann, *The Coming of God: Christian Eschatology,* trans. Margaret Kohl (Minneapolis: Fortress, 1996), pp. 302-06.

[24]It is encouraging to see evidence of an increase in cooperative efforts among mission organizations, such as in the Alliance for Saturation Church Planting.

[25]Wayne Grudem, "Do We Act As If We Really Believe That 'the Bible Alone, and the Bible in Its Entirety, Is the Word of God Written'?" *Journal of the Evangelical Theological Society* 43, no. 1 (2000): 13-14.

[26]As Charles De Gaulle said about the challenge of uniting the French, "Nobody can simply bring together a country that has three hundred sixty-five kinds of cheese."

[27]Cf. Stanley J. Grenz, *Renewing the Center: Evangelical Theology in a Post-theological Era* (Grand Rapids, Mich.: Baker, 2000).

Subject Index

abstract ideas expressed in metaphor, 60, 64, 72
acclamation, 97, 202, 220
Ahab, 135, 143-44, 147-51
Ahijah, 45, 139, 141-42, 147-50
Alexander the Great, 104-6, 112-14, 151
    successors of, 105, 114-15, 118
ancient Near Eastern treaties, 76, 83, 89
angels, 153
antichrist, 116
Antiochus Epiphanes, 106, 116
apocalyptic, 13, 49, 97, 103-28, 168, 170-71, 196-99
    definition of, 106
apocalypticism, 168-69
apostasy, 42, 46, 91, 130, 141-42
Aristotle, 59
Assyrians, 46, 54, 109, 144-45, 150, 152, 193
Baruch, 52
Babylon, 96-97, 165-66
Babylonians, 47, 54-55, 98, 109, 146
battle between good and evil, 111
beast, 121-26, 198
birth, metaphors of, 60-61
blessing, language

of, 21, 23, 28, 44, 47, 71, 79-80, 83, 85-91, 97, 152, 180, 206
blood, 167-68
Bullinger, E. W., 66
captivity, 55, 119, 142, 152
chosen people, 21, 130, 161, 206
cognitive dissonance, 168
comfort, 108, 111
community, 65
covenant, 44-46, 89-91, 95-96, 98, 130, 161, 198
    Abrahamic, 45, 196
    Davidic, 45
    Mosaic, 45
crowns, 28, 182
cultural differences, 56, 65
Daniel, 48, 103-4, 111-20
Darius, 114
David, 98, 100, 137, 140, 148, 150
Davidic dynasty, 46
day of judgment, 167
death, metaphors of, 60-61
descendants, 92, 216-17
desolation, 96, 218-20
determinism, 108
Diaspora. See captivity; dispersion
dictation, 52-53
disobedience, 45-46
dispensationalism, 12, 155, 188
dispersion, 93-95, 142-44, 150, 152, 217-18
dragon, 120-22, 125-26
dualism, 109, 186

Egypt, 54, 106, 151-52
Eli, 137-38
Elijah, 136, 143-44, 147, 150, 153
endurance, patient, 123-24, 126, 188
Esarhaddon, vassal treaties of, 84
eschatology, 11, 34, 156, 163, 205-6, 210
ethics, ethical teaching, 108, 111, 122, 124, 174, 187, 199, 202
euphemism, 61
everlasting, 42, 46
exile. See captivity
exodus, 97, 190
exposure, 97, 221-22
false prophets, 45
forever, 42, 44, 46, 98-101, 222
Former Prophets, 136
genre, 157
    apocalyptic, 106, 127
    narrative, 26
    prophecy, 27
    treaties, 83
goat, 111-12, 117-18
God
    attributes of, 20, 56, 80, 195
    grace of, 56
    indescribable qualities of, 27, 71
    intervention of, 109-10
    judgment of, 136-38, 142, 169
    love of, 23, 27, 56, 76, 79, 131, 160, 196
    presence on earth, 31
    revelation of, 25,

27, 185, 205
    sovereignty of, 186-87
    transcendence of, 78, 170, 198, 224
    union with creation, 30
    wrath of, 19, 21-23, 27, 42, 48, 56, 76, 78-80, 95, 124, 130-31, 133, 141, 143, 160, 175, 180, 184, 188, 195-96, 207
Greece, 104, 112-14, 118-19
heaven, 26-27, 30, 111, 228
Hellenistic kingdoms, 106, 151
Hezekiah, 144-45, 150
highways, 97, 221
horn, 111-14, 116-18, 120
hyperbole, 24, 41, 43-44, 46-47, 56, 87, 90, 92-93, 95, 99-102, 113, 158-60, 196-97, 199
idolatry, 41, 44
illocution, 80-82, 94, 100, 102, 196, 206
imagination, 24-25, 50, 95, 109, 118, 124, 184
imminence, 101, 173-75
inspiration, 11-12, 53, 103
interpretation, literal, 37, 39-40, 159, 164
interpreter, heavenly, 109, 112
Isaiah, 50, 136, 144, 150
Israel, kingdom of, 43, 46, 55, 142-45, 148-50, 152, 190